International Financial Co-operation

The 1988 Basel Accord – now commonly referred to as "Basel I" – has exerted a strong influence on prudential financial sector regulatory policy and international financial politics, yet controversy has always surrounded the Accord's impact on the safety and competitiveness of the world's largest financial institutions and the evolution of transnational regulatory convergence.

The author provides a comprehensive examination of the impact of the 1988 Basel Accord on the capital adequacy regulations of developed economies. This study seeks to understand if the Accord affected broad or isolated convergence of 18 developed states' bank credit risk regulations from 1988 to 2000 and also to understand what political economic variables influenced observed levels of regulatory convergence. Quillin creates a quantitative database of developed countries' interpretations of the Basel rules which shows that many persistent distinctions remained in the way they implemented the Accord. This book also explores why convergence emerged among a subset of states, yet not others, by testing a battery of political economic explanations.

This book is very timely in providing guidance on many of the challenges that the second Accord faces as it moves into the implementation phase. It also contributes to a broader understanding of the implementation of international financial regulatory regimes and the process of transnational policy convergence and divergence. It will appeal to those studying International Finance and Banking, International Economic Relations and Political Economics.

Bryce Quillin is Economist at the World Bank, USA.

Routledge international studies in money and banking

1 **Private Banking in Europe**
   Lynn Bicker

2 **Bank Deregulation and Monetary Order**
   George Selgin

3 **Money in Islam**
   A study in Islamic political economy
   Masudul Alam Choudhury

4 **The Future of European Financial Centres**
   Kirsten Bindemann

5 **Payment Systems in Global Perspective**
   Maxwell J. Fry, Isaak Kilato, Sandra Roger, Krzysztof Senderowicz, David Sheppard, Francisco Solis and John Trundle

6 **What Is Money?**
   John Smithin

7 **Finance**
   A characteristics approach
   Edited by David Blake

8 **Organisational Change and Retail Finance**
   An ethnographic perspective
   Richard Harper, Dave Randall and Mark Rouncefield

9 **The History of the Bundesbank**
   Lessons for the European Central Bank
   Jakob de Haan

10 **The Euro**
    A challenge and opportunity for financial markets
    Published on behalf of *Société Universitaire Européenne de Recherches Financières (SUERF)*
    Edited by Michael Artis, Axel Weber and Elizabeth Hennessy

11 **Central Banking in Eastern Europe**
    Edited by Nigel Healey and Barry Harrison

12 **Money, Credit and Prices Stability**
    Paul Dalziel

13 **Monetary Policy, Capital Flows and Exchange Rates**
Essays in memory of Maxwell Fry
Edited by William Allen and David Dickinson

14 **Adapting to Financial Globalisation**
Published on behalf of *Société Universitaire Européenne de Recherches Financières (SUERF)*
Edited by Morten Balling, Eduard H. Hochreiter and Elizabeth Hennessy

15 **Monetary Macroeconomics**
A new approach
Alvaro Cencini

16 **Monetary Stability in Europe**
Stefan Collignon

17 **Technology and Finance**
Challenges for financial markets, business strategies and policy makers
Published on behalf of *Société Universitaire Européenne de Recherches Financières (SUERF)*
Edited by Morten Balling, Frank Lierman and Andrew Mullineux

18 **Monetary Unions**
Theory, history, public choice
Edited by Forrest H. Capie and Geoffrey E. Wood

19 **HRM and Occupational Health and Safety**
Carol Boyd

20 **Central Banking Systems Compared**
The ECB, the pre-Euro Bundesbank and the Federal Reserve System
Emmanuel Apel

21 **A History of Monetary Unions**
John Chown

22 **Dollarization**
Lessons from Europe and the Americas
Edited by Louis-Philippe Rochon and Mario Seccareccia

23 **Islamic Economics and Finance**
A glossary, 2nd edition
Muhammad Akram Khan

24 **Financial Market Risk**
Measurement and analysis
Cornelis A. Los

25 **Financial Geography**
A banker's view
Risto Laulajainen

26 **Money Doctors**
The experience of international financial advising 1850–2000
Edited by Marc Flandreau

27 **Exchange Rate Dynamics**
A new open economy macroeconomics perspective
Edited by Jean-Oliver Hairault and Thepthida Sopraseuth

28 **Fixing Financial Crises in the 21st Century**
Edited by Andrew G. Haldane

29 **Monetary Policy and Unemployment**
The U.S., Euro-area and Japan
Edited by Willi Semmler

30 **Exchange Rates, Capital Flows and Policy**
Edited by Rebecca Driver, Peter J.N. Sinclair and Christoph Thoenissen

31 **Great Architects of International Finance**
The Bretton Woods era
Anthony M. Endres

32 **The Means to Prosperity**
Fiscal policy reconsidered
Edited by Per Gunnar Berglund and Matias Vernengo

33 **Competition and Profitability in European Financial Services**
Strategic, systemic and policy issues
Edited by Morten Balling, Frank Lierman and Andy Mullineux

34 **Tax Systems and Tax Reforms in South and East Asia**
Edited by Luigi Bernardi, Angela Fraschini and Parthasarathi Shome

35 **Institutional Change in the Payments System and Monetary Policy**
Edited by Stefan W. Schmitz and Geoffrey E. Wood

36 **The Lender of Last Resort**
Edited by Forrest H. Capie and Geoffrey E. Wood

37 **The Structure of Financial Regulation**
Edited by David G. Mayes and Geoffrey E. Wood

38 **Monetary Policy in Central Europe**
Miroslav Beblavý

39 **Money and Payments in Theory and Practice**
Sergio Rossi

40 **Open Market Operations and Financial Markets**
Edited by David G. Mayes and Jan Toporowski

41 **Banking in Central and Eastern Europe 1980–2006**
From communism to capitalism
Stephan Barisitz

42 **Debt, Risk and Liquidity in Futures Markets**
Edited by Barry A. Goss

43 **The Future of Payment Systems**
Edited by Stephen Millard, Andrew G. Haldane and Victoria Saporta

44 **Credit and Collateral**
Vania Sena

45 **Tax Systems and Tax Reforms in Latin America**
Edited by Luigi Bernardi, Alberto Barreix, Anna Marenzi and Paola Profeta

46 **The Dynamics of Organizational Collapse**
The case of Barings Bank
Helga Drummond

47 **International Financial Co-operation**
Political economics of compliance with the 1988 Basel Accord
Bryce Quillin

International Financial Co-operation
Political economics of compliance with the 1988 Basel Accord

Bryce Quillin

LONDON AND NEW YORK

First published 2008
by Routledge
2 Park Square, Milton Park, Abingdon, Oxfordshire OX14 4RN

Simultaneously published in the USA and Canada
by Routledge
711 Third Avenue, New York, NY 10017

First issued in paperback 2014

Routledge is an imprint of the Taylor and Francis Group, an informa business

© 2008 Bryce Quillin

Typeset in Times by Wearset Ltd, Boldon, Tyne and Wear

All rights reserved. No part of this book may be reprinted or reproduced or utilized in any form or by any electronic, mechanical, or other means, now known or hereafter invented, including photocopying and recording, or in any information storage or retrieval system, without permission in writing from the publishers.

British Library Cataloguing in Publication Data
A catalogue record for this book is available from the British Library

Library of Congress Cataloging in Publication Data
A catalog record for this book has been requested

ISBN 978-0-415-77288-4 (hbk)
ISBN 978-1-138-80542-2 (pbk)
ISBN 978-0-203-93028-1 (ebk)

Contents

List of figures	ix
List of tables	x
Acknowledgments	xii
List of abbreviations	xiii
1 Introduction	1

PART I
Historical and theoretical perspectives on the 1988 Basel Accord — 9

2 The political economy of the negotiation of the 1988 Basel Accord as a soft law agreement — 11

3 Theorizing degrees of compliance with the Basel Accord — 28

PART II
Quantitative studies — 47

4 Measuring implementation and explanatory variables — 49

5 Explaining implementation-quantitative tests — 74

PART III
Case studies — 93

6 Implementation of the Basel Accord in the United States — 101

7 Implementation of the Basel Accord in Europe: the case of France and Germany — 123

8	Implementation of the Basel Accord in Japan	145
9	Conclusions and extensions	165
	Notes	179
	Bibliography	191
	Index	205

Figures

1.1	The evolution of the Basel Committee and capital adequacy regulation	7
2.1	G-10 banks' capital asset ratios, 1970–1985	14
3.1	Convergence and divergence effects with a differentiated compliance variable	32
3.2	Convergence and divergence effects with a binary compliance variable	33
3.3	Dynamic convergence and divergence effects with a differentiated compliance variable	34
5.1	CREG and PREBASEL index comparisons	77
6.1	Capital-to-assets ratios for the leading ten US banks: 1900–1980	104
6.2	Unweighted Tier1 capital-to-assets ratios for leading ten US banks: 1988–2000	116
7.1	Unweighted Tier1 capital ratios for the leading ten French and German banks, 1988–2000	143
8.1	Averages for G-10 countries' major banks cost of equity, 1993–2001	148
8.2	Nikkei 225 index: 1985–2000	153
8.3	Aggregate market value of Japanese bank shares: 1985–2000	154
8.4	Capital adequacy ratios: 1988–1996	158

Tables

2.1	Comparison of 11 states' pre-Basel Capital Adequacy Regulations	16
2.2	Comparison of US/UK Accord and Basel Accord Capital Regulations	19
3.1	Hypotheses on the implementation of the Basel Accord	46
4.1	Areas of permitted discretionary implementation with the 1988 Basel Accord	51
4.2	Comparative descriptive statistics for CREG indexes	54
4.3	Comparative descriptive statistics for CREG components (t)	55
4.4	Tier2 capital definitions (t)	56
4.5	Tier1 capital definitions (t)	57
4.6	Comparative descriptive statistics for CREG index components ($t + 1$)	59
4.7	Univariate analysis of hegemonic hypothesis	61
4.8	Univariate analysis of regional effects hypothesis	62
4.9	Variance of CREG scores: EU versus non-EU	63
4.10	Pre-Basel capital regulatory index	64
4.11	Descriptive statistics: explanatory variables	64
5.1	Correlation coefficients: independent variables	76
5.2	Correlation coefficients: CREG (t)	76
5.3	Correlation coefficients: CREG components	79
5.4	OLS regression results: CREG (t)	80
5.5	OLS regression results: CREG (PREBASEL excluded)	81
5.6	OLS regression results: CREG (PBRATIO PROXY)	83
5.7	Correlation coefficients: STABILITY 1989–1995	84
5.8	Correlation coefficients: CREG ($t + 1$)	85
5.9	Correlation coefficients: CREG ($t + 1$) components	86
5.10	OLS regression results: CREG ($t + 1$)	87
5.11	Ordered Probit regression results: CREG ($t + 1$) component results	88
5.12	Correlation coefficients: ΔCREG	90
III.1	Chronological ordering of comparison case studies	90
III.2	Comparison of CREG scores for case-study countries	92
III.3	Comparison of explanatory variables values for case-study countries	92

6.1	Comparison of FDIC and Basel Accord capital regulations	106
6.2	Comparison of 1982 FDIC–Fed/OCC capital definitions	107
7.1	Capital-to-assets ratios of the leading ten French banks, 1988	127
8.1	Estimated effects of the Nikkei 225 on Japanese city banks' capital ratios	155
8.2	Reformulated capital-to-assets ratios of major Japanese banks, March 1998–September 2000	160

Acknowledgments

This book joins most pieces of research in being the product of the contributions of many individuals and institutions. In particular, I benefited from the research training and academic environments at McGill University and the London School of Economics.

I particularly acknowledge the advice and guidance of Kern Alexander, David Stasavage, William Wallace, Andrew Walter, and two reviewers at Routledge. Also, no amount of praise can exaggerate the contribution of my doctoral adviser, Daphné Josselin. Her persistence, patience, and insightful criticisms undoubtedly improved this piece of research.

I would also like to thank those financial services practitioners who generously gave of their time to assist my research. In particular, appreciation is held for dozens of financial regulators throughout the G-10 economies who provided me with information, data, and advice concerning their respective banking environments. In addition, John Tattersall at PriceWaterhouseCoopers provided useful advice and tracked down some impossible to find documents that aided my research at every turn.

Finally, I thank Jessica K. Quillin. She is the love of my life and my partner in learning the "cause of things."

All errors and inaccuracies are the full responsibility of the author.

Abbreviations

AFEC	Association Française des Etablissements de Crédit
BAC	European Union Banking Advisory Committee
BCBS	Basel Committee on Banking Supervision (G-10 plus Luxembourg)
BDB	Bundesverbank deutscher Banken
BHCs	Bank Holding Companies
BIS	Bank for International Settlements
BNP	Banque Nationale de Paris
C & I	Commercial and Industrial Loans
CAD	EC Capital Adequacy Directive
CAR	capital adequacy ratio
CEC	Comité des Etablissements de Crédit
CRB	Comité de la Réglementation Bancaire
CREG	Capital Regulation Index
EC	European Community
EU	European Union
FBAJ	Federal Bankers' Associations of Japan
FDIC	US Federal Deposit Insurance Corporation
FBSA	German Federal Bank Supervisory Authority
GAAP	Generally Accepted Accounting Practices
IMF	International Monetary Fund
ILSA	International Lending Supervision Act of 1983
IOSCO	International Organization of Securities Commissions
LDP	Japanese Liberal Democratic Party
LDCs	lesser-developed countries
NPLs	non-performing loans
OBS	off-balance sheet
OECD	Organization for Economic Cooperation and Development
OPEC	Organization of Petroleum Exporting Countries
OCC	US Office of the Comptroller of the Currency
OTS	US Office of Thrift Supervision
REITS	real-estate investment trusts
RWA	risk-weighted assets
S & Ls	Savings and Loans
SPVs	special purpose vehicles

1 Introduction

Book overview

In 1988, the G-10 states agreed to a series of prudential capital adequacy guidelines for the credit risks of their internationally active commercial banking institutions. These rules, called the Basel Accord, endeavored to increase the soundness and stability of their largest financial intermediaries and ameliorate the competitive regulatory advantages conferred by some G-10 regulators to their domestic banks.[1]

Though, by the late 1990s, a major international effort was initiated to fundamentally amend the agreement, the original Basel Accord ostensibly produced a highly successful international regime. Initially created by a small group of industrialized states, the Basel Accord ("Accord") has become the worldwide prudential standard, or benchmark, for the commercial banking industry. The Accord was negotiated by an informal organization of G-10 central bank governors and financial services regulators, now known as the Basel Committee on Banking Supervision (BCBS).[2] The ambitions of the Committee were to create a common definition of bank regulatory capital, formulae for weighing the relative credit risks of banks' assets, and to enforce uniform capital-to-assets minima. The agreement was concluded in 1988 and was to be fully implemented in the G-10 economies by 1992. Yet, the goal of the Committee was to extend the Accord's influence beyond the G-10 and the Accord was "circulated to supervisory authorities worldwide with a view to encouraging adoption of [the] framework in countries outside the G-10 in respect of banks conducting significant international business."[3] This ambition was fully realized as the Accord was adopted by the European Community (EC), Australia, Ghana, Hong Kong, New Zealand, Norway, Saudi Arabia, and Singapore during the late 1980s and early 1990s.[4] Over the next decade, this number increased exponentially so that over 100 states had unilaterally committed to the Basel standards by 1999.[5]

This global diffusion of the Basel rules has been accompanied by an enormous production of research by political scientists, international lawyers, and financial economists eager to examine the political origins and economic impacts of the Accord. Tomes of research have been dedicated to understanding the effects of the Accord on the banking sector and broader economies of implementing countries. Economists have questioned whether the Accord increased, or indeed decreased, the safety and soundness of country banking systems, influenced the long-run competitiveness of multinational banks, or contributed to downturns in macroeconomic growth during the 1990s.[6] Scholars of international relations and law have similarly produced much research to understand how such a successful inter-state regime could have emerged in an issue area – financial services – in which very little international cooperation had occurred before the 1990s.[7]

Yet, before academic attention shifts away from the 1988 Basel Accord to its successor Basel II Accord, there are several important dimensions of the 1988 Accord that have yet to be systematically investigated and which, ex ante, appear to have ramifications for a full evaluation of the Accord's significance.[8] Such research could have crucial implications for the results of previous findings on the politics of the Accord's negotiation and its micro- and macroeconomic effects. This research could also contribute to a broader understanding of the implementation of international financial regulatory regimes and the process of transnational policy convergence and divergence.

In particular, little empirical evidence has been produced that illustrates how the Accord was implemented in some or all of the 100 adhering states. Minimal academic attention has been given to understanding how domestic political actors interpreted the Basel Accord rules when creating the regulatory guidelines and legislation that implemented the Accord. This is a critical handicap to bear when gauging the political economic effects of the agreement. Though a key goal of the 1988 Accord was to level the regulatory playing field for banking risks, the agreement is an example of "soft law." National regulators were given extensive discretionary powers for determining the exact manner in which the Accord was operationalized and enforced in their domestic banking space.[9] This discretion was established, explicitly, by laying out a minimum regulatory baseline that national policymakers were invited to exceed in critical issue areas. Also, the Accord implicitly provides for high levels of discretionary policy by not seeking to harmonize cross-national tax and accounting standards and other prudential regulatory policies that are believed to bear upon the stringency of prudential banking regulation.[10]

The importance of understanding the implementation of the Basel rules was recognized in research by banking practitioners and economists during the first several years after the Accord's negotiation. The results of these studies suggested that the Accord was implemented in widely different fashions by the core group of industrialized states in the G-10 and EC that adopted the agreement shortly after its completion.[11] Some states implemented very strict or "super-equivalent" interpretations of the Basel rules while others implemented loose, barely in compliance or non-compliant, interpretations. Econometric research has provided support for the view that these disparities matter as the domestic rule interpretations may have financially advantaged some banks at the expense of others.[12] In other words, the Accord may have failed in its objective to level elements of the banking regulatory playing field and allowed or exacerbated the problem of competitive regulation in the area of capital adequacy.

Yet, this book argues that previous research is not extensive enough to draw firm conclusions about the effects of the Basel Accord. The research on the Accord that has progressed over the last decade lacks attempts to operationalize its implementation in such a way that we can measure it across a wide range of cases over a period of time. Research has generally focused on implementation in two or three states and most of this work was completed with late 1980s data.

This book will address this empirical lacuna. Subsequent chapters analyze the Accord's implementation with the preliminary aim of answering the question of how were the baseline Basel rules interpreted in the core implementing countries and how, if it all, did such interpretations change over time? In so doing, two specific questions will be addressed:

1   Did the Accord produce or contribute to transnational convergence or divergence in industrialized states' capital adequacy policies shortly after the Accord's negotiation?
2   Did the Accord produce or contribute to transnational convergence or divergence in industrialized states' capital adequacy policies during a 12-year period (1988–2000) after the Accord's negotiation. Put differently, did initial levels of convergence or divergence alter over time?

Addressing this set of questions permits a unique study of comparative political economy. Looking at the implementation of the Accord provides an opportunity to conduct a yardstick comparison of the way that states make bank regulatory policy in relation to a common, baseline standard. Before the Basel Accord, cross-sectional bank regulatory capital comparisons were almost impossible because of the distinctions in regulatory approach and vocabulary utilized among countries. It was common for academics to observe that if State A's banks maintained an average capital adequacy ratio (CAR) of 7 percent and State B's banks maintained a 5 percent ratio, then the latter were less sound and, by virtue of being less severely regulated, maintained a competitive advantage.[13] Yet, such statements ignore the rules that underpin how banks are required to tabulate such ratios and thus ignore one of the key areas of cross-border regulatory advantage – or "non-market" advantage – that banks may compete for when interacting with their domestic supervisors. From a positive political economy perspective, the absence of a common regulatory approach and language made the detection of capital adequacy policy convergence and divergence very difficult and confounded efforts to learn if financial internationalization produced a global "race to the bottom" through the adoption of a common, lax regulatory standard or increased prudential oversight.

Two methodologies will be employed to address these questions. First, univariate statistical analysis will be employed to determine the degree of implementation severity that emerged in a large sample of industrialized states that committed to the Basel Accord in 1988. A quantitative index of implementation will be constructed to provide numerical comparisons of the degrees of implementation stringency for the sample states. This index is constructed from two under-utilized studies of Accord's implementation produced by PriceWaterhouse (1991) and Murray-Jones and Gamble (1991) and documentation provided by G-10 and European Union (EU) regulators. In addition to presenting data for a cross-section of states, the index will provide implementation data across a period of time. It will thus be possible to judge whether there has been a convergence in Basel rule interpretations from 1988 to 2000, about the time that the Basel II discussions launched.

Qualitative case studies will accompany this quantitative analysis. These cases allow for a much more empirically detailed examination of rule implementation. This will be provided in a selection of focused, comparison case studies of the United States (Chapter 6), France and Germany (Chapter 7), and Japan (Chapter 8). Each case country study will provide data of the country's pre-Basel Accord capital adequacy rules and their interpretations of the Accord from 1988 to 2000. Though the quantitative indicators seek to be exhaustive in capturing the empirical phenomena of rule implementation, there are several regulatory issue areas that are difficult to capture with quantitative measures. As will be made clear, the implementation of the Basel rules, and capital adequacy regulation more generally, is quite complex. Some elements that can affect the severity of capital regulation are difficult to directly observe. Moreover, as Tamura (2003a:2) observed, evaluating implementation "requires a considerable element of judgment about compliance – the degree to which national regulators adhere to the spirit of an international regulatory accord." The case studies afford such a close "on the ground" inspection of some of the more complex elements of Basel rule implementation.

Beyond providing these descriptive data on the content of Basel rule interpretations, however, this book endeavors to address the question of why did some countries adopt strict interpretations of the Basel Accord while other countries adopted more lax approaches. Another way to address this question is why has there been convergence among some states' capital adequacy regime rules over time but not others? Adding to the two questions posed above, the two questions addressed here are:

3   Why did states adopt loose or strict interpretations of the broad "soft law" provisions of the Accord?
4   What led states to increase or reduce the stringency of their initial interpretations of the Accord over a 12-year period of time (1988–2000)?

As before, quantitative and qualitative methodologies will be employed to address these questions. Econometric tests of a battery of hypotheses will be made in an effort to understand some explanations for the uneven amounts of implementation over the sample time period, 1988–2000. In these analyses, the implementation index, described above, will constitute the dependent variable and measures of statistical association will be generated between it and a number of explanatory variables generated by the hypotheses.

These "why" questions will also be investigated in the case studies of the United States, France, Germany, and Japan. Given the difficulties in determining the convergence of results from different research strategies in studies employing triangulation techniques, the case studies will not test the exact theories tested in the quantitative exercise but will use the regression results as a guide to exploring the rich empirical detail behind the implementation of the Basel Accord.

The hypotheses are drawn from a wide spectrum of approaches to public policy implementation. Relying on a previous study of the implementation of the Accord, a battery of hypothesis is collected that predicts implementation will vary by four domestic and international attributes:[14]

1 domestic bank preferences;
2 macroeconomic environment;
3 domestic political institutions;
4 international imitation effects.

By addressing the *why* questions, this book is positioned to generate insights into two significant political economy problems. By providing an understanding of the conditions for strict versus liberal forms of interpretation of the Basel rules, it highlights those variables that might be significant for understanding the implementation of international regimes. Second, by looking at the extent of rule convergence over time, this book sheds light on the applicability of policy convergence and divergence theories. The key theoretical contribution of this book is the testing of theories from these distinct, though highly related, political economics research programs.

Moreover, this book suggests that some improvement is necessary to the study of international regime implementation. Most existing approaches to the topic seek to understand why states commit or defect from their international commitments. The process of compliance is characterized as a binary phenomenon: states either comply or they do not. Little consideration is paid to whether states substantially fail to comply or fail in small respects, or whether committed states simply meet the minimum international standards or adopt superequivalent interpretations. I suggest that implementation studies may have failed to come to grips with some of the key issues of regime implementation through this dichotomy.

For many international agreements, it is necessary to focus less on *whether* states comply and more on understanding *how* they comply. This shift in perspective would probably yield important empirical and theoretical insights for all forms of international agreement. Yet, it is mandatory in the study of non-binding agreements or what have been termed "international soft law." Such agreements very often do not require states to implement a discrete series of rules, but suggest a vague string of "best practices" to be adopted on a voluntary basis. For such agreements, discussing compliance in terms of commitment or defection is not as empirically useful as understanding how states have interpreted such agreements and in what way such agreements are operationalized in domestic law and regulatory statute.

This book concurs with previous research in concluding that the Basel Accord is an example of such soft law.[15] The Accord is not enforceable by law. It does not create a discrete selection of hard and fast rules. Rather, it provides a minimum regulatory baseline that states should follow and invites states to implement stricter interpretations. It is thus necessary to look at *degrees* of compliance with the Accord rather than *if* the Accord has produced commitment.

In sum, the book thus hopes to contribute to the corpus of empirical data concerning the effects of the Basel Accord and international and comparative political economic theories of regime implementation and cross-border policy convergence and divergence. Specifically, the book endeavors to enumerate the following empirical and theoretical innovations to the study of banking regulation and political economy:

- Present the first cross-sectional comparison of the ways that the Basel rules were interpreted with a quantitative measure that permits a clear study of areas of regulatory convergence and divergence.
- Lay out the ways in which the interpretations of the Basel rules have changed over time with data not utilized in previous studies of the Basel implementation process.
- Test theories of international regime implementation and policy convergence in an issue area – finance – that has not been extensively considered in previous academic studies.

It is also necessary to enumerate what the book will not attempt to accomplish. In laying out these areas of potential empirical investigation, it should be made clear that it is not claimed that this study will not touch upon these areas in some respects. In the process of investigating the implementation of the 1988 Accord, these areas may well come under direct or indirect study. Yet, these areas of research are not involved in the central questions of interest to this book and no effort is made to thoroughly "tie up all the loose ends" as far as these areas of study are concerned.

First, the book will not attempt to systematically judge the effects of degrees of compliance on commercial bank behavior or profitability nor on systemic financial stability and soundness. With regards the former, some qualitative analysis will be provided on the effects of the Accord on internationally active banks. Yet, sorting out the relative importance of capital adequacy policy to the day-to-day decision-making of banks and their profitability is complex.[16] Econometric studies devoted solely to this question have failed to produce robust results that are stable across various specifications.[17] Similarly, it is difficult to measure the independent impact of the Accord generally (much less individual state's interpretations) on financial stability or macroeconomic soundness.

Second, it will not extensively address the major amendments that have been made to the Accord. The Basel Committee and the EU have issued numerous

Introduction 7

updates and regulatory interpretations and re-interpretations to the original 1988 agreement. As the timeline in Figure 1.1 illustrates, three amendments were made from 1991 to 1996 until the Basel II negotiations commenced in 1999. The first two of these amendments (1991 and 1995) were relatively minor adjustments to the original Accord. They did not alter the original 1988 formulation to any great degree nor court political controversy. However, the 1996 decision to expand the scope of the Accord to international banks' market risk exposures was significant. In addition to incorporating a whole new area of bank activity into the Accord's purview, this amendment deviated from the 1988 document by permitting some (quite sophisticated) banks to utilize their own risk management modeling systems to establish their own, tailor-made risk charges, subject to stringent regulatory parameters.[18]

Despite the importance of this amendment, it will be generally ignored for three reasons. First, some research indicates that the 1988 Accord effected a much larger change on existing regulator and bank practice than the 1996 amendment. In a Bank of England study entitled "Fallacies about the Effects of Market Risk Management Systems," it is argued that the market exposure requirements did not pose so large a challenge to bankers as it often believed.[19] Second, financial regulators and practitioners are mostly in agreement that credit risk is by far the largest nominal risk in banking and focusing solely on such a

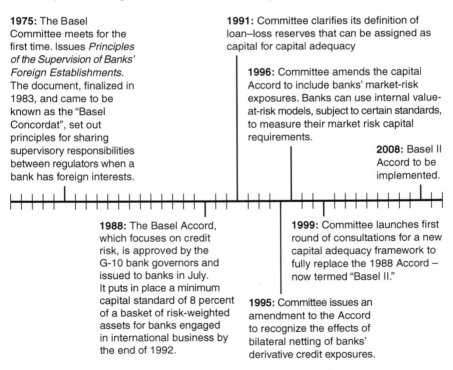

Figure 1.1 The evolution of the Basel Committee and Capital Adequacy Regulation (source: adapted from Ferry (2003: 54–55)).

risk is justified.[20] Finally, the focus remains firmly on credit risk in order to keep this study tractable. The aim here is to complete a tight comparison of the effects of the 1988 Accord on capital adequacy policy in developed economies. This goal is facilitated by focusing on one international agreement over a fixed period of time. Introducing a second agreement with a shorter implementation time period (1996–2000) may confound the comparative tightness being sought.

Book organization

The research results will be presented in a cumulative fashion. Chapter 2 provides a brief history of the Basel Accord's negotiation. The aim will not be to simply retell these events, but to re-cast them from a new perspective. It is argued that previous considerations of the Accord's negotiation have, implicitly, assumed that the Accord created a hard law standard. By taking account of the Accord's soft law nature, a novel conclusion may be reached on the politics of the agreement's negotiation. Thus, in addition to laying a historical base for the remainder of the research findings on implementation, Chapter 2 contributes to a more empirically accurate account of the agreement's negotiation than has been presented in some of the political economy literature.

Chapter 3 presents a theoretical discussion of the implementation of international soft law. It suggests that existing approaches to international cooperation are unnecessarily crude by dichotomizing the implementation process and a method of assessing degrees of compliance is proposed. This method permits researchers to bring together disparate hypotheses of policy implementation and transnational policy convergence and divergence together in a single, theoretical platform. This method will then be employed to present a number of hypotheses concerning the implementation of the Basel Accord.

Chapters 4 and 5 will subject these hypotheses to statistical examination. Chapter 4 will operationalize and generate descriptive statistics for quantitative measures of implementation with the Accord and a variety of explanatory variables that are suggested by the hypotheses. The descriptive statistics will be utilized in the univariate testing of a number of the hypotheses. Chapter 5 will provide econometric tests.

Chapters 6–8 will utilize the aggregate results to guide structured, focused comparison case studies of implementation in the United States, France, Germany, and Japan. The case studies will use the econometric results as a guide to exploring the rich empirical detail behind compliance with the Basel Accord. Applied in sequence, the quantitative and qualitative studies each contribute differing strengths to the testing of the hypotheses that have been laid out. The quantitative element provides a broad understanding of implementation and permits the forming of generalizable conclusions about the types and correlates of implementation that have occurred. Yet, given the crude operationalization of many social science variables, it is useful to have a more refined account of implementation in a number of states. Though conclusions made about each case may not necessarily be generalizable, it will be possible to elaborate on the quantitative tests.

Part I
Historical and theoretical perspectives on the 1988 Basel Accord

2 The political economy of the negotiation of the 1988 Basel Accord as a soft law agreement

Introduction

The 1988 Basel Accord established an extraordinary international financial regime. Though negotiated by the G-10 states, and Luxembourg and Switzerland, the Accord had been implemented in over 100 countries by the late 1990s.[1] This diffusion of the Basel capital adequacy standard proceeded in developed and developing economies despite the absence of an enforcement mechanism or a systematic political effort to encourage the Accord's wide-spread adoption.[2] Though bankers and economists have criticized the Accord since its inception, it has become a qualitative and quantitative standard that financial services regulators worldwide want to be seen to be enforcing, and with which banks want to be in compliance.[3]

Yet, the creation of the Accord was an arduous seven-year process that nearly did not succeed. Discussions among the G-10 central bankers, meeting as the BCBS, persisted for over a decade before the agreement was concluded in July 1988. A consensus was difficult to reach as the negotiating states maintained very distinct capital adequacy regimes with divergent definitions of capital, unique capital regulatory vocabularies, and diverse national goals for their bank regulatory policies that were difficult to reconcile. In addition to these technical impediments, the members of the Basel Committee were placed under enormous political pressures by their constituent commercial banks to negotiate a position consistent with their economic interests – in most instances, this was a path-dependent position that would allow the maintenance of their regulatory status quo.

Political economists' explanations for the successful conclusion to the Basel negotiations have fallen into two groups. The first suggests that the Accord solved an international market failure resulting from the increasing internationalization of the banking business. By the late 1980s, it was clear that regulators were less able to effectively ensure the prudential security and international competitiveness of their domestic banks and thus needed to establish an inter-state agreement to reinforce their regulatory competence. This line of thought concludes that the Accord provided joint gains to all G-10 states.[4]

The opposing argument suggests that the Accord resulted from the exercise of financial power by the United States and, to a lesser degree, the United Kingdom. These two states grew impatient with the slow negotiation process and they gave dissenting states, especially France, Germany, and Japan an ultimatum in 1987: if they did not agree to their version of the Accord, then their domestic banks may find themselves unable to secure or renew operating licenses in New York or London. In this scenario, the Accord produced wealth gains for American and British banks at the expense of their international competitors. Drawing from theories of regulatory capture, this argument concludes that the Accord produced a wealth re-distributive regime.[5]

This chapter suggests that both of these perspectives are empirically inaccurate and provides a third account that is more consistent with the painstaking compromises that permitted the Accord's negotiation. Following the arguments of international legal scholars, I show that extant political economy explanations fail to consider the "soft law" characteristics of the Basel Accord.[6] The joint-gains and wealth distribution arguments implicitly assume that the Accord created a discrete selection of rules that committing states were required to meet. In practice, the Accord only set out a minimum selection of baseline regulations and permitted national regulators to exercise wide discretion for interpretation and implementation. States had the possibility of "fitting" their existing regulatory structure within the Accord's wide parameters and comply with the agreement without undergoing as much reform as some have suggested. I argue that by not considering these soft law characteristics, the existing approaches present a misleading picture of the Accord's history and draw erroneous conclusions about the agreement's ability to distribute symmetrical or asymmetrical gains. In doing so, I recommend that studies of international regime implementation turn their attention to the diverse "degrees of compliance" that can emerge from non-binding agreements.

This chapter begins by briefly describing the Accord's negotiation process and enumerating the distinct negotiating positions of the Basel Committee members. These negotiating positions, it will be shown, were highly influenced by the Committee member states' desires to maintain their extant capital adequacy regulations and ensure that the Accord required as little domestic regulatory change as possible. In presenting these negotiating positions, this chapter makes the first academic effort to systematically compare the pre-Basel Accord capital adequacy regulations of the G-10 economies.

Next, this chapter will challenge both political economy explanations for the Accord's negotiation. The rudiments of the joint-gains and wealth redistribution arguments are presented and challenged by explicitly considering the Accord's "soft law" characteristics. It is suggested that by looking at the way the agreement structured the implementation process, it is necessary to re-cast the story of the Accord's negotiation. By considering the potential for compliant states to maintain widely differing capital adequacy regimes, the existing theories must be qualified. This conclusion will be supported through the presentation of comparative legal and econometric studies.

Negotiation of the 1988 Basel Accord

The Basel Accord was negotiated by the G-10 central bankers and bank supervisors to accomplish two objectives.[7] First, it endeavored to increase the stability and financial soundness of these countries' internationally active commercial banks. Second, it sought to induce inter-state regulatory convergence and moderate sources of competitive regulatory advantages for commercial banks. Concerns for the former arose from the intensification of international bank competition from the late 1970s. During this time, the coalescence of technological, political, and market factors increased the opportunity costs of providing traditional financial intermediary services exclusively to the domestic marketplace. Though variations persisted among industrialized states, large commercial banks expanded their geographical and product offerings. Branching extended internationally as banks followed their multinational clients abroad, pursued foreign market shares, and sought to arbitrage the inter-state regulatory regime in search of competitive advantages.[8] Banks diversified their income streams through the issue of new products, many of which did not appear on the balance sheet ["off-balance sheet" (OBS) business] and were consequently unaccounted for in many states' regulatory exam procedures.[9]

The result was the increasing fragility of the G-10's largest banks. The intensification of trans-border competition squeezed profit margins and pressured bank managers to seek out riskier investments in order to increase revenues.[10] In the best of market environments, commercial banks seek out risky investments to remain competitive and solvent. As financial analyst Dominic Casserley observed:

> Most businesses shun risk ... they try and pass on their financial risk to others so that they can concentrate on making and selling their products. To succeed, however, financial firms must seek out risk. In nearly all their businesses, by being able to separate well-priced from underpriced risks, they can prosper. By avoiding all risk, however, they cease to be financial firms at all and will wither away.[11]

Yet, the competitive environment of the late 1970s and 1980s led international commercial banks to engage in a wide range of, what could now be regarded as, poorly priced risk-taking.

In particular, this has been observed in the types and extent of loans advanced to lesser-developed economies during the 1970s. The recycling of Organization of Petroleum Exporting Countries' (OPEC) petrodollars through the Eurocurrency markets left G-10 banks with large loan exposures to lesser-developed country (LDC) governments by the early 1980s. American banks generated the largest exposures, ranging from about 100–200 percent of their capital. British and Japanese banks were second and third with exposures of 80 percent and 50 percent of their capital, respectively.[12] As Figure 2.1 shows, the ratio of capital-to-assets, an important measure of bank soundness, steadily decreased in many industrialized states in the decade leading up to 1988, though the broader picture

14 Historical and theoretical perspectives

is fairly mixed. Banks' capital levels are neither an indicator of financial health nor a sufficient measure of bank stability, yet they have become a key benchmark with which the market and regulators judge financial institutions' ability to withstand adverse economic shocks and manage risks.[13] As a result, the BCBS issued a paper concluding:

> that in the current and prospective environment further erosion of capital should, on prudential grounds, be resisted and that, in the absence of common standards of capital adequacy, supervisors should not allow the capital resources of their major banks to deteriorate from their present level, whatever those levels may be.[14]

The second objective of the Accord was to ameliorate many of the prudential regulatory distinctions between states. The multi-nationalization of banking complicated the task of prudential bank regulation. Domestic bank supervisors

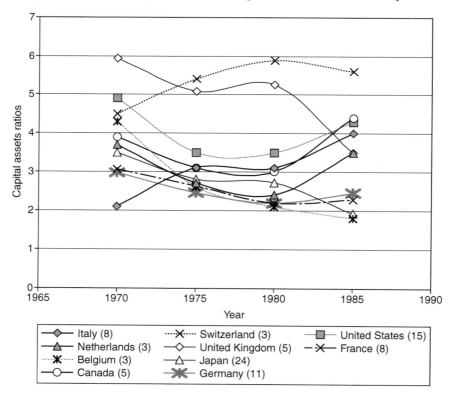

Figure 2.1 G-10 banks' capital asset ratios, 1970–1985 (source: compiled from data in *The Banker*, various issues).

Notes
Numbers in parentheses refer to the number of banks sampled; capital defined as common stock, disclosed reserves, and retained earnings.

could now inspect and regulate only a limited part of an international banking network.[15] As Peter Cooke of the Bank of England observed in 1981, "supervisors were still very much domestically oriented within the framework of different national banking systems."[16] The absence of an international institution to facilitate information exchange between bank regulators is believed to have conferred information asymmetry advantages to banks. With this superior information, many banks may have been able to build large risk exposures that no single regulator was able to detect.

In addition, many G-10 regulators believed that the absence of a supranational regulatory regime permitted states to confer regulatory advantages upon their domestic banks.[17] In this view, some states' regulators, commercial banks, and perhaps politicians, colluded to implement comparatively lax prudential standards that permitted their banks to outperform their international competitors. Though evidence for this position is difficult to establish, many American politicians and bankers believed that the Japanese and French banks were successfully leveraging relatively weak credit risk regulations to build positions unattainable in the United States due to the more demanding solvency requirements imposed by the American regulators. Thus in an effort to address this source of regulatory competitive disadvantage, the United States supported the creation of a multilateral standard to create a level regulatory playing field.

In order to address these concerns, the G-10's central bankers initiated discussions for an international capital adequacy standard in 1981. They met, with representatives of Luxembourg and Switzerland, as an informal group now termed the BCBS at the Bank for International Settlements (BIS) in Basel, Switzerland. This committee set to work devising a multilateral bank capital standard. Though capital adequacy regulation is among the most critical component of any state's prudential regulatory system, there were and remain great distinctions in the way states implement such rules.[18] Recognizing this, the BCBS did not attempt formal legal harmonization but "greater convergence among its members with regard to national definitions of bank capital for supervisory purposes."[19]

This initiated a seven-year negotiation process. During this time, the Committee established numerous complex methodologies for constructing a common standard able to incorporate the particularities of each G-10 state's capital adequacy regime into a unified framework. Establishing a "functional equivalents" scheme presented many technical difficulties.[20] As Table 2.1 shows, there were sharp distinctions in the G-10 states' definitions of capital and the way they derived capital regulations. The Basel Committee does not have any formal enforcement authority and approves of measures on the basis of unanimity and it was thus necessary to construct an agreement that did not diverge too significantly from any one state's extant regime to secure approval. The result was a slow and deliberate negotiation process. Resolution was confounded by the technical difficulties of constructing a common standard and the intense political pressure that domestic banks placed on their regulators to adopt a standard convergent with their current practices and interests.

Efforts to conclude an agreement were boosted by the urgency created by the

Table 2.1 Comparison of 11 states' pre-Basel Capital Adequacy Regulations

	Belgium	Canada	France	Italy	Japan
Definition of capital	• Common equity • Published and hidden reserves • Retained earnings • General provisions • Limited subordinated debt	• Common equity • Permanent preferred stock • Convertible preferred stock • Limited subordinated debt	• Share capital • Reserves • General provisions • Unlimited subordinated debt	• Disclosed reserves • General provisions • Subordinated debt for some banks	• Equity capital • Reserves
Are assets risk-weighted?	Yes	No	Yes	No	No
Minimum capital ratio	Varies between 5–7.5%	Gross assets should not exceed 30–20 times total capital	5% requirements	Variety of different debt	No minimum ratio

	Luxembourg	Switzerland	UK	US	West Germany
Definition of capital	• Share capital • Reserves • Retained earnings • General provisions debt • Limited subordinated debt	• Paid up capital • Published reserves • Limited subordinated debt • General bad debt provisions	• Share capital • Reserves • Limited subordinated • Contingency rights capital reserves • Limited subordinated	• Common stock • Preferred stock • Profits • Profit participation	• Equity capital • Retained surpluses • Silent capital contributions
Are assets risk-weighted?	No	Yes	Yes	No	Yes
Minimum capital ratio	Range of 3–10%	Varies	Varies	5% requirement	Variety, including a 5.6% minimum

Source: Derived from data in Dale (1984).

LDC debt crisis, beginning in August 1982. This crisis prompted much criticism of the BCBS for its failure to anticipate and prevent the expansion of G-10 lending that led to the crisis. Most importantly, the crisis was partly responsible for the US Congress' decision to issue the International Lending Supervision Act (ILSA) in 1983 that demanded that its banking regulators arrange for the conclusion of the multilateral capital adequacy negotiations while implementing a stricter domestic capital code. With this new political impetus, US Federal Reserve chairman Paul Volcker placed pressure on the Committee to conclude some sort of agreement. The initial effect was continued delay. An October 1986 Committee paper concluded that, "[o]ver time, *it is hoped* that the exercise will assist in determining the *divergence* between the capital positions of different national banking systems."[21] This lack of progress did not impress Volcker or the US Congress.

The US–UK Accord

The result of the deadlock in Basel was Volcker's decision to establish a bilateral capital adequacy agreement with the United Kingdom in July 1986. Volcker approached the Bank of England governor, Robin Leigh-Pemberton, regarding a bilateral accord that circumvented the Basel negotiation processes. The United Kingdom was in the process of overhauling their domestic capital rules to incorporate banks' OBS risks and quickly agreed to establish a bilateral standard. The process of coordinating these two states' capital adequacy standards was relatively straightforward. Beyond the fact that coordinating two states' policies is more easily accomplished than coordinating those of 12, the US and the UK rules had several common features. In particular, each state's regulators recognized the need for a risk-weighted capital adequacy standard.[22] Though the United States did not have a risk-weighting approach in place during the Basel negotiations, such an approach had been utilized in the past and was under consideration after the LDC crisis.[23]

The remaining distinctions between the US and the UK practices were dealt with through a mutual recognition compromise. Each state allowed its domestic banks to maintain some forms of capital that the other did not recognize. In particular, Table 2.1 shows that the Bank of England included general bad debt provisions while some American regulators recognized almost unlimited preferred stock as regulatory capital. Neither regulator would expand its definition of regulatory capital to incorporate the other's idiosyncrasies. A solution was found by creating a two-tier capital measurement scale. The first tier (termed "capital included without limits") included those capital elements that the United States and the United Kingdom agreed were of a high quality and thus readily available to meet bank losses. The second ("capital included with limits") included capital instruments that could meet bank losses, yet not as readily as top-tier items. To ensure that banks' capital bases contained more high-quality capital, it was stipulated that Tier2 capital could not exceed 50 percent of the total items included in Tier1. The disputed capital instruments were, for the most

18 *Historical and theoretical perspectives*

part, allocated to the second tier and each state was free to interpret the agreement as they chose within the parameters, see Table 2.2.[24] In this way, the United States and the United Kingdom agreed on a capital accord that emphasized a common and high-quality definition of capital and yet allowed each state to include its own unique forms of capital.

Looked at strategically, the key importance of the US/UK Accord was the political economic pressure it exerted on BCBS members to conclude a multilateral agreement. The announcement of the bilateral accord was described as a "bombshell" by one regulator.[25] In particular, EC member states were concerned that the United Kingdom was circumventing parallel efforts to construct a common European solvency standard within the EC Banking Advisory Committee (BAC). Also, many Europeans resented the fact that they had been informed of the agreement only one day before it was made public; some even argued that Britain could be in violation of the 1958 Rome Treaty.[26]

Such fears were exacerbated when Japan initiated discussions to opt into the standard in late 1986. The US Congress had long expressed fears that Japan's weak capital standard had facilitated their banks' success in penetrating the US financial services market in the 1980s. It is not unambiguously clear that Japan's definition of capital supports this view, yet their capital-to-assets ratios were among the lowest in the G-10. The leading Japanese banks' ratios averaged just over 2 percent in the mid-1980s compared to a 5 percent average ratio for American banks, when these ratios are constructed with common definitions of capital as in Figure 2.1. Perhaps fearing that this US–UK agreement could result in the sanctioning of banks that did not comply with it, the Ministry of Finance (MOF) and the Bank of Japan (BOJ) sought to opt-in on the assumption that elements of their unique capital regulations would be incorporated into the two-tier structure, just as the United States' and the United Kingdom's rules had been fused. In particular, Japan sought to include its unrealized capital gains into the agreement, an important component of Japanese banks' capital base. Negotiations on this point were prolonged as the United States and the United Kingdom resisted these reserves' inclusions given the potential volatility of their value. Yet, by September 1987, the capital regulation philosophies of the United States, the United Kingdom, and Japan converged sufficiently for them to adopt a single negotiating position at Basel.

Negotiation of the Basel Accord

The first draft of the Basel Accord was issued three months after the announcement of the bilateral accord. There has been some debate on the effects of the bilateral (and with Japan, the trilateral) Accord on the Basel process. Some argue that the Accord was a catalyst for the finalization of the international negotiations,[27] while others suggest that the December 1987 announcement would have been forthcoming without the bilateral standard and that the US/UK proposal served only to aggravate tension and disagreement.[28] It may be difficult to definitively conclude which position is correct, yet there seems to be little doubt that the 1986 accord significantly shaped the way that a Basel, and Brussels, solution emerged.

In particular, the Basel Accord resolved committee disagreements by adopting a two-tiered mutual recognition framework. The final Basel Accord was issued in July 1988 after several rounds of industry and inter-state consultation. The agreement entered a transition stage from 1988 to 1992 and was to be fully implemented from 1 January 1993. The agreed definition of allowable capital, see Table 2.2, was bifurcated into two tiers with the same 50 percent restrictions imposed on the quantity of Tier2 versus Tier1 capital as the 1986 standard. The most noticeable distinction between the two accords is that while the two standards roughly permit the same number of capital instruments (about seven), most of the 1986 Tier1 items were relegated to Tier2 status. It is generally held that this reorganization is the result of the German Bundesbank's objection that the 1986 Accord permitted an excessively weak definition of capital. German banks were subject to a very strict definition of capital and German regulators worried that they would have to loosen their standards or be competitively disadvantaged. The compromise was to include the various "weaker" capital types, yet limit their use through the Tier2 classification.[29]

Also, this two-tiered framework permitted a resolution to be reached by allowing each regulator to "fit" their extant regulatory practices into the international code. By comparing the pre-Basel regime capital practices with the Basel standards, see Table 2.2, it is clear that nearly every state's idiosyncratic capital definition qualified for the Basel standard. The Accord went to great lengths to bring about this congruence. Some elements of hybrid Tier2 capital are included to incorporate the instruments of just one state's capital regime – for example, French *titre participatif* and German *Genusscheine*. For the remaining capital instruments, states were left to include or exclude these instruments at their discretion. The Accord essentially produced a "mutual recognition" framework similar to that produced by European efforts to create a Single Market; this permits states to exercise discretion for implementing policy

Table 2.2 Comparison of the US/UK Accord and Basel Accord Capital Regulations

US–UK Accord	Basel Accord
Capital without limits • Common stock • Retained earnings • Minority interests • General reserves • Hidden reserves	Tier 1 • Common stock • Preferred stock • Disclosed reserves • Retained profits • Minority interests
Capital included with limits • Preferred stock • Subordinated debt	Tier 2 • Undisclosed reserves • Revaluation reserves • General provisions • Subordinated debt

20 *Historical and theoretical perspectives*

tailored to their national circumstances within the confines of a minimalist standard, thus ensuring some degrees of transnational harmonization.

Beyond capital definitions, however, it is not clear to what extent the Accord required significant BCBS change in other areas of capital regulation. The Accord required regulators to comply with three additional standards pertinent to capital adequacy assessment. Banks were required to maintain 4 percent of the value of their assets in Tier1 capital and 8 percent in total (Tier1 + Tier2) capital. Banks were required to multiply their assets (e.g. loans extended to counterparties) by a pre-established multiplier whose value corresponds to the ex ante determination of a counterparty's default risk. These multipliers or "risk-weights" were set out in the Basel Accord. Risk-weights apply for both on-balance sheet and OBS asset classes. To determine how much capital to set aside for a particular loan (on-balance sheet) or letter of credit or derivatives contract (OBS) bank managers determine the product of an asset's value in relation to its risk-weight. A $100 credit to a private sector corporation requires a 100 percent risk-weighting and a bank needs to hold $8 of the value of this loan as a capital adequacy cushion.[30] The 100 percent weight requires that the full value of the 8 percent capital requirement be imposed. Another way of expressing this is to indicate that a corporate loan has to be supported by 8 percent regulatory capital.[31] Yet if the counterparty is a bank domiciled in an Organization for Economic Cooperation and Development (OECD) country, the $100 credit would require only $1.6 regulatory capital as these assets have a 20 percent risk-weighting or a 1.6 percent capital requirement.

Yet, like the definition of capital, some latitude for regulatory discretion was provided for these required ratios and risk-weightings. In particular, the Accord explicitly deemed a selection of asset classes subject to national discretion. Also, like capital definitions and minimum ratios, the Accord encouraged states to implement beyond minimum interpretations wherever possible.

The ability of states to arbitrage these discretionary areas and "fit" their extant capital adequacy regimes into these other areas of the Accord's rules may not be as clear-cut as in the case of capital definitions, yet some elements of this may have indeed been possible. This will be discussed further in later chapters, but many states did not have risk-weighted capital standards before the Basel Accord, but required banks to maintain assets against a less risk sensitive measure of their balance sheets. It is difficult to estimate the regulatory burden of generating a risk-weighting framework across jurisdictions. Yet, many states may not have tinkered too finely with their regimes and indeed Dale's (1984) study of 11 developed economies revealed that about half had implemented risk-capital standards in advance of the 1988 agreement.

Theoretical perspectives on the Basel Accord

As the Accord was one of the first international financial regulatory agreements, it has attracted considerable attention by academics. Political economists have developed two explanations to explain the successful negotiation of the Basel

Accord. Both sets of theory argue that the Accord was successfully negotiated because of the exercise of American – and to a lesser extent, British – financial market power over other G-10 states. Yet, one standpoint argues that the Accord was successfully negotiated because it allowed states to share in joint gains. This argument posits that only an international agreement would allow regulators to meet their twin goals of creating a safe prudential regulatory environment without paralyzing the international competitiveness of their banks.[32] Opposing this conclusion is Oatley and Nabors's (1998) argument that the agreement was purely the result of US economic hegemony. The agreement disadvantaged the majority of the G-10 states and advantaged the United States; the agreement did not produce joint gains.

Joint-gains theory

A common approach to explaining the successful negotiation of the Basel Accord has been to emphasize the mutual benefits realized by all BCBS states from the agreement. This argument draws from Institutionalist theory in International Relations and concludes that the Accord distributed gains for all G-10 states.[33] This argument is grounded in the reasoning that international financial integration had both increased systemic financial risk and reduced the ability of domestic supervisors to ensure the soundness of their banking systems. The result had been the emergence of an international market failure evinced by the LDC debt crisis and the meltdown of the American commercial banking and thrift industries during the 1980s.

Moreover, financial integration increased the opportunity costs for unilateral prudential standard setting. Before the 1980s, cross-country differences in capital adequacy policy were not only justifiable given states' unique financial histories and markets but of little practical relevance so long as banking remained a mostly domestically oriented business. Yet, the internationalization of banking may have caused previously benign distinctions in capital policy to become a new source of competitive advantage or disadvantage. This created the need for a multilateral capital adequacy standard.[34]

The only way to solve this market failure was through collective regulatory action that would be mutually beneficial. Structural forces in the international financial economy created a regulatory demand that required a collective international political response. As Kapstein argued, "[t]o the extent that the payments system had the character of a public good, it was reasonable to ask every state to contribute to its maintenance."[35]

Kapstein (1989) and Singer (2002) argued that the Accord helped G-10 states resolve a common "regulator's dilemma." Each bank regulator must solve a policy dilemma emerging from their conflicting twin objectives: rules must be sufficiently stringent to induce prudential behavior from regulated banks and yet sufficiently lax to prevent domestic banks from losing international competitiveness. The only way that a state can balance these demands is through an international agreement that sets a minimum level of prudential regulatory stringency. This international standard should protect against systemic instability while providing a minimum regulatory floor that permits domestic regulators to set necessary prudential standards without fear of creating competitive disadvantage. In this way, the Basel Accord resolved a mutual problem of the G-10 states and thus the agreement was pareto-optimal.

Redistributive theory

A paper by Oatley and Nabors (1998) disagrees that the Accord benefited all Basel Committee members. They suggest that the United States leveraged upon its large financial markets to impose the Accord on the G-10, particularly Japan and France. The United States designed an international agreement consistent with its interests in order to support the competitive position of its commercial banks, at the expense of their G-10 competitors.

Oatley and Nabors begin by observing that states may wield asymmetric negotiating authority in international negotiations. They concur that inter-state regimes can produce joint gains, yet only if two conditions hold: the agreements must be approved by unanimity and no state has the ability to manipulate the choice set of its negotiating partners. Drawing from public choice theory, they advance Mueller's argument that, "an individual who can control the agenda of pair-wise votes can lead the committee to any outcome in the issue space he desires."[36] States propose and support international agreements only if they benefit their domestic interests, in this way regimes produce joint gains or they do not exist. Yet if a state can successfully manipulate the choice set of another negotiating state, or establish a punishment mechanism for non-cooperation, it can force the others to join regimes contrary to its domestic interests. These regimes have the potential to redistribute gains from one state to another and are thus pareto-inoptimal for some committing states.

This logic is best explained through empirical application. Oatley and Nabors argue that the Accord was not in the interests of many BCBS members. To empirically establish this position, they conduct a comparative analysis of the pre-Basel CARs of a panel of French, Belgian, German, Italian, British, American, and Japanese banks from 1981 to 1987. It is argued that the Accord set a minimum ratio more in line with those of American banks than French or Japanese banks. In their panel, US banks have an average capital ratio of 4.31 percent, while French and Japanese ratios averaged 1.87 and 2.52 percent, respectively. From this, the authors conclude that, "[h]armonized capital adequacy therefore represented a negative transfer of banking income."[37] The empirical puzzle for these authors is, how did such a redistributive outcome emerge?

The answer is that the United States successfully coerced France, Japan, and other recalcitrant G-10 states to agree to the Accord. American regulators had to solve a regulator's dilemma that was created by the need to implement stricter capital standards, after the LDC crisis, without disadvantaging the competitiveness of US banks. When the Basel Committee's negotiations stalled in the mid-1980s, the Federal Reserve responded with the formation of a regulatory duopoly, as Pattison (2006) termed it, with the Bank of England by negotiating the bilateral Accord.[38] Given the importance of the New York and London financial markets, this Accord narrowed the choice sets of other G-10 states so that they did not have any option but to agree to sign the Basel agreement.

If French, Japanese, and other G-10 regulators failed to acquiesce to a multilateral capital standard, they risked their banks' exclusion from the British and American markets. Oatley and Nabors note that "[b]y concluding a stringent bilateral accord with Great Britain and threatening to apply the terms of this accord to foreign banks operating in the U.S. market, American policymakers effectively eliminated the regulatory status quo from G-10 policymakers' choice sets."[39] The only choice thus left for the Committee was to agree to a multilateral standard that would enable them to moderate the terms of the US/UK standards in a way that would not entirely disadvantage them.

This strategy was successful. Japan was first to succumb, given their already rocky relations with US regulators. Shortly thereafter, the Accord was concluded as France, Germany, and others agreed to a compromise solution to avoid US and UK sanctions. The result was the creation of an international regulatory regime that provided asymmetric gains for a subset of the G-10 at the expense of others.

Basel Accord as international soft law

Yet, the joint gains and redistributive views of the Basel Accord both fail to take stock of the soft law nature of the agreement. They implicitly assume that the Accord established a discrete selection of "hard law" bank regulatory guidelines that counterparties to the agreement must implement to be in compliance. This position provides an inaccurate portrayal of the way the Accord was structured and the rules that guided its implementation. A more empirically faithful exposition of how the Accord was negotiated must directly address its soft law qualities, particularly those relating to the high level of discretion permitted in the 1988 agreement. Research must be focused on the way the Accord was to be implemented to more fully appreciate its negotiation.

The failure of most political economists to address the Accord's soft law characteristics may be the result of the ambiguities inherent in the soft versus hard dichotomy. Generally, the term "soft" is employed to refer to those forms of domestic or inter-state law or simply norms that are non-binding or are not enforced with some form of punishment mechanism. More simply, Alexander (2000b:3) observes that, "[s]oft law generally presumes consent to basic standards and norms of state practice, but without the *opinio juris* necessary to form binding obligations under customary international law." Yet very often, soft law will be employed in tandem with "harder" or enforced norms or used as a "precursor to hard law or as a supplement to a hard law instrument ... [s]oft law instruments often serve to allow treaty parties to authoritatively resolve ambiguities in the text or fill in gaps."[40] The distinction between the two may blur in such cases. The vagueness of the term may be pronounced in the study of international law as the absence of a supranational political structure may render all agreements soft to one degree or another.[41]

Yet, there are some standard indicators with which to classify international law as possessing more "soft" versus "hard" characteristics. Alexander (2000b) highlights that legalization is better characterized as a multidimensional continuum rather than a dichotomous quality.[42] Domestic and international legal standards vary from the ideal types "no law" to full "hard law." Placement in this continuum, between these end points, is determined by the extent to which a law *obligates* agents to adhere to *precise* standards and *delegates* a third-party authority (i.e. a court) to resolve disputes and issue rule interpretations. These three variables are maximized in full hard law, fully absent in the instance of no law, and present in varying degrees and combinations in softer legalization types.

By these standards, the Basel Accord represents a fairly "soft" example of soft law. The Basel Committee does not possess any legal enforcement authority and states comply with the Accord at their own discretion. Beyond this, the Accord created, what could be termed, a soft law set of norms. The Accord established what a World Bank study termed a "minimum harmonization" or baseline of rules that states must adopt, yet provided a high degree of national discretion for interpreting these rules into their national banking regulations and codes.[43] In this sense, the Accord achieved what Woolcock (1996) referred to as "constructive ambiguity" in the context of EU standard setting. Like European standards permitting "subsidiarity," the Accord is constructive in the sense of enabling states with very different policies to sign up for a single unifying standard. A balance is struck between the harmonization and persistent competition of rules.[44] As a result, the Accord is perhaps not only a soft law in the sense of being non-binding but a "softer" version of soft law for not establishing a clear criterion by which to measure implementation.[45]

Woolcock (1996) highlighted a number of practical advantages to such soft law agreements. In a discussion of the rules underpinning the European effort to create a Single Market, he observed that providing high levels of national discretion within international agreements permits a "constructive ambiguity" by allowing governments with very different views of the role of regulation to agree to some form of common framework. In some instances, this form of loose confederation of rule making may represent a "radical, open-ended alternative to harmonization which allows a market for regulation to reflect divergent national (or sub-national) preferences for public goods" while allowing some degree of international rule competition.[46]

In addition, explicitly considering such "soft law" characteristics permits the advancement of a key theoretical challenge to the conclusions reached by orthodox political economy explanations for the Accord's negotiation. A necessary assumption of the regulator's dilemma model is that the Accord produced some transnational regulatory convergence. If this assumption is violated and states adopt widely distinct interpretations of the Accord's provisions, the dilemma persists. Measuring how much convergence is required to qualify as sufficient to affect a successful escape from the dilemma is probably neither possible nor necessary. The regulator's dilemma is more a theoretical exercise than a tool subject to empirical falsification: operationalizing the constituent variables such as too much regulatory stringency or laxity are likely impossible except through ex post empirical analyses. Therefore, it is not possible to conclude that persistent divergence in the Accord's application would exacerbate the regulator's dilemma. This would provide a key qualification to the joint-gains argument.

Similar qualifications can be applied to the redistributive argument. Concluding that the Accord distributed wealth from one subset of the G-10 to another seems to again assume that a common standard was imposed. Yet if the Accord did not substantially alter the risk-capital regulations of the French or Japanese authorities, how can this argument be justified? Moreover, the Accord did not address many policy elements that influence the stringency of capital adequacy regulation. Scott and Iwahara (1994) and Scott (1995) illustrate that the Accord could not create a level playing field as it failed to harmonize regulations concerning the way banks provision for doubtful loans, the accounting and tax procedures with which banks measure capital, the way that capital adequacy policy is enforced, and the implicit or explicit government bail out policy for troubled banks. They found that achieving convergence in the definition of capital and a common capital-to-assets policy could ultimately produce a more uneven regulatory playing field if these other policy areas were not also harmonized.

Oatley and Nabors do not support their position with detailed econometric estimations of the determinants of cross-national bank profitability under the Accord's procedures. In fact, the only statistical component of their analysis is a cross-national comparison of the capital assets ratios of an extremely small sample of 14 G-10 banks. The authors drew conclusions about the relative capitalization of the BCBS banks through the data of one French bank, three Japanese, and three American. I will argue later that this small sample is empirically unrepresentative and leads to the drawing of inaccurate inferences. Yet, if persistent divergence were found, it would also present some severe qualifications and perhaps a theoretical challenge to the hegemonic argument of the Accord's negotiation.

Admittedly, stronger support for these conclusions about the influence of the soft law provisions would require evidence that the uneven implementation of the Accord independently influenced banks' balance sheets. It would be helpful to know if there has been convergence and whether degrees of convergence of divergence matters for bank profitability and lending decisions. Do banks actually win or lose from the implementation of strong or lax capital adequacy rules?

Theoretical and empirical treatments from financial economics literature have concluded that capital standards can influence the profitability of banks. One of the crucial goals of bank managers is to maximize their asset profitability, or return on assets. The value of this profitability may be derived from the expression:

$$P/A = P/E \times E/A$$

where P = profits; A = average level of assets; E = equity capital base.

26 *Historical and theoretical perspectives*

If banks are required to hold more equity per their average level of assets (E/A) – or a strict interpretation of a capital adequacy standard – this will require the increase in the return-on-assets (with implications for product pricing) or lower the return on equity to the disadvantage of shareholders and the future supply of equity capital. As a consequence, the imposition of a stricter definition of Tier1 capital or a higher capital requirement can impair the profitability of banks and the smooth functioning of a banking system.

Econometric studies of these theoretical propositions have produced mixed results. A Basel Committee review of six studies on the effects of the Basel Accord on commercial banks' stock prices indicated that about half found significant effects.[47] Yet four of these studies employed panel data of US banks only. Among the two that incorporated banks from a variety of BCBS members, both found that asymmetric interpretations of the Basel rules may have produced wealth gains for some states.[48] Wagster's (1996) study provided the interesting conclusion that Japanese banks realized a cumulative wealth gain of 32 percent.

Yet there are empirical weaknesses in these econometric studies. First, these studies only look at the implementation of the Accord up to the very early 1990s. As such, these studies do not address the effects of the Basel rules over the majority of the implementation period and do not consider the impact of reformulations of Basel rule interpretations over time. Also, these studies employ crude indicators of states' interpretations of the Basel Accord's provisions. The common method has been to rely on newspaper and financial periodicals databases to collect data on the content of states' interpretations of the Basel rules. A more precise indicator is needed to more fully account for the various ways that regulators can interpret the Accord. Many elements of great importance to capital adequacy regulation are quite detailed and complicated. From existing studies, it is difficult to conclusively understand whether the Accord produced uneven implementation and what the impact of this may have been for bank profitability, and to test the veracity of political economy explanations of the Accord's negotiation.

Still, the very concept that the Accord did not produce high levels of international rule convergence challenges the existing models. It may be suggested that the empirical results of the implementation process are not relevant so long as BCBS negotiators *thought* they were producing joint or asymmetric gains. Yet, all regulators were well aware of the broad boundaries set by the Accord. Comparing the state of the BCBS members' pre-Basel Capital Adequacy Rules with those of the Basel Accord suggests that all states gained from this arrangement – including the United States and its drive to have preferred stock included in the list of allowable capital. Highlighting the soft law nature of the Accord permits the inference that the Accord was not designed to redistribute bank wealth. There are simply too many avenues for allegedly disadvantaged states (namely France and Japan) to "fit" their existing capital practices into the Basel framework.

The remainder of the book will work toward contributing to understanding these questions in more detail through the close measuring of the levels of convergence and divergence among the G-10 states over time and weighting of the political and economic explanations for these rule interpretations. The joint and redistribution gains hypotheses will be reviewed in light of this study's findings in Chapter 9. It is hoped that this study will contribute to a resolution of this debate on the Basel Accord and suggest fruitful avenues for future research on international financial regime implementation.

Conclusion

This chapter presented a review of existing research on the negotiation of the 1988 Basel Accord. It has argued that existing political economy explanations for the Accord's successful negotiation have failed to come to grips with the rudiments of the Accord's content. The 1988 capital adequacy agreement did establish some minimum guidelines for the G-10 states' prudential regulatory practices, but it also allowed wide areas of discretionary policymaking in the implementation of these standards. The empirical veracity of existing approaches to understanding the creation of the Accord was called into question by their failure to endogenize these "soft law" qualities of the Accord.

This chapter has also justified the necessity of a new empirical and theoretical research program. Though economic studies have addressed the discretionary policy-setting nature of the Accord, they have not found good indicators of the ways that the Accord was implemented by industrialized states. Did states "fit" existing capital adequacy practices into the broad regulatory confines established in Basel? Did regulatory convergence or divergence emerge from the Accord? What variables explain these empirical patterns? Existing research cannot provide good answers to these questions.

The next chapter initiates this research program by considering how international and comparative political economic theories relate to understanding the implementation of international financial regimes. It is suggested that most existing approaches fail to address the idiosyncratic empirical questions raised by "soft law" regimes and methods are proposed to address these theoretical lacuna.

3 Theorizing degrees of compliance with the Basel Accord

Introduction

This chapter develops a series of testable propositions about the conditions under which states can be expected to implement a non-compliant, minimalist, or strict interpretation of the 1988 Basel Accord rules. The propositions endeavor to provide probabilistic statements that explain why states that were committed to the Accord chose to implement the strict or loose interpretations that they did and why, or why not, those interpretations may have converged or diverged over time from 1988 to 2000. This chapter aims to contribute to a broader theoretical perspective in which to understand the effects of an international regime on state behavior in an issue area – financial services – that has not been extensively considered in previous research. The hypotheses derived in this chapter will receive a quantitative testing in Chapters 4 and 5 and will form part of the qualitative analyses of implementation in Part III.

By addressing the question of understanding *degrees* of state compliance or convergence with the Basel Accord, this chapter moves into a relatively unexplored area of international and comparative political economy research. The overwhelming majority of existing studies into the influence of internationally agreed rules on state behavior center on the conditions amenable to the successful implementation of regime rules into national law. The effects of international agreements are generally treated as a static, dichotomous process: the rules are implemented or not. In the study of the implementation of the Basel Accord, this dichotomization is empirically inappropriate given that national policymakers were given extensive discretionary powers for determining the exact manner in which the Accord was to be operationalized in their domestic banking rules. Attention needs to be given to the effects of the Accord on convergence or divergence with particular interpretations of the Basel rules. As over 100 countries claim to be implementing the Accord, the interesting empirical and theoretical question is not *if* states have complied with the standard but *how*.

This chapter suggests ways in which to answer this question through the enumeration of eight hypotheses. These hypotheses seek to contribute to the cumulation of knowledge about the effects of international rules on state behavior by drawing from, and extending, existing theoretical propositions of political economy. Yet, this chapter will put a novel spin on these hypotheses by considering their applicability to understanding degrees of compliance.

This section commences by considering the distinct methodology of considering a differentiated rather than dichotomous implementation process. It is argued that existing theoretical approaches to understanding compliance with a soft law regime are heuristically inappropriate. The next section defines and describes the hypotheses and indicates what evidence would allow for their falsification when given empirical test.

By conducting these modeling and hypotheses-generating exercises, this chapter seeks to make a number of innovative contributions to the understanding of the implementation of international public policy. First, as mentioned, it seeks to judge the influence of an international "soft law" financial regime on state behavior. Few studies have explicitly considered the post-negotiation phase of inter-state agreements in this issue area. Second, it develops hypotheses that aim to understand patterns of convergence and divergence of state responses to an international agreement, rather than look solely at a dichotomous question of regime implementation.

Theorizing about degrees of compliance

Existing approaches to implementation

The study of the impact of international regimes on state behavior has become an important and increasingly well-researched topic. The systematization and codification of inter-state norms since World War II has naturally led to a basic and applied interest in the utility of international regimes to independently or indirectly explain state policies.[1] The variation of academic opinion is now quite wide.

Looking at the field of International Relations, the Realist and rationalist Institutionalist schools argue that state compliance with international rules is dependent upon the presence of a punishment mechanism for defectors. This so-called Enforcement School does not consist of a homogenous body of theory, owing to fundamental disagreements between Realist and Institutionalist theorists. The general Realist position asserts that international institutions, or regimes, do not independently influence state behavior. If states with heterogenous ex ante preferences alter their behavior in accordance to a regime this reflects the underlying power structure of the international system. Regimes reflect the interests of their most powerful members, or a hegemonic member. Widespread compliance reflects the exercise of great state power or indicates that the regime resolved a coordination problem in which states maintained homogenous ex ante preferences.[2]

Conversely, Institutionalists argue that international organizations can exert independent influence on state behavior or act as intervening variables between power and state behavior. In this regard, regimes may influence state behavior by minimizing the transactions costs of cooperating, reducing uncertainty by providing a forum for future cooperation, and establish a mechanism by which information can be exchanged and regime defectors exposed and punished.[3] Thus, despite their distinctions, these two system-level International Relations approaches are classified as a single Enforcement School as they each conclude that more enforcement is correlated with more compliance.

The more law-based Management School provides the chief opposition to the Enforcement School. This approach adopts the somewhat counterintuitive assumption that, "almost all nations observe all principles of international law and almost all of their obligations almost all of the time."[4] In this view, instances of non-compliance generally reflect states' inability rather than unwillingness to comply. For example, states' apparent defection may result from the ambiguity of regime rules making compliance difficult to judge, or a state may simply not have had enough time to fully implement an agreement, or a state may not possess an administrative apparatus capable of implementation. The solution to curbing defection is not enforcement, which creates prohibitively high political and economic costs, but the international political management of those impediments to compliance.[5]

A final group of theories includes the extensive range of middle range hypotheses and theoretical frameworks generated by comparative politics and public policy research. This heterogeneous body of research has developed at least since Pressman and Wildavsky (1973) and has been so extensive so as to confound easy summary.[6] More will be said of the approaches later, yet at present it is sufficient to highlight that this research has identified a wide array of generally domestic-level variables, such as political institutions, market institutions, and ideas, associated with compliance with inter-state regimes. Promising lines of research have been recently innovated in the study of the influence of democracy and diverse legal traditions, regional imitation effects,[7] and the dynamic study of regime implementation change.[8]

These three approaches constitute the core body of political economy research into regime implementation. Though they adopt distinct simplifying assumptions and often focus on divergent independent variables, the theories converge in their dichotomous conceptualization of implementation. They each treat the implementation-dependent variable in a binary fashion in which state behavior takes on one of two values: states comply or defect with their international commitments. Whether a quantitative or qualitative research methodology is employed, the aim of most policy compliance research is to discern variables correlated with an implementation dummy variable. As Botcheva and Martin argue, "[t]his crude dichotomization of the vast variety of state behavior has perhaps obscured as much as it has revealed."[9]

In particular, this dichotomization abstracts away many of the nuances involved in the process of regime implementation. It does not allow for the investigation of why some states may over-comply with regime rules while others defect. A binary compliance variable can only record one of two possibilities. This variable is not exhaustive enough to capture the empirical possibility that a state implements a regime in excess of the minimum requirements. To capture such a possibility requires the abandonment of the dummy variable concept in favor of an indicator capable of taking on three or more values: for example, defection or compliance or over-compliance. Addressing over-compliance would seem to be as useful a question as understanding defection, especially for testing Enforcement hypotheses that seem to assume that states will, ceteris paribus, seek to defect from their international obligations. If there are empirical instance of over-compliance, they could be an anomaly for Enforcement theory, especially if there is an enforcement mechanism that applies to all states equally, and it would be important to capture this empirical possibility.[10]

Also, it would be useful to categorize those states that defect substantially from those that fail to comply in a few minor issue areas. Understanding the degrees of regime defection would again be an interesting phenomenon for the Enforcement School to explain and perhaps a mandatory phenomenon for managerialist studies. Two of the key proponents of the Managerial School, Abram Chayes and Antonia Handler Chayes, argue that a "regime as a whole need not and should not be held to a standard of strict compliance but to a level of overall compliance that is 'acceptable' ..." and "questions of compliance are often contestable and call for complex, subtle, and frequently subjective evaluation."[11] A binary understanding of compliance would seem ontologically inconsistent with making these nuanced judgements about compliance and operationalizing "acceptable" compliance thresholds.

Further, an Institutionalist paper by Botcheva and Martin (2001), suggests that eschewing the binary conception allows for an assessment of the differential impact of regimes over time. By adopting a more nuanced understanding of compliance, it is possible to move beyond the general debate of international cooperation studies – Do Institutions Matter? – to ask more specific questions of How Do Institutions Matter? Although it may be possible to capture some of this How question with a binary variable, it is not possible to assess the conditions in which regimes will produce convergence, divergence, or have no impact at all. Yet by looking at cases of over-compliance and degrees of defection from regimes, it is possible to create studies in which we can more clearly observe the differentiated impacts of regimes and combine studies of regime compliance with those of transnational policy convergence and divergence with inter-state rules.[12]

As illustrated from an adaptation of Botcheva and Martin's example of international trade regime effects (see Figure 3.1), a fuller understanding of compliance permits us to judge the impact of an international regime to create policy convergence or divergence. The solid diagonal line represents the stringency of the pre-international regime policy in Countries A–C and the solid horizontal line, at M, represents the minimum policy stringency floor established by an international agreement. The dashed and dotted diagonals represent distinct options that the sample states have in implementing the regime. Looking first at the dotted line, States A and B choose to increase the stringency of their policies

32 *Historical and theoretical perspectives*

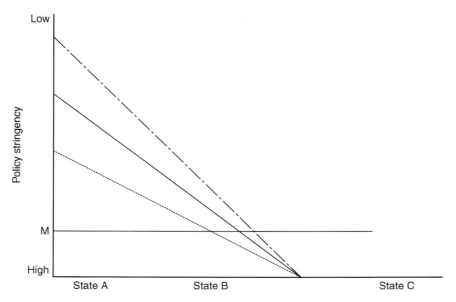

Figure 3.1 Convergence and divergence effects with a differentiated compliance variable (source: adapted from Botcheva and Martin (2001)).

Note
Solid line represents the stringency of a country's policy prior to the implementation of an international regime. The dotted and dashed lines represent alternative interpretations that a country can make of the regime during implementation.

in accordance with the regime while State C maintains its pre-regime policies that were already above the regime's minimum targets. Though State B implements a tougher policy than State A, the overall regime effect is to tighten policy globally and produce convergence among the three states' policies, even if State A does not fully comply with the regime rules. If we were to derive univariate statistics for the figure, the variance among the three state's policy levels would decline from the pre-regime period to the post-regime period. The dashed line, by contrast, illustrates the decisions of States A and B to defect from the regime. Though State A defects more substantially than B, this implies that the regime perversely produces a divergence effect.

It would not be possible to draw similar conclusions from a binary compliance variable. This may be illustrated through a modification to Figure 3.1 so that a dummy variable replaces the policy stringency scale on the vertical axis (see Figure 3.2). With a binary conceptualization, each state's response to the regime is classified as either Compliant or Non-Compliant (Yes or No). Though this figure illustrates the influence of the regime on state compliance, it does not really inform on the extent of convergence or divergence produced by the regime. The solid line represents compliance by all three states and is equal to the M horizontal. The dotted line indicates that States A and B defect from the

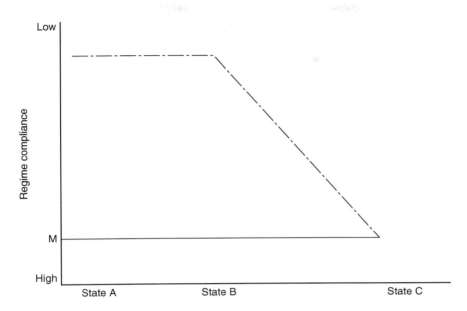

Figure 3.2 Convergence and divergence effects with a binary compliance variable.

Note
Dotted line represents whether states successfully implement the international regime.

agreement while State C complies (as would be the case for the dashed line in Figure 3.1). In neither instance, however, are we informed about the extent of compliance. Did States A and B fail to comply by a small margin, did State C meet the minimum compliance standards or implement substantially more changes in policy stringency. We are informed about the behavior of states in response to regime rules more than about their actions in accordance with the goals of the international regime. If all states substantially increase the stringency of their policies, along the dotted line, then even with States A and B's defections we can conclude that the regime achieves some success. Measures of dispersion that conveyed useful information with the differentiated variable in Figure 3.1 do not provide any information for the binary conception.

If the analysis of implementation is extended over a considerable period of time, the weaknesses of the binary approach multiply further. As Figure 3.3 illustrates, if the period of analysis includes a snap shot of the policy stringency levels during pre-regime period $(t-1)$, the initial implementation period (t), and a second implementation period at some point in the future $(t+1)$, it is possible to observe changes in the interpretations that states make to the way they are implementing the tariff regime. The solid line in Figure 3.3 represents the pre-regime $(t-1)$ period while the dotted line represents the initial (t) period of implementation when States A and B tightened policy in accordance with the regime. Yet, the broken line now represents an extended implementation $(t+1)$ period. This line indicates that State A has, over time, opted to revise the way the regime is implemented in its domestic political economy and has adopted a less stringent, non-compliant, policy. Perhaps the initial policy had a deleterious consequence on domestic interests and a revision was made to the initial implementation decision or there was a change in the government that elected a party that supported a defection from the international agreement. Though the new policy remains in compliance with the agreement, as indicated by (M) on the y-axis, there is now less convergence in the second implementation period. If we construct a similar dynamic analysis with a binary variable, no change is indicated from the initial to the extended implementation periods. State A's policy reformulation changes over time, yet it remains in compliance (below M in Figure 3.3) with the regime so no change can be recorded on the binary indicator.

The differentiated conception of compliance thus seems to heighten the ability of international cooperation studies to understand the process of regime implementation. It should be conceded that, in many issue areas, the binary indicator captures as much of the empirical reality as a more nuanced indicator. Underdal (1995), for example, asserts that many security pacts, such as arms agreements, may not allow any room for state discretionary policymaking while remaining compliant to a regime. If there were no room for domestic maneuver

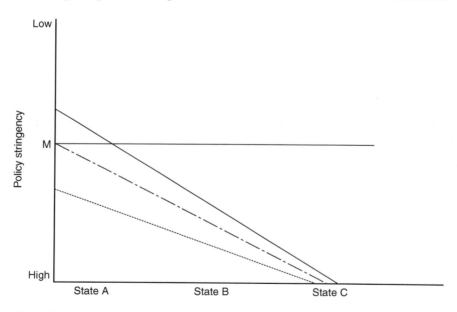

Figure 3.3 Dynamic convergence and divergence effects with a differentiated compliance variable.

Note
The solid line represents the stringency of a country's policy prior to the implementation of an international regime ($t-1$). The dotted line represents policy stringency during the time in which the regime is to come into effect (t), while the dashed line shows stringency in a second, extended period, after implementation is required ($t+1$).

within the confines of regime rules, then the binary conception would seem to capture the compliance phase of international cooperation adequately. Even though for such regimes, a fuller account of the pre-regime period may seem useful. Yet, as will be discussed in the next section, for the study of international financial agreements the differentiated approach seems most appropriate as these agreements often provide wide room for discretionary policy by constructing international "soft law" or by prescribing a fairly vague collection of "best practices."[13] In these instances and for those regimes that do permit elements of discretionary state behavior, studying degrees of compliance, "directs our attention away from process tracing to consideration of variation in outcomes ... [i]t allows us to specify conditional hypotheses rather than the broad and undifferentiated claim that 'institutions matter.'"[14] Moreover, "soft law" regimes highlight Alexander's (2000b:7) argument that legalization is not properly captured by a binary conception (no law versus law) but a multi-dimensional continuum. Our measures of state compliance with such agreements require the same qualities.

Degrees of compliance and the 1988 Basel Accord

The Basel Accord falls within the category of international regimes that would be best studied with a differentiated compliance indicator. As Chapter 2 discussed, the Accord is widely cited as a "soft law" regime.[15] The agreement is not legally binding on the negotiating states and responsibility for regime enforcement is delegated to domestic bank supervisors. Most importantly, however, the Accord provides domestic authorities with wide discretionary powers for determining how the Accord is operationalized in their own regulations and bank codes. This is accomplished by allowing a wide range of bank capital adequacy regulatory practice to qualify as "compliant" with the Accord and then allowing domestic supervisors to pick and choose among these practices when interpreting the rules for their own banks. The Accord creates a regulatory baseline and invites states to exceed this baseline.[16] The 1988 Accord provides states with a wide range of discretionary maneuvers and represents an excellent opportunity to analyze degrees of compliance. By adopting a compliance measure capable of capturing the G-10 states' various interpretations of the Basel rules, it is possible to address the differentiated impact of the Accord and measure the extent of convergence or divergence (if any) that the Accord produced.

Previous research into the Accord's implementation confirms the importance of analyzing degrees of compliance with the Basel rules. In particular, Ho (2002) endeavored to identify variables associated with a binary indicator of Basel regime compliance with a logistical regression model. Drawing from a recent World Bank database, his study coded the capital adequacy regulations of 122 states so that they score a "1" if they implemented the Accord and "0" if they did not.[17] Yet because about 90 percent of the sample states claimed to be in compliance with the Accord, Ho was left to explain defection by only nine states. There is thus very little information conveyed by viewing the implementation of the Basel Accord with a binary measure. Ho acknowledges this and

36 *Historical and theoretical perspectives*

suggests that the "dependent variable may ultimately be even better captured by measuring the degree of convergence or divergence."[18]

Yet, Ho's study remains useful as he successfully aggregates a wide range of extant compliance theories into a single research design. Drawing from many of the analytical frameworks and models discussed above, Ho tests the association of 26 independent variables with his dummy compliance variable. The section that follows will draw from Ho's body of theory to fashion 12 hypotheses that may be reasonably argued to be associated with a differentiated measure of compliance. Thus, while not all of Ho's variables are useful for looking at degrees of compliance, the majority provide some insight and by testing these explanations' utility in Chapters 4–7, this book will assess the ability of his theories to explain how states complied and use the results to try to determine why they complied.

Theories of compliance with the Basel Accord

Introduction

This section will indicate how a study of degrees of compliance with an international agreement may be employed in practice. The simple approach adopted here involves reinterpreting existing hypotheses that were designed to explain a binary compliance phenomenon in a fashion that enables us to make predictions about types of compliance. In practice, this section aims is to design testable, probabilistic propositions that explain why some states may have implemented very strict interpretations of the Basle rules, why some adopted a loose interpretation, and why there was convergence or divergence in interpretations over the 1988–2000 period. The theoretical statements described here will be tested in subsequent chapters.

Piecing together a battery of theories of implementation involves drawing from disparate theories that have been developed in various areas of political economy and economics. This is a difficult task for as one study concluded:

> [t]he rate of compliance is a function of a web of factors ... [i]t is unlikely that a specific formula can be discovered for all norms that would allow one to control the rate of compliance or allow one to fashion all norms to optimize compliance.[19]

The same is true for hypothesizing on kinds of compliance. This section thus endeavors to contribute to theory building in the study of the implementation of soft law by providing a platform in which to bring numerous disparate approaches to implementation and convergence together for comparison and testing against a common empirical phenomenon.

In order to facilitate the platform for this theory testing exercise, the following section will rely heavily on Ho's study of the implementation of the Basel Accord. Here I draw together a battery of hypotheses on the macroeconomic, political and economic institutional, and societal preferences that could be reasonably expected to explain why a state would implement the Accord. As the objective of this study is to understand distinctions in state behavior in response to a common external event, the Basel Accord, this comparative focus seems to be appropriate. Ho's theory can be organized in four categories with each category containing a number of hypotheses to explain why a state would choose to implement the Accord. Each of the categories, and thus their hypotheses, explain that state implementation behavior is a function of a vector of domestic attributes and systemic or external political and economic variables. These categories will be fully described in the next section, yet they include:

1   domestic bank preferences;
2   macroeconomic environment;
3   domestic political institutions;
4   international influences.

In testing Ho's hypotheses, however, several innovations are advanced. First, these hypotheses will be adapted in a number of ways to address variations in implementation rather than rates of implementation. Second, the hypotheses will be employed dynamically. Ho's study explains why a cross-section of states implemented the Accord at one period of time, roughly the late 1990s. As will be explained below, this study will seek to understand changes in the Basel rule interpretations of a cross-section of states, over a 12-year period of time. Accounting for these changes will involve innovating a few new hypotheses that fit within Ho's categories.

Finally, not all of Ho's hypotheses will be employed. This book does not necessarily seek to replicate Ho's study with a new dependent variable so much as leverage upon this work to fashion an organizational scheme around which to arrange hypotheses of implementation. Though replication is an interesting by-product of this approach and will be conducted to some extent, not all of these hypotheses can be reasonably presumed to be related to the differentiated compliance variable.

Theories of implementation

This section will lay out the hypotheses of implementation. Each hypothesis' simplifying assumptions will be clearly identified as will its expected relationship (positive, negative, indeterminate) to the endogenous variable – degrees of compliance. By enumerating these attributes clearly, it is hoped that the internal consistency of the hypotheses will be assured and that it will be clear under what circumstances the hypotheses fail to predict the actual implementation outcomes.

38 *Historical and theoretical perspectives*

Bank preferences

This section outlines a number of hypotheses on the preference of a given sample state's banks toward a lax or stringent interpretation of the Accord. Clearly, such preferences do not influence policy in isolation. These preferences are filtered through distinct sets of domestic political institutions before public policy emerges. These variables will be investigated in due course. Here, we lay out propositions regarding bank preferences with the assumption that these influence policy. This "demand side" model of the policymaking process is rooted in the Chicago view of interest group or "capture" theory.[20] This suggests that as the costs of stringent capital adequacy regulations are concentrated on domestic banks while the prudential benefits diffused among consumers, banking organizations have an incentive to lobby policymakers for a favorable interpretation of the Accord. Studies of banking politics in industrialized economies have observed that the style of banking regulations after World War II (i.e. segmentation laws, credit ceilings, etc.) made credit policy a target to rent-seeking by banks anxious to prevent the capping of their credit.[21]

So what may determine the preferences that banking organizations attempt to project into the policy process? First, Ho (2002) suggests that this depends on how well-capitalized banks were when the Accord was adopted. Banks with relatively low capital-to-assets ratios may support a lax interpretation of the Accord's rules. As Chapter 2 discussed, it is expensive for banks to raise capital. Doing so requires painful portfolio alterations that may involve raising new equity, selling off assets, or foreclosing particular lending projects. These actions can raise shareholder ire (in the case of publicly-held banks) by diluting equity and thus reducing the return on their shares in the bank. Foreclosing lending options may drive away relationship customers to other banks or other forms of funding. Selling off assets can advantage other, well-capitalized, banks and other financial institutions that can purchase these assets at attractive prices.[22]

Conversely, of course, well-capitalized banks may well seek a strict interpretation of the Accord. Banks in this position could seek to leverage a strict interpretation of the Accord as a form of "non-market" competitive advantage against poorly capitalized domestic competitors or foreign competitors subject to domestic practices.[23] For example, such banks could seek to use the domestic application of the Accord to manipulate the domestic regulatory playing field to their advantage and disadvantage foreign competitors. Such banks could increase the value of their equity if demand is increased for banks already in compliance with the Accord and increase their share of the domestic lending market through the acquisition of new customers and the purchase of assets sold by their lesser-capitalized competition.

Similarly, banks subject to relatively stringent capital adequacy regulations before the Accord may favor an interpretation consistent with their current practice. Banks that were subject to limited definitions of capital or risk-weighted asset (RWA) requirements prior to the Accord may well seek to gain a non-market advantage through encouraging a strict domestic, and likely cross-national, standard. This suggests:

Hypothesis 1. Banks with relatively lax (strict) pre-Basel CARs or subject to weak capital adequacy standards will be more likely to support a lax (strict) interpretation of the Accord

This hypothesis advances one element of a broader "path dependence" theory of inter-state regime implementation. The main observable implication of the hypothesis is that the Basel Accord did not produce much actual change in the capital adequacy regulations of the states that originally agreed to the rules in 1988. This conclusion may seem counterintuitive in light of research suggesting that the Accord contributed to recession in the early 1990s and effected fundamental changes in the financial intermediary business.[24] After its negotiation, the Accord was described as a "landmark in international supervisory cooperation" by the Governor of the Bank of England and a "breakthrough" by the Chairman of the US Federal Reserve Bank.[25] Yet, much regime implementation literature emphasizes the possibility that the Accord may not have changed many elements of the G-10 state's capital regulations. The behavior of domestic regulators and the preferences of domestic banks could have been heavily path dependent; their dominant preference may, ceteris paribus, have been to minimize differences between their interpretation of the Basel rules and existing capital adequacy rules and practices. As Morgan and Knights (1997) concluded, "national approaches to regulating banks are slow to change."[26]

The broader logic behind this hypothesis has been the subject of analysis in studies of regime and public policy implementation. Specifically, domestic-level analysts have observed that path dependence can be expected to characterize the response of actors to policy change. In the public policy literature, there has been extensive debate regarding the relationship between new and extant rules and regulations in policy implementation. A hypothesis that has been widely tested, and found some support, is that the probability of effective implementation is inversely related to the extent of departure from the status quo.[27] At the international level, Underhill (1992) observed that the rules and norms prescribed by the regime enter each implementing state's "regulatory space" which is occupied by historically and institutionally conditioned policy strategies, inter-governmental turf battles, and, "constellations of private interests joined in alliances with constellations of public interests."[28] Likewise, Baron (2000) argued that theories of regulation must model that, "as regulation is applied to on going economic activity, [the] status quo can be important to legislative choice."[29] Though, as indicated in Chapter 2, most states' interpretations of the Basel rules occur in a more de-politicized environment in which banking regulatory bureaucracies are more likely to interpret the Basel rules than a legislature, the same logic would seem to apply.

In fact, the path-dependence hypothesis would seem to be especially pertinent when applied to the case of the Basel Accord and study of degrees of compliance, more generally. As Chapter 2 argued, the negotiation of the Accord was made possible through allowing G-10 states to "fit" elements of their own capital adequacy regime into the new multilateral standard. For example, French negotiators refused to support the Accord if the unrealized appreciation in physical assets were not distinguished as an allowable component of bank capital. These were allowed by French banks' regulations before the Accord's negotiations and were an important component of many French banks' capital base. Though the inclusion of this capital instrument was opposed by Germany at the Basel Accord negotiations and the EC Own Funds Directive negotiations, it was ultimately allowed in both standards in order to secure unanimous approval from the negotiating parties.[30] Many elements of the Accord's rules, especially the definitions of capital, took shape in this manner and thus reflected the interests of one or two negotiating states. As a result, we should expect that domestic regulators and banks of implementing states would have the opportunity to interpret the Accord so as to minimize any major disruptions to the regulatory status quo. A state's existing capital adequacy rules were probably the product of a regulatory compromise and were designed perhaps in coordination with other elements of prudential regulation (such as official government bank bailout policies) or idiosyncrasies of the states' financial system (e.g. costs of capital). Also, as Simmons (2001:2) suggested, "national regulators typically prefer to avoid rules that raise costs for national firms or that encourage capital financial activity to migrate to under regulated jurisdictions." Maintaining the existing rules would thus minimize the costs of re-negotiating bank regulations for supervisors and banks.[31]

Of course, a state's pre-Basel Capital Adequacy Regulations could cut both ways. If the Accord is implemented with asymmetric stringency among industrialized states, banks subject to relatively strict standards may demand that their domestic supervisors loosen their regulations in an effort to level the playing field. Oatley and Nabors (1998) and others suggested that it was American bankers' demands that Japanese banks be subject to stricter capital standards that led the United States to fervently pursue the Accord's negotiation. Elements of this view will be further discussed later as the influence of International Factors.

One possible counter to this criticism is that banks may seek to utilize their capital adequacy practices as a signal of stability to the international market. Rather than seeking a tit-for-tat race to the lowest possible regulatory standard, banks may use the Accord to heighten their reputation. Ho cites a wide range of research concluding that "international law serves to increase the reputational harm of non-compliance, serving the function of a stamp of approval for the conduct of international business."[32] Complying with an international financial standard, even one with negative distributional costs in the short run, is thus beneficial as this compliance signals a state's financial stability and competitiveness to international investors and depositors.[33] It thus may be possible to hypothesize that a state's banks will prefer to maintain or depart from a lax status quo and demand that their regulators implement a strict interpretation of the Basel rules as such a signal irrespective of their pre-regime rules. Extant research has not yet examined the relationship between international signaling effects and *types* of compliance. Is the mere announcement to comply with the Basel Accord sufficient to serve as a credible signal? Is it necessary for a state to signal a particular type of compliance for its banks to glean any reputational advantages (or avoid any disadvantages)? These questions have not been previously addressed.[34]

I argue that banks' perceptions of the relative reputational effects of compliance types will depend upon their exposure to international markets. In many instances, banks may be expected to lobby for a loose interpretation of the Accord, as the benefits of capital adequacy regulation are diffuse while the costs are heavily concentrated on banks' borrowers.[35] Banks that are subject to a high level of market or private "supervision" may be induced to follow standards that are more demanding than their regulators mandate, in order to earn competitive credit ratings and earn competitive returns in capital market issues. A 1990 Basel Committee review of the Accord's effects advanced a similar point by arguing that the "market itself has imposed its own discipline ... [b]anks have found a distinct advantage in being able to satisfy the rating agencies and the market generally that their capital was adequate in terms of the final Basle standard."[36] Moreover, an empirical study by the US Federal Reserve Bank concluded that the market had led US banks to maintain regulatory capital well in excess of the minimum 8 percent requirement. Thus, banks subject to such market pressures may want to augment their international reputation by adhering to strict capital adequacy standards and may thus lobby their regulators for the adoption of a relatively strict interpretation of the Basel rules or not fight the discretionary implementation of tough standards. This leads to the proposition:

Hypothesis 2. Banks subject to a high degree of market supervision will favor a relatively strict interpretation of the Basel Accord

Banks' preferences could also be conditioned by their international ambitions. Banks with extensive international operations may need to adhere to the Accord in order to conduct business in other Basel complying states. For example, banks aiming to conduct business in the United States must provide the Federal Reserve with evidence of compliance with their national regulators' interpretation of the Basel rules or, if they are domiciled in a non-compliant state, must provide balance sheet information that suggests compliance with the Accord's provisions.[37] On this basis, Ho concludes that banks with international ambitions will lobby their supervisors to implement the Accord to ease their entry into foreign markets. Though his results are statistically insignificant in the test of this hypothesis, it seems reasonable to advance that banks with extensive international ambitions may have preferences for stricter domestic regulations as such banks may be subject to strict market governance and to provide them with greater flexibility for entering foreign market places.

Hypothesis 3. Banks with large international exposure will favor a relatively strict interpretation of the Accord

Macroeconomic environment

In addition to the factors outlined in the previous section, the preferences of political economic actors are linked to the current climate of the financial and broader market economies in which they operate. There are a wide variety of macroeconomic variables that could be reasonably assumed to contribute to a state's interpretation of the Basel rules. The hypotheses discussed in this section are useful as the macroeconomic environment conditions domestic preferences toward degrees of capital adequacy rule severity and are useful control variables in order to assess the influence of domestic bank preferences and institutions. In particular, periods of economic instability and financial sector distress should influence a state's decision to implement the Accord. It may be argued that this instability conditions the preferences of regulators and commercial banks toward the reform of the regulatory regime. Yet, it is not equally clear what the causal directions of such effects are, should macroeconomic instability be associated with a loose or strict interpretation of the Basel rules?

Ho explicitly addresses this question and is unable to find a clear, theory-based answer. First, he advances the argument that perhaps instability should be associated with states' decision to not implement the Accord. The financial crises would make bank compliance with a stricter capital code more costly and perhaps exacerbate the effects of the crises on domestic banks. His regression analyses find that instability is negatively correlated with implementation and statistically significant in one of the two models in which the variable is employed.[38] This same logic would seem to hold for looking at degrees of compliance with the Accord. A state would probably seek to implement a fairly minimal interpretation of the Basel rules to allow domestic banks to take advantage of a wide range of capital instruments in order to combat the effects of the crisis on their balance sheets.

Alternatively, an equally logical argument may be advanced to predict a tightening of a state's capital adequacy guidelines. Perhaps the macroeconomic instability could be endogenized into the argument so that we are left with the proposition that regulators would implement the Accord *because* of macroeconomic instability. Equally, regulators may choose to tighten solvency ratio standards in reaction to instability. This hypothesis would seem to be consistent with Walter's (2002) observations that financial reform in the United States during the 1980s and in East Asia during the 1990s followed rather than preceded the onset of banking crises in these regions.[39]

A final way of conceptualizing the importance of this variable is generated from the regulator's dilemma model, discussed in Chapter 2. Kapstein (1989, 1991, 1994) and Singer (2002) argue that macroeconomic instability or microeconomic distress in the banking sector contributes to the decisionmaking processes of regulatory authorities. Their model assumes that the onset of eco-

Theorizing degrees of compliance 43

nomic instability may require the intervention of political authorities. While seeking to maximize votes, politicians will seek to shift blame to market actors' irresponsible behavior or imprudent regulatory oversight. In both events, regulatory authorities may experience a loss of autonomy, prestige, and budget.[40] As a result, we may expect that economic crisis will be strongly associated with a tightening of regulatory policy.

In associating economic instability to a degree of compliance variable, the theoretical literature does not provide a clear guide to predicting outcomes. The literature is sufficiently robust, however, to advance that the variable does seem important.

Hypothesis 4. The presence of economic instability will be associated with a state's decisions to implement a strict or lax interpretation of the Basel rules

Political Institutions Theory

Studies of policy implementation have universally acknowledged the importance of domestic political institutions to determine the likelihood of compliance with public policy. If the macroeconomic environment conditions banks' and regulators' preferences, the political institutional environment structures the way these preferences interact with one another in the production of policy. Ho's study of the determinants of state commitments with the Basel Accord found considerable support for hypotheses gauging that the likelihood of compliance covaried with distinct configurations of domestic political regimes and practices.[41] In particular, his logic regression analysis found robust statistical association between the likelihood of compliance and:

1 Fragmentation in the political decisionmaking regime;
2 Degree of respect for the rule of law, the level of corruption, and the presence of democracy.

When indicators of the phenomena were added to strict macroeconomic explanations of implementation, the number of correctly predicted cases of implementation increased from 87.72 percent to 96.97 percent.[42]

In applying Ho's hypotheses to this study, it seems that only the first requires explicit enumeration here. The second, concerning the rule of law and democracy, is controlled for here as our sample includes only high-income states that exhibit high degrees of convergence in measures of corruption and democracy. If we measure the democracy scores of our sample with the 10-point scale from Polity III data, we derive a standard deviation of 0.476, with only two states failing to achieve the maximum score of 10.[43]

Looking at the first of these hypotheses, that the likelihood of implementation can be expected to decrease as the fragmentation of a sample state's political institutions increases, seems highly applicable to this study.[44] In this instance, political fragmentation was measured as federalism, bicameralism, or a strong

44 *Historical and theoretical perspectives*

opposition party or parties, to the executive, in parliamentary government. Though the latter of these is not strictly an institutional variable, these features constrain the ability of a small number of actors (the cabinet, for example) from wielding unchecked power through the multiplication of the veto players in the policymaking process and provide a role for particularistic interests to influence the policymaking process. Ho noted that, "[a]s such constraints increase, politicians are more likely to face opposition from regional and local governments, and more likely to satisfy concentrated banking groups that may be negatively affected by the Basle Accord."[45]

If we first assume that domestic banks will seek to influence their domestic regulators to adopt a relatively lax interpretation of the Accord that is consistent with their pre-Basel rules, then their ability to affect this policy outcome will depend upon the institutional structuring of the supply-side of the regulatory equation. This leads to the proposition that:

Hypothesis 5. States will be more likely to adopt a lax interpretation when their political system is fragmented

A second political institutional variable concerns the impact of government ownership of the banking sector. A high level of state ownership infers that the state would have to bear part of all of the costs for the implementation of the Accord. If banks' capital were derived from state funding, then public coffers would need to contribute to capital injections necessary to raise CARs above the Basel Accord's minima. Barth *et al.* (2001c) find that greater government ownership is associated with less efficient and profitable banking systems. It thus seems unlikely that the government would, ceteris paribus, opt to implement a Basel interpretation stricter than their current regime and would implement a relatively weak implementation of the Basel rules.

Hypothesis 6. States with a high level of government ownership of domestic banks will implement a relatively weak interpretation of the Basel Accord

International influences

Another set of influences relates to the impact of variables in the international political economic space. First, the existence of regional norms seems pertinent. Ho argues "[b]anks and regulators within a region may have similar management philosophies, similar attitudes towards risk, and face similar competitive environments (i.e. shareholder expectations), leading to similar preferences towards the Basle Accord."[46] This follows the results of Beth Simmons' (2000) finding that states are more likely to comply with international monetary "soft law" if states in their region comply. Simmons argues that states voluntarily comply with unenforced norms to realize the signaling and reputational effects discussed earlier. Such effects, she advances, will be stronger in the event that other states in the region comply with a monetary standard. The same could well be advanced for degrees of compliance with the 1988 Accord.

Hypothesis 7. States will be more likely to adopt a strict (weak) interpretation of the Accord if states in their region adopt a strict (weak) interpretation

In a separate study, Simmons (2001) tests another international influence that may affect patterns of compliance. In a study of the negotiation of international financial regulation, Simmons suggests that the United States wields hegemonic power in the negotiation of financial standards due to the size and importance of its capital markets. In fact, she argues that the United States has a "first mover" advantage as other states are subject to market pressures to emulate American regulatory innovations – perhaps even in the absence of a multilateral agreement. In other words, "there are strong incentives to emulate a U.S. regulatory innovation involving capital adequacy standards ... there is very little incentive to reduce standards and risk developing a reputation as 'poorly regulated.' "[47]

These arguments seem to resonate in Realist International Relations approaches. Recalling earlier sections of this chapter, Realists conclude that it is powerful states, not international regimes, which influence compliance. If regimes produce convergence among states with heterogeneous ex ante preferences, powerful states' punishment mechanisms were effectively exercised. Part of this punishment could evolve through the Federal Reserve's requirement that foreign banks adhere to American solvency standards and some through the market's punishment of banks not adhering to the US guidelines. According to this point of view, there should be convergence on the Basel interpretation adopted by the United States.

Hypothesis 8. States will be more likely to adopt a strict (lax) interpretation of the Accord rules if the United States adopts a strict (lax) interpretation

Conclusion

This chapter aimed to accomplish two tasks. First, it set out to justify why studies of international cooperation need to amend the way they model the process of regime implementation. It was shown that, for the majority of international agreements, conceptualizing compliance as a dichotomous process produces empirically uninteresting or misleading results. A great deal of rich empirical detail concerning instances of over-compliance and degrees of under-compliance are obscured.

Second, this chapter presented eight hypotheses explaining why states might implement one of several various degrees of compliance with the 1988 Accord. A key hypothesis is that states would, ceteris paribus, resolve to adopt a roughly path-dependent interpretation of the Basel rules. Other hypotheses lead to investigations into what political and economic variables may condition this direct relationship between path dependence and Basel

Table 3.1 Hypotheses on the implementation of the Basel Accord

No.	Description	Abbreviation	Predicted sign
1	Pre-Basel regime	PREBASEL	+
2	Market supervision	MARKET	+
3	International exposure	EXPOSURE	+
4	Economic instability	STABILITY	Indeterminate
5	Political fragmentation	CAPTURE	−
6	Government ownership	GOV	−
7	Regional influences	REGION	+
8	Hegemonic influences	HEGEMON	+

interpretations. These hypotheses suggest that different variables may condition the implementation process at different points of time. These hypotheses are summarized in Table 3.1. The expected relationship of this variable on severity of implementation with the Accord is also indicated.

Part II
Quantitative studies

4 Measuring implementation and explanatory variables

Introduction

The preceding chapters explained that the Basel Accord provided the G-10 states with fairly wide discretionary powers for determining how the agreement was operationalized in their banking laws and regulatory codes. Though the Accord's text expressed the hope that the credit risk rules "be applied as uniformly as possible at the national level," the responsibility for interpreting and enforcing the agreement was delegated to the national-level policymakers.[1] Chapter 3 presented a variety of theoretical propositions regarding the conditions in which we would expect states to implement strict or lax interpretations of the Basel rules and thus effect transnational capital adequacy rule convergence or persistent divergence.

The present chapter advances this line of discussion by operationalizing the explanatory variables discussed in Chapter 3 and developing a measure of implementation. This chapter also presents descriptive statistics for these variables, using data from cases of Basel Accord implementation for 1988 and around 2000. In Chapter 5, these quantitative measures of implementation are utilized in econometric tests of explanations for why we observe particular patterns of compliance and convergence with the baseline Basel rules. Yet even before the statistical measures are applied, these descriptive statistics provide some insight into the empirical side of the Basel Accord's implementation in around 20 countries. Previous research on the Accord has, in nearly all cases, utilized very small samples of countries and not presented much data on its implementation. This has led to the formation of a form of conventional wisdom about the Accord based on limited or incomplete data. One theory permeating the international political economy literature is that the Accord resulted from the exercise of US–UK financial market hegemony in order to eliminate regulatory advantages created by Japanese, and to a lesser degree French, regulators at the expense of American and British banks.[2] Yet, the descriptive data demonstrate that it is the United States and the United Kingdom that, among these four states, have adopted the strictest forms of implementation. This leads to the question of how the Basel implementation stage contributed to the US–UK goals if these states continued to have much stricter capital regulatory standards after 1988?

Also, the descriptive statistics allow for a quantitative measurement of convergence with Basel rules over time. There has not yet been a study that investigates the transition of capital adequacy rules over time, though the financial press has continually discussed alterations in risk capital rules since 1988. This lacuna may be partly justified by the dearth of an easily assessable or centralized source for capital adequacy regulatory data. This chapter builds a quantitative indicator that aims to capture change in Basel rule interpretations over time through the deductive coding of the credit risk regulations of a large sample of states.

These data will also be utilized in a univariate statistical assessment of three of the hypotheses discussed in the previous chapter. By illustrating the degrees of capital adequacy rule convergence and divergence among industrialized states from 1988 to 2000, it will be possible to investigate the hegemonic and regional effects hypotheses. These predict that we will see states' interpretations of the Accord converge to those of the United States or regional partners' definitions. It is concluded that these hypotheses are of limited use in understanding patterns of strict and lax compliance. The operationalization of the capital adequacy regulatory variables also permits an assessment of the "path dependence" hypothesis through a comparison of the severity of states' pre- and post-Basel capital practices. This comparison provides some support for this hypothesis, though further statistical testing is administered in the next chapter.

The next section begins by describing the methodology employed to create the quantitative measures of Basel rule implementation. It will then proceed to provide univariate statistical analyses for the statistical indicators. The third section will operationalize the independent variables. The last section concludes.

Measurement and description: implementation

The extensive research on the Basel Accord that has progressed over the last decade lacks attempts to operationalize its implementation in such a way that we can measure it and test explanatory hypotheses across a wide range of cases. There has been no rigorous effort to analyze and explain degrees of implementation with a large population sample. The majority of implementation studies involving the Accord have been exercises in comparative financial law, generally involving comparisons of two or three states' interpretation of the 1988 Basel rules.[3]

The two major exceptions to this trend are 1991 research projects by Murray-Jones and Gamble and PriceWaterhouse.[4] These studies were conducted independently of one another yet both rigorously compare about 20 states' domestic interpretations of the Basel and EC capital adequacy regulations. This information is useful in assessing the extent of rule compliance during the first year of the Accord's implementation phase. Yet, the studies do not include data after 1990 and do not seek to code their samples' capital regulations so that they may be easily comparable across cases.

The econometric analyses in Chapter 5 will rely on five new measures of implementation that aim to fill these empirical gaps by providing generalizable indicators to measure implementation across a large sample of states and facilitate statistical analysis. Given the difficulties of effectively measuring implementation in unambiguous fashion, it is necessary to utilize multiple indicators of the implementation phenomenon when judging degrees of compliance.[5] The implementation process with the 1988 Accord is highly complex and measuring a state's implementation of the 1988 standard requires some subjective judgements and interpretations.

This subjectivity is exacerbated by two factors. The absence of a central repository for collecting states' capital adequacy requirements means that data must be collected from each state's regulator on a case-by-case basis. This has the effect of making it arduous to collect data for an extremely large sample of states and, second, introducing elements of error in the process of quantitatively coding states' regulations. Though the Accord sought to link the disparate G-10 capital adequacy guidelines by providing a common regulatory language, many states continue to utilize distinct, national terms for banking assets and credits. That many of these terms do not translate very efficiently into the English language (assuming that English translations are available), without some critical loss of information, further frustrates cross-sectional comparisons. As a result, utilizing multiple methods of measurement is necessary to ensure the content validity of the Capital Regulation Index (CREG).[6]

Methods of construction

The dependent variable is an index of implementation severity that attempts to capture the extent to which any given state has adopted a strict, lax, or non-compliant interpretation of the 1988 Basel Accord rules. Measurements are made in each of the six capital adequacy policy areas addressed by the Accord. These six capital adequacy policy elements have been identified as the primary areas of discretionary policy setting by previous studies of the Accord's implementation and are thus a logical starting point for developing this variable.[7] These policy areas were discussed in some detail in Chapter 2, yet Table 4.1 provides a brief review of each policy and, in parentheses, presents the

Table 4.1 Areas of permitted discretionary implementation with the 1988 Basel Accord

- Definition of allowable Tier1 or primary capital elements, within established parameters (TIER1)
- Definition of allowable Tier2 or supplementary capital elements, within established parameters (TIER2)
- Specification of deductions to be made from either Tier1 or Tier2 capital elements before their inclusion in the regulatory-defined capital base (DEDUCT)
- Required minimum percentage of risk-weighted Tier1 and Tier2 assets divided by total capital, with the minima set at 4 percent of Tier1 and 8 percent of total capital (RATIO)
- Assignment of credit risk weights to on-balance sheet assets (RW)
- Assignment of credit-risk weight conversion factors to off-balance sheet assets (OBS)

52 Quantitative studies

quantitative code term that will be utilized to abbreviate each area in the quantitative analyses.

A 1–4 ordinal scale was constructed for each of these six indicators, with higher values indicating greater regulatory stringency. The scale aims to capture the degree to which a sample state's implementation of the Basel Accord was a below-minimum interpretation (score = 1), a minimum interpretation (score = 2), a reasonably strict interpretation (score = 3), or a highly strict interpretation (score = 4). Based on these categories, a state's interpretation for each of the six policy areas was scored from 1 (below-minimum) to 4 (highly strict interpretation). EU member states' definitions of implementation are matched against EU, not Basel, regulations to the small extent that they diverge (see Appendix 4.1 for a comparison of the two regimes).

To aid statistical testing, these six variables are agglomerated into an index. CREG was simply constructed by summing the values of the six policy area values, with each composite variable receiving equal weight. The index thus ranges from 1 to 24, with higher values indicating greater stringency.

Three measures were taken to ensure the reliability of the CREG and its constituent variables.[8] First, to ensure the mutual exclusivity of each of the ordinal coding categories, a detailed mapping scheme was constructed (see Appendix 4.3).[9] The origins of the mapping procedure are derived from the Basel implementation coding categories in Murray-Jones and Gamble (1991), PriceWaterhouse (1991), and Hall (1993). These three studies largely agree on the policy areas that should be addressed when assessing sample state's levels of compliance with the Accord. The PriceWaterhouse study, in particular, was especially useful in the engineering of the mapping scheme as the authors created a table that listed the sample state's implementation methods that were divergent from the Basel baseline rules.

The second reliability measure employed was a test–retest method for each of the three capital adequacy policy variables. This method involves applying the measuring instrument to the sample population at different times and then computing the correlation between the two sets of observations, to obtain a reliability estimate. This method indicated that the measuring instrument provides a high degree of reliability as a robust correlation was achieved in the two measurements and no major distinctions emerged between the two applications of the coding procedures.

Finally, the constituents of the CREG were subjected to a Cronbach alpha examination. This reliability test measures how well a set of variables measure a single, unidimensional latent construct. The alpha score can range from 0.0 to 1.0 with higher values indicating that the constituent variables of an agglomerated index measures a consistent construct. The CREG alpha score was 0.35, which indicates that the constituent variables are not highly correlated with one another and do not measure a unified construct very consistently. It will thus be useful to disaggregate the index at periods in order to assess how individual variables perform.[10]

The data for these variables were obtained from a variety of sources at two

Measuring implementation and explanatory variables 53

points of time. First, data were obtained for the original counterparties to the 1988 Accord and ten states that signaled their intention to implement the Accord from 1988. This yields a sample size of 18 states that includes members of the BCBS and members of the EC. Data for these states' original interpretations of the Basel rules were obtained from PriceWaterhouse (1991) and Murray-Jones and Gamble (1991), who obtained their data from national regulatory authorities directly and financial law attorneys practicing in the sample states. These two sources independently report identical results concerning the sample states' interpretations to the Accord, thereby contributing to the reliability of the coding process. These data indicate capital adequacy practices from around 1988 to 1990 for each sample state. I label the variables constructed from these data as "First Period Implementation" measures.

Next, the most recent capital adequacy regulations were obtained for this same sample of states. Capital adequacy regulations may often be re-evaluated by states and thus it is necessary to directly measure these changes rather than extrapolate from 1991 data in determining current standards. Unfortunately, data limitations make it presently impossible to conduct year-by-year comparisons of states' capital practices across a large sample. This study attempts to obtain the next best objective by measuring states' most recently published capital adequacy practices, which are here labeled "Second Period Implementation" measures. These standards were obtained from bank supervisor websites, publications, and by direct interviews. For replication purposes, details of the documents from which these data were obtained are listed in Appendix 4.3.

One of the key weaknesses of this variable comes from this manual data collection method. Having to collect data for each sample state individually makes it difficult to find data for a larger sample of states. Ultimately, it would be optimal to locate capital adequacy regulatory data changes, for each sample state, for each year from 1988, and conduct a dynamic analysis of the determinants of capital adequacy regulatory stringency. Unfortunately, the data for such a project are lacking. A year-by-year study of regulatory changes will, however, be made for a much reduced sample of states in the case study analyses in Part III – thus partly justifying the coordination of a qualitative addition to a quantitative study of implementation.

First period of implementation

The descriptive statistics for the CREG are presented in Table 4.2. As mentioned, the descriptive statistics present the index scores for two points of time: the late 1980s (t) and recent regulations ($t + 1$). The table also derives the degree of regulatory change that occurred in the sample states between the two points of observation through $(t + 1) - (t)$. Finally, the table presents generally utilized measures of central tendency (arithmetic mean) and dispersion (standard deviation).

In looking at the sample states' initial interpretations of the Accord (t) for which data are available, it seems the Accord may have successfully established

54 *Quantitative studies*

Table 4.2 Comparative descriptive statistics for CREG indexes

	t	t+1	Change[a]
Australia	15	16	+1
Austria	14	13	−1
Belgium	14	14	0
Canada	15	17	+2
Denmark	15	15	0
Finland	11	13	+2
France	13	13	0
Germany	17	15	−2
Ireland	15	12	−3
Japan	13	14	+1
Luxembourg	14	15	+1
Netherlands	13	13	0
New Zealand	16	16	0
Spain	14	15	+1
Sweden	14	14	0
Switzerland	18	16	−2
United Kingdom	14	16	+2
United States	16	15	−1
N	18	18	18
Mean	14.50	14.50	−0.05
Standard deviation	1.61	1.38	1.48

Source: Murray-Jones and Gamble (1991), PriceWaterhouse (1991), and regulatory authorities listed in Appendix 4.3.

Note
a Change = $(t+1) - (t)$

a regulatory floor. Most states implemented a well above minimum interpretation of the Basel rules during the late 1980s. If one takes, as a benchmark, the view that a pure minimal interpretation of each dimension of the Accord would result in an index score of 12 (2 × 6 policy areas), it is striking to observe that every state, save for one (Finland), earned a score between 13 and 18. More striking still, is that the mean for first period (t) data (14.5) indicates that the average state implemented the Accord with considerable stringency above the minima.

Examining the regulatory stringency of the composite variables of the CREG in Table 4.3 supports this conclusion. Looking at the marginals of Table 4.3, the mean for five of the six policy areas is above 2 (the baseline minimum). Each sample state, again save for Finland, implemented a stricter than minimum, or "superequivalent," interpretation in at least one policy area while half of the sample adopted a very strict interpretation (coded as 4) in at least one dimension of the Basel rules. There were, however, several areas in which the sample states failed to comply with the Basel minima (coded as 1). Yet, even among this group of non-complying states (Finland, Japan, Spain, and the United States), three implemented superequivalent interpretations in at least two policy areas

Table 4.3 Comparative descriptive statistics for CREG index components (*t*)

	Tier1	Tier2	Deduct	RW	Ratio	OBS	Total (CREG)
Australia	2	3	2	4	2	2	15
Austria	3	3	2	2	2	2	14
Belgium	2	3	3	2	2	2	14
Canada	2	3	3	3	2	2	15
Denmark	3	3	2	2	3	2	15
Finland	1	2	2	2	2	2	11
France	2	3	2	2	2	2	13
Germany	4	4	2	3	2	2	17
Ireland	2	2	2	4	3	2	15
Japan	2	3	1	3	2	2	13
Luxembourg	2	4	2	2	2	2	14
Netherlands	3	2	2	2	2	2	13
New Zealand	3	2	4	3	2	2	16
Spain	2	4	2	3	2	1	14
Sweden	3	3	2	2	2	2	14
Switzerland	2	4	3	4	2	3	18
United Kingdom	2	2	2	4	2	2	14
United States	1	4	3	4	2	2	16
Mean	2.28	3.00	2.28	2.83	2.11	2.00	14.65
Standard deviation	0.751	0.767	0.660	0.857	0.323	0.343	1.631

while the regulators of one (United States) implemented superequivalent interpretations in three policy areas.

Looking more closely at the degrees of compliance in individual policy areas, it is interesting to observe that the strictest interpretations were clearly in the defining of Tier2 capital. The mean for supplementary capital (3.00) was noticeably higher than other areas of the Accord and five states adopted a very narrow definition of supplementary capital so as to earn a 4 in the Tier2 category (Germany, Luxembourg, Spain, Switzerland, and the United States).

As was discussed in Chapter 2, Tier2 or supplementary capital essentially includes a variety of accounting reserves that are not as permanent or available to meet losses as equity, yet provide some protection in the event of counterparty default. The Basel Accord allowed five items to be included in Tier2 capital for all G-10 states, yet as with other items of the Accord, invited states to exceed the minimum requirements.

The severity of the sample states' interpretation of the Basel Accord is not surprising as one of the key purposes behind the decision to construct a Tier2 capital measurement was to provide counterparty states with a wide open category of capital within which they could include numerous forms of capital, sometimes of questionable quality, that had been a traditional component of their banking regulations. The objective in doing so was to ensure the Accord's acceptance by regulators who were under severe domestic pressure to defend their idiosyncratic practices at the Basel Committee negotiations. The tier thus

56 Quantitative studies

includes numerous capital instruments (such as revaluation reserves and general loan loss provisions) that were not legally allowed in many of the negotiating states but were a key component of the capital regulations of other states. Thus, the decision to exclude these instruments in many states may well reflect a sample state's pre-Basel status quo rather than a strict interpretation per se. This status quo, or path dependency, hypothesis will be investigated in subsequent chapters.

At this stage, however, analyzing the raw data used to construct the Tier2 variable can develop useful insights. If we chisel the Tier2 indicator down into the individual response frequencies (see Table 4.4), it is interesting to note that general provisions or general loan loss reserves were restricted or excluded (as indicated by an "X") by more states than they were permitted as only five states allowed their inclusion (as indicated by a "*") without significant limitations being imposed on their use. Conversely, subordinated debt was widely permitted without restriction as only two states (Australia and Germany) limited their inclusion in permitted capital while only four states prohibited the use of undisclosed reserves, and five prohibited hybrid capital instruments (which includes cumulative preferred stock).

Yet, while the strict interpretation of Tier2 capital is not altogether surprising, the narrowness with which the counterparty states interpreted Tier1 (or primary) capital is not as expected. This tier of capital is considered to be the highest grade "cushion" against bank insolvency in the face of credit risks. Thus while

Table 4.4 Tier2 capital definitions (t)

	Undisclosed reserves	Revaluation reserves	General provisions	Hybrid instruments	Subordinated debt
Australia	*	X	X	*	X
Austria	*	*	X	*	*
Belgium	*	*	X	*	*
Canada	*	X	X	*	*
Denmark	*	*	X	*	*
Finland	*	*	*	*	*
France	*	X	*	*	*
Germany	X	X	X	X	X
Ireland	*	*	*	*	*
Japan	*	X	*	*	*
Luxembourg	*	X	X	X	*
Netherlands	*	*	*	*	*
New Zealand	*	*	*	*	*
Spain	X	*	X	X	*
Sweden	*	X	X	*	*
Switzerland	*	*	*	*	*
United Kingdom	*	*	*	*	*
United States	X	X	X	*	*
$N(*)$	15	10	8	15	15
$N(X)$	3	8	10	3	2

Tier2 capital was designed to be broad, to placate competing demands by negotiators, the Tier1 capital definition was made intentionally narrow. The instruments permitted in this tier, by the Accord, must be permanently and quickly available for banks to draw upon in the face of financial difficulties. As a result, this is the most expensive capital for banks to maintain and we would thus expect banks to lobby for a fairly broad definition of Tier1 capital so as to maintain international competitiveness vis-à-vis their international competitors.

Looking at the index marginals, in Table 4.3, however it seems that domestic policymakers held a relatively strict line on the Tier1 definition. The mean (2.28) is the third highest of the policy area variables and six states (Austria, Denmark, Germany, New Zealand, the Netherlands, and Sweden) implemented superequivalent interpretations of Tier1 capital while one (Germany) implemented a very strict definition in the late 1980s. Looking at the disaggregated data in Table 4.5, it is interesting to note that the vast majority of the restricted interpretations concerned the inclusion of current year profits and funds for general banking risks in regulatory capital. Regarding the former, five states opted to exclude or heavily restrict the inclusion of current year profits. Keep in mind that the EC Own Funds Directive forced all European member states to adhere to a stricter interpretation than that enumerated in the Basel Accord by requiring all current year profits to be certified by an external auditor. Beyond this, five EU member states went even further by excluding profits entirely from regulatory capital.

Table 4.5 Tier1 capital definitions (*t*)

	Equity	Disclosed reserves	Minority interests	Current year profits	General risk funds
Australia	*	*	*	*	—
Austria	*	*	*	X	*
Belgium	*	*	*	*	*
Canada	*	*	*	*	—
Denmark	*	*	*	X	X
Finland	*	*	*	*	*
France	*	*	*	*	*
Germany	X	*	X	X	*
Ireland	*	*	*	*	X
Japan	*	*	*	*	—
Luxembourg	*	*	*	*	*
Netherlands	*	*	*	*	X
New Zealand	*	*	*	X	—
Spain	*	*	*	*	*
Sweden	*	X	*	X	*
Switzerland	*	*	*	*	—
United Kingdom	*	*	*	*	X
United States	*	*	*	*	—
N (*)	17	17	17	13	8
N (X)	1	1	1	5	4

58 *Quantitative studies*

It is also important to observe, however, that two states defected from their commitments to comply with the Tier1 requirements. In particular, Finland adopted an especially broad definition of primary capital that permitted banks to include 50 percent of the value of trading assets and investments, a capital item that should probably fall under the category of a revaluation reserve and be classified as supplementary capital. Also, the United States diluted the stringency of its primary capital requirements by permitting bank holding companies (BHCs) to tally cumulative preferred stock in their Tier1 capital base. This practice is expressly forbidden by the Accord as these instruments, unlike non-cumulative preferred equity, do not allow banks to omit dividend payments, but simply forego the dividend whose value cumulates into a future payment. As a result of the fixed costs that these cumulative instruments carry, the Accord relegates them to Tier2 status.

Beyond the definition of supplementary capital, it is interesting to observe that the specification of risk-weight categories was also subject to a strict interpretation by the sample. The risk-weights category, in Table 4.3, indicates that the mean index score was 2.83, and five states implemented an extremely limiting risk-weighting regime and earned 4. This is an intriguing result, given that the RWAs approach was a novelty for many implementing states, as will be discussed below.

Second implementation period

The univariate statistics for the second period ($t + 1$) in Table 4.2 illustrate that some significant degrees of change occurred to these initial Basel rule interpretations over a roughly ten-year period of time. First, Table 4.2 illustrates that the capital adequacy regulatory stringency of the entire sample remained largely constant over time. The sample mean remained 14.5 for the (t) and ($t + 1$) periods. More telling, however, is that the standard deviation decreased from 1.61 to 1.38. The decrease in the variance over time suggests that the sample states' capital adequacy regulations converged between our two sampling periods.

The data contained in the Change column illustrates that this greater convergence was created through 12 states' revisions of their credit risk regulations. Thus, over half the sample modified their capital adequacy regulations in a way that affected a change in their CREG scores.[11] Of the 12 CREG scores that changed, five weakened their interpretations over time while seven increased the severity of their Basel interpretations.

Looking first at cases of weakening, Table 4.2 reveals that Austria, Germany, Ireland, Switzerland, and the United States each reduced their capital adequacy rule severity in ways measured by the index. Of these, Ireland affected the most dramatic loosening of their capital regulations over the sample period as their CREG score dropped from 15 to 12. This reduction was, as indicated in Table 4.6, mostly the product of the Irish regulator's decision to significantly water down their risk-weighting framework to the minimum standards set out in the

Table 4.6 Comparative descriptive statistics for CREG index components ($t + 1$)

	Tier1	Tier2	Deduct	RW	Ratio	OBS	Total (CREG)
Australia	2	3	3	4	2	2	16
Austria	2	3	2	2	2	2	13
Belgium	2	3	3	2	2	2	14
Canada	2	3	3	3	4	2	17
Denmark	3	3	2	2	3	2	15
Finland	2	2	2	2	3	2	13
France	2	3	2	2	2	2	13
Germany	3	3	2	3	2	2	15
Ireland	2	2	2	2	2	2	12
Japan	2	3	2	3	2	2	14
Luxembourg	3	4	2	2	2	2	15
Netherlands	3	2	2	2	2	2	13
New Zealand	3	2	4	3	2	2	16
Spain	2	3	4	3	2	1	15
Sweden	3	3	2	2	2	2	14
Switzerland	2	2	3	4	2	3	16
United Kingdom	2	3	4	3	2	2	16
United States	1	4	3	2	3	2	15
Mean	2.22	2.78	2.72	2.56	2.22	2.00	14.50
Standard deviation	0.548	0.647	0.752	0.705	0.548	0.343	1.383

European Own Funds Directive. Ireland initially required some bank credits to domestic government and public sector entities to carry much higher capital asset charges than those set out in the Basel and European accords. For example, fixed rate Irish government stock, with a maturity of one to five years, and domestic public sector entities were assigned a 10 percent risk-weighting as opposed to the 0 percent set out in the Basel/EC rules. The Irish regulators also required their domestically domiciled banks to maintain a capital-to-risk assets ratio of greater than 8 percent. Yet, by the late 1990s, these strict standards had been brought in line with the Basel minima and the Irish CREG score dropped from 15 to 12.

More surprising than the magnitude of the Irish CREG score decrease, however, is the large reduction created by the German bank supervisors during the sample period. As Chapter 2 discussed, Germany's bank regulators, and their domestic banks, were highly critical of the capital adequacy negotiations in Basel for producing multilateral standards that were too lax and, in particular, permitted too many instruments to qualify as regulatory capital that were not permanently available to meet bank funding needs. Germany's initial implementation of the Accord (t) was congruent with their criticisms of Basel and excluded most capital instruments, save for common equity and some current-year profits. Yet, by the late 1990s, Germany's CREG score of 15 puts its capital adequacy standards more on par with states that criticized the severity of the Accord's standards, especially France and Japan. More unexpected still, is that

Table 4.6 reveals that the reduction of Germany's CREG score was almost entirely the product of an expanded definition of Tier1 and Tier2 capital from the highly restrictive definition that German negotiators had fought for in Basel.

Though not as surprising in the context of the Basel negotiations, the American's regulatory loosening is noteworthy. The index score for the United States in the second time period was the result of a loosening of the state's highly restrictive risk-weighting framework. The United States constructed, perhaps, the most punishing risk-weighting scheme for its internationally active banks in the months following the Accord's negotiation. The US rules required a 10 percent charge for claims collateralized by cash or OECD securities (Basel minimum: 0 percent), a 50 percent charge for domestic bonds (Basel minimum: 0 percent), and a 100 percent charge for home mortgage loans (Basel minimum: 50 percent). Yet, like Ireland, by the end of the 1990s, all of these superequivalent interpretations had been reversed and US rules were at the Basel minima.

What did not change, over time, however was America's non-compliance with the Basel Tier1 capital requirements. As discussed above, the US regulators agreed to permit BHCs to hold cumulative preferred stock as primary capital. Though this practice attracted severe criticism by its Basel Committee peers, the practice continues to be maintained.

Looking now at those states that strengthened the severity of their capital adequacy regulations over time, several interesting cases stand out. On the whole, seven states increased the stringency of Basel rule interpretations from the (t) to the ($t + 1$) periods. Two of these states (Australia and Canada) initially implemented capital regimes that were well above the CREG sample mean and tightened relatively strict regimes even further. The remaining five (Finland, Luxembourg, Japan, Spain, and the United Kingdom) tightened Basel interpretations that were at, or just below, the sample mean.

Of these five, Canada and Finland stand out as the only states to tighten their minimum capital-to-asset ratio requirements. Though the ratio requirement is the most easily measured of the Basel policy areas, and has thus received the bulk of attention in studies of the Accord,[12] only Canada and Finland absolutely require their domestic banks to maintain overall ratios greater than 8 percent. Though I classified five states as either 3 or 4 on the Ratio scale, three of these assignments were made because of the nature of the restrictions placed on the ratio requirements, rather than a hard and fast rule that ratios must exceed the 4 percent and 8 percent minima (see Tables (Figures-Components t and $t + 1$)). For example, Denmark requires a 10 percent ratio if banks hold subordinated debt as Tier2 capital. The supervisors of Finland and Canada, however, have established trigger ratios above 8 percent and will take action against those banks whose ratios, in the case of Finland, fall to 8 percent and, for Canada, fall below 10 percent.

The regulatory changes of the United Kingdom also stand out, though not only because of the increases in regulatory stringency that were made. The United Kingdom's CREG score increased fairly significantly from 14 to 16. This increase was affected through Britain's decision to exclude undisclosed reserves from regulatory capital and the adoption of a long list of deductions to be made from regulatory capital. Yet, what the aggregate CREG score hides is that the United Kingdom loosened their restrictive risk-weight framework during the ten-year period and had a reduction of their risk-weight ranking from 4 to 3. Like the United States, a large part of this reduction was the result of the Bank of England's decision to move mortgage loans from the 100 percent to 50 percent risk bucket. The reasons for this are not indicated in these data, of course, yet the vast reductions evinced in the risk-weighting schemes of the sample states – even those that strengthen their overall capital adequacy regime over time – is clearly in need of investigation in the chapters to follow.

Testing hegemony and regional imitation hypotheses

The data presented above permit the testing of two of the hypotheses laid out in Chapter 3. In particular, the predictions of convergence among regional partners and with the American interpretations may be partly assessed with descriptive statistics. A cursory glance at Table 4.6 suggests that little hegemonic or regional imitation effects were in operation. Yet, it is necessary to subject these hypotheses to more rigorous univariate statistical tests.

Support for the hegemonic hypothesis is to be found if non-US CREG scores converge with the US score for either time period. Given the predicted effect of path dependence, we may expect to find increased convergence with the American rules from the first to the second period, yet any evidence of convergence with US rules will provide grounds to reject the hegemonic null-hypothesis.

Testing the hypothesis involves a comparison of the mean CREG scores of non-US CREG scores with the US score for both periods. The results are presented in Table 4.7. Little support is found for the hegemonic hypothesis in either time period. The mean for non-US CREG scores in the first sample period was 14.41 while the US score was considerably higher at 16. Considerable CREG score convergence emerged in the second sample time period, yet in the opposite direction to that predicted by the hypothesis. The non-US CREG ($t + 1$) score remained constant while the US score decreased to 15. This result suggests support for the null-hypothesis: it was the United States that converged with other states' interpretations rather than the opposite effect predicted by the hegemonic hypothesis.

Table 4.7 Univariate analysis of hegemonic hypothesis

Period	Sample group	N	Arithmetic mean
t	US CREG	1	16
	Non-US CREG	17	14.41
$t + 1$	US CREG	1	15
	Non-US CREG	17	14.52

62   Quantitative studies

Looking now at the hypothesis that industrialized states' interpretations converged on a regional basis, support for this hypothesis would be provided if the variance in states' CREG scores was less within their region than with states outside of their region. Relying on standard classifications, the 18 sample states may be divided into three regions:

- **Europe** (Austria, Belgium, Denmark, Finland, France, Germany, Ireland, Luxembourg, the Netherlands, Spain, Sweden, Switzerland, the United Kingdom).
- **Asia Pacific** (Australia, New Zealand, Japan).
- **North America** (Canada, the United States).

The comparison of the intra-regional dispersion of CREG scores is presented in Table 4.8. The results provide mixed support for the regional effects hypothesis. In the first time period, the two states of North America and three of Asia adopt interpretations more convergent with one another than with those in other regions. European states were less likely to experience convergence among one another as Europe's coefficient of variation ("Coefficient of Var.") was 0.12, compared with 0.08 for other regions. In the second time period, the opposite effect emerged as Europe was the only one of three regions to feature greater relative convergence.

These results do not suggest that regional effects were unimportant. Regional imitation effects may have been important for Asian and North American states in the two time periods. In particular, Canada and the United States experienced much greater convergence with one another's interpretations in the first period

Table 4.8 Univariate analysis of regional effects hypothesis

Period	Sample group	N	Mean	Coeff. of var. (%)
t	Europe	13	14.31	0.12
	Non-Europe	5	15.00	0.08
t	North America	2	15.50	0.04
	Non-North America	16	14.38	0.12
t	Asia Pacific	3	14.67	0.10
	Non-Asia Pacific	15	14.47	0.12
$t+1$	Europe	13	14.15	0.09
	Non-Europe	5	15.60	0.07
$t+1$	North America	2	16.00	0.08
	Non-North America	16	14.38	0.12
$t+1$	Asia Pacific	3	15.33	0.08
	Non-Asia Pacific	15	14.40	0.10

Measuring implementation and explanatory variables 63

Table 4.9 Variance of CREG scores: EU versus non-EU

Period	Sample group	N	Mean	Coeff. of var. (%)
t	European Union	12	14.00	0.10
	Non-EU	6	15.50	0.10
t+1	European Union	12	14.00	0.08
	Non-EU	6	15.67	0.07

than non-North American states. Though not part of the hypothesis test, it is also interesting to note that these two states' mean CREG scores were considerably higher than the rest of the samples in the two periods.

Though not an explicit part of the regional hypothesis, Table 4.9 assesses whether EU states experienced greater convergence among one another than non-EU states. Though EU states were permitted to apply subsidiarity principles in their interpretation of the Own Funds and Solvency Ratio Directives, we might expect that the institutional networks binding European states and the drive toward a Single European Market might affect greater convergence. Given the elements of the set of "Europe" states above, assessing this hypothesis involves calculating a Europe versus non-Europe variance examination with Switzerland moved out of the European category.

The results of this simple exam indicate that little EU convergence effects emerged. In the first period, the variance of EU states' CREG scores was equal to that of non-EU states. Over time, EU states' scores converged yet not as closely as that of the non-EU. Moreover, in both sample periods, EU states' interpretations were considerably looser than those outside the organization.

Measurement and description: explanatory variables

This section details methods of empirically measuring the explanatory variables that were discussed in previous chapters. Chapter 3 described five possible categories of variables that could be expected to have an impact on the implementation of the Basel Accord. These categories included:

1. bank preferences;
2. macroeconomic environment;
3. political institutions;
4. international Influences.

I utilize a number of well-tried and tested and new measures as quantitative proxies of the theoretical propositions corresponding to these four categories. The one exception is International Influences. Given the relatively weak hegemonic and regional imitation effects detected in the previous section and the difficulties of designing adequate multivariate tests of these hypotheses, these variables will not receive further quantitative examination. These hypotheses

64 *Quantitative studies*

Table 4.10 Pre-Basel capital regulatory index

	PBTIER1	PBTIER2	PBRW	PBRATIO (%)	PREBASEL
Belgium	2 (2)	3 (3)	1 (2)	2.83	8.83 (14)
Canada	4 (2)	4 (3)	0 (3)	5.00	13.00 (14)
France	2 (2)	3 (3)	1 (2)	2.60	8.60 (13)
Germany	4 (4)	4 (4)	0 (3)	2.81	10.81 (17)
Japan	2 (2)	3 (3)	0 (3)	2.37	7.37 (13)
Luxembourg	2 (2)	3 (4)	0 (2)	3.48	8.48 (14)
Netherlands	2 (3)	3 (2)	1 (2)	3.76	9.76 (13)
Switzerland	2 (2)	4 (4)	1 (4)	5.24	12.24 (18)
United Kingdom	2 (2)	3 (2)	1 (4)	6.17	12.17 (14)
United States	2 (1)	4 (4)	0 (4)	4.92	10.92 (16)
Mean	2.4 (2.3)	3.4 (3.0)	0.5 (2.8)	3.92	10.20 (14.5)
Standard deviation	0.84 (0.77)	0.52 (0.82)	0.53 (0.83)	1.42	1.90 (1.71)

Note
Corresponding CREG (*t*) policy values in parentheses for comparison.

Table 4.11 Descriptive statistics: explanatory variables

Variable	Mean	Std Dev	N
PRIVATE	7.29	1.16	17
EXPOSURE	7.00E+10	8.23E+11	18
STABILITY1	0.278	0.461	18
STABILITY2	0.444	0.511	18
CAPTURE	0.485	0.160	17
GOV	6.33	11.799	15

will return for full consideration in the qualitative studies in Part III. The subsections below present the empirical operationalization of the hypotheses under review. The descriptive statistics for these variables are shown in Tables 4.10 and 4.11.

Bank preferences

The bank preference "path dependence" hypothesis suggested that the content of states' pre-Basel Accord rules influenced how the Accord was implemented. Deriving cross-sectional data for a large sample of states' pre-Basel capital adequacy standards is challenging given the low level of regulatory disclosure in many states before the creation of the Accord. Also, comparison is confounded by the vast diversity of capital regulation terminology and practice before the Accord. For example, many states required banks to ensure that capital was a minimum multiple of assets (i.e. capital must be five times greater than assets) rather than a percentage of assets (i.e. the Basel 8 percent minimum). It may be impossible to reliably convert such multiple requirements into a percentage requirement across a range of unique banking systems. A key purpose of the

1988 agreement was to provide a common regulatory vocabulary and framework, thus indicating the difficulties of pre-Basel comparisons.

It is thus necessary to rely on fairly crude indicators of pre-Basel rules. Four measures are constructed and presented on a country-by-country basis in Table 4.10. Relying on Dale (1984) and Pecchioli's (1987) comparative analyses of capital adequacy regulation, a pre-Basel capital definition is measured. Utilizing the sample coding procedure as for the CREG (see Appendix 4.2), two variables measuring the severity of Tier1 and Tier2 capital definitions were constructed. Though many states did not employ a two-tier capital structure before the Accord, it is possible to separate the pre-Basel regulatory capital elements into two tiers and determine what elements allowed in the Accord were included or excluded from the definition of regulatory capital. The coding of pre-Basel Tier1 produces the PREBASEL(1) measure while Tier2 produces PREBASEL(2).

Second, I measure whether each state's pre-Basel capital adequacy standards required the risk weighting of assets (PREBASEL(RW)). This is measured with a dummy variable scored as unity in those instances in which a risk-weighting system was in place prior to the Accord and "0" otherwise.

Finally, I seek to measure the relative severity of pre-Basel minimum capital-to-assets ratios by measuring each state's average level of capitalization prior to the Accord. The variable (PBRATIO) is constructed by taking the average, unweighted capital-to-assets ratio for each sample state's leading ten banks for the five years leading up to the Accord (1983–1987). A full decade is sampled to ensure that the variable measures the average capitalization levels of a state – if one really exists – rather than ratios influenced by short-term macroeconomic concerns. These data were taken from *The Banker*'s Top 500 and Top 1000 global bank reviews over the sample period as this publication measures capital adequacy levels with identical definitions of capital across states. The definition is more limited that permitted by most regulators and by the Accord and includes common stock, disclosed reserves, and retained earning. Measuring states with this uniform, though limited, definition of capital and the use of unweighted ratios permits comparisons of capitalization while controlling for the effects of distinct capital definitions and risk-weighting approaches.

These four indicators are summed into a composite index of pre-Basel capital severity. The index (PREBASEL) is constructed by summing the constituent variables. Table 4.10 presents the results of this variable's construction in comparison with the CREG results presented above. Unfortunately, detailed pre-Basel data were only available for ten sample states. Yet, among these states, a strong comparison may be drawn among definitions of capital and total index scores from the pre- to post-Basel implementation phases. The means for the Tier1 and Tier2 definitions of capital are very similar. Interestingly, however, the standard deviation for the Tier2 definition is considerably larger in the post-Basel implementation phase. This suggests the possibility that states' definitions of secondary capital were more similar before the Accord than afterwards. This will serve as an interesting avenue of research in the chapters ahead.

66 Quantitative studies

The influence of private market governance on bankers' preferences (Hypothesis 2) is measured with the Private Monitoring Index from Barth et al. (2001a). This index is constructed through the summation of the results of seven questions distributed directly to the banking supervisors of over 100 states:

1 Are certified audits of banks required?
2 What percentage of banks are rated by international credit ratings agencies?
3 Does the income statement include accrued or unpaid interest or principal on non-performing loans (NPLs); are banks required to produce consolidated financial statements?
4 Is there an explicit deposit insurance regime?
5 Are OBS items disclosed to the public?
6 Is subordinated debt an allowable (required) part of regulatory capital?
7 Must banks disclose their risk management procedures to the public?

The index (PRIVATE) varies from 0 to 7 with each question being scored a "1" if yes is the supplied answer. Question (2) is scored as unity if 100 percent of banks are rated. Higher values of the index indicate more private monitoring. The aggregate results of this variable's construction – and the variables discussed below – are presented in Table 4.11.

It was also expected that bankers' preferences would be shaped by the quantity of exposure to foreign competition at home (Hypothesis 3). This variable is drawn from the World Development Indicators (2001) and measures the total import value of the insurance and financial services. The measure takes the average of this data for 1985–1988.

Macroeconomic environment

One macroeconomic variable was predicted to influence implementation: the presence of a major episode of instability or crisis in the banking market. Instability is operationalized as the incidence of severe banking crisis. This phenomenon is measured by two dummy variables constructed from data provided by Caprio and Klingebiel (1996). The first variable (STABILITY1) is scored "1" if a state experienced a major systemic bank insolvency from 1985 to 1988 and "0" otherwise. The second (STABILITY2) is scored the same way for banking crises occurring from 1989 to 1995. Unfortunately, these data are limited to a 1995 endpoint. I am not aware of an aggregate indicator that measures banking crises beyond this date.

Political institutions

Two hypotheses suggested that implementation varied by different elements of the political institutional environment. The first suggested that political fragmentation would influence implementation outcomes. A key element of this hypothesis was that fragmentation would permit commercial banks to exercise greater political power. Ho (2002) suggests a quantitative measure of overall "bank power" that combines the number of veto points or political institutional constraints of a state's political system and relative economic strength of the domestic banking sector. The first of these phenomena is measured with Henisz's (2000) well-known veto points metric. The second with a measure of bank concentration from Demirgüç-Kunt and Levine (2001b). This measures the percentage of national deposits held by the three largest banks. These two measures are multiplied together, thus permitting the construction of an index of regulatory capture potential (CAPTURE). The value of constructing this index is that it permits the simultaneous measurement of these two variables' influence on implementation, which increases the theoretical leverage of these course proxies for a complex concept.

Second, it was predicted that the level of state ownership of the banking sector would influence that implementation. The level of a government's ownership is measured as the fraction of a state's banking assets that are 50 percent or more government owned. These data are taken from Barth *et al.* (2000a).

Conclusion

This chapter has taken the first empirical cut at understanding the implementation of the 1988 Basel Accord and its credit risk-related amendments. It presented a method for coding the way the 1988 Basel Accord was implemented across a range of states. It applied this method to a sample of 18 industrialized economies for two periods of time: 1988 and around 2000. The results suggested that the Accord might have successfully established a regulatory floor that few states violated. Yet, numerous distinctions remained in these states' capital adequacy practices after 1988, though some level of regulatory convergence emerged from 1988 to 2000.

Second, this chapter conducted an empirical examination of the viability of the two International Influences hypotheses enumerated in Chapter 4. It found little support for either the hegemonic or regional imitation explanations. These hypotheses will not be given further quantitative testing, though will be discussed in the qualitative studies in Part III.

Finally, the chapter presented the descriptive statistics for the explanatory variables. Aggregate descriptive statistics were presented for the variables whose coding procedures were drawn from existing research. More extensive descriptive statistics were presented for the pre-Basel Accord Capital Regulatory index (PREBASEL) constructed here. The results of comparing this index's results with the post-Basel Accord Capital Regulatory Index (CREG) indicated that "path dependency" might be a viable explanation of observed degrees of compliance with the Accord. This hypothesis will receive further quantitative testing with the other hypotheses in Chapter 5.

Appendix 4.1 Differences between the Basel framework and the EU directives

Regulation	Basel framework	EU differences from Basel
Tier1 definitions	• Paid-up share capital/common stock; perpetual non-cumulative preference shares • Disclosed reserves • Minority interests in equity of subsidiaries less than wholly owned • Current year profits	• Current year profits included only if verified by auditors • Funds for general banking risks included without limits as a separate category
Tier2 definitions	• Undisclosed reserves • Asset revaluation reserves (including latent reserves) • General provisions/general loan loss reserves • Hybrid (debt/equity) capital instruments • Subordinated term debt	• Latent revaluation reserves not allowed • Commitments of cooperative members specified as included
Deductions	• From Tier1: goodwill • From Tier2: investments in unconsolidated banking and financial subsidiaries; investments in capital of other banks and financial institutions and financial institutions under certain conditions	• From Tier1: goodwill and other intangibles; own shares held at book value; current year losses • From Total: investments in capital of other banks
Ratio	• Minimum 8% capital to risk-adjusted assets • Tier2 limited to maximum of 100% of Tier1	

Appendix 4.2 Coding of the Capital Regulatory (CREG) Index

This appendix presents the methodology used to create the quantitative indicator of states' interpretations of the 1988 Basel Accord. The Capital Regulatory (CREG) Index ranges from 0–24 with higher values indicating higher levels of capital regulatory stringency in areas addressed by the 1988 Basel Accord. It is constructed through the summing of five variables which correspond to the key five capital adequacy policy areas addressed by the Accord (see Table 4.1).

Each of the five policy variables is an ordinal scale that ranges from 1–4 with higher values indicating greater stringency. The coding procedures for each policy variable follows:

Definition of Tier1 capital

Code	Description
1	Tier1 standard has been implemented, but at a below-minimum interpretation. More than the minimum four Tier1 capital elements permitted.
2	Tier1 standard implemented, the four Tier1 capital elements allowed by the Accord are fully allowed without restriction.
3	Tier1 standard implemented so that a slightly more stringent interpretation has been made. This will include the subtraction of one or two allowable Tier1 items from the domestic definition of regulatory capital – save for the definition of equity capital, which has remained intact.
4	Tier1 standard implemented so that three or more non-equity Tier1 items are subtracted from the domestic definition of regulatory capital or the definition of equity capital has been made more stringent.

Definition of Tier2 capital

Code	Description
1	Tier2 standard has been implemented, but at a below-minimum interpretation. More than five of the five allowable Tier2 capital instruments permitted or at inflated discount factors.
2	Tier2 standard implemented, base five Tier2 capital elements permitted (four in EC) in the domestic definition of regulatory capital at specified discount factors.
3	Tier2 standard implemented so that one or two capital elements or discount factors has been subtracted from the domestic definition of regulatory capital or been implemented in a superequivalent fashion.
4	Tier2 standard implemented so that three or more capital elements or discount factors have been subtracted from the domestic definition

of regulatory capital or been implemented in a superequivalent fashion.

Deductions from capital

Code   Description

1   No deductions from capital required or deduction standards have been implemented, but not all baseline deductions are required to be made from the domestic definition of regulatory capital.
2   Deduction standard has been implemented; all baseline deductions are required.
3   Deduction standard has been implemented, yet domestic regulators require one more than the minimum baseline deductions to be made from the domestic definition of regulatory capital.
4   Deduction standard has been implemented, yet domestic regulators require two or more than the minimum baseline deductions to be made from the domestic definition of regulatory capital.

On-balance sheet risk-weights

Code   Description

1   Risk-weight standard has been implemented, yet several assets are assigned a lower risk-weight than required or risk-weighting scheme not implemented.
2   Risk-weight standard has been implemented with all assets assigned to their minimum required risk-weight.
3   Risk-weight standard has been implemented, yet one of the two discretionary risk-weighting assignments has been to a higher than required weight.
4   Risk-weight standard has been implemented, yet both of the two discretionary risk-weighting assignments have been to a higher than required weight.

Off-balance sheet risk-weights

Code   Description

1   Risk-weight standard has been implemented, yet several assets are assigned a lower risk-weight than required or risk-weighting scheme not implemented.
2   Risk-weight standard has been implemented with all assets assigned to their minimum required risk-weight.
3   Risk-weight standard has been implemented, yet one of the two discretionary risk-weighting assignments has been to a higher than required weight.

4   Risk-weight standard has been implemented, yet both of the two discretionary risk-weighting assignments have been to a higher than required weight.

Minimum capital-to-risk weights-assets ratio requirement

Code   Description
1   No minimum capital-to-assets ratio requirement or minimum ratio assigned but at levels below the specified minima.
2   Minimum ratio assigned but at levels required by the Accord.
3   Minimum ratio assigned but at levels 100–200 basis points above the minimum levels required by the Accord.
3   Minimum ratio assigned but at levels over 200 basis points above the minimum levels required by the Accord.

Appendix 4.3 Sources of regulatory data for quantitative database

This appendix presents bibliographical references for the regulatory documents, web sites, agencies and individuals that contributed data for the construction of the quantitative measures presented in Chapter 4. Data for the Capital Regulatory (CREG) Index was obtained for all countries in PriceWaterhouse (1991) and Murray-Jones and Gamble's (1991) surveys of implementation of the Basel Accord in a large sample of countries. Yet these studies only provide data for the initial interpretations made of the Accord's rules by industrialized economies. In order to corroborate the findings of these two surveys and extend the scope of coverage to the most recent interpretations of the Accord, it was necessary to obtain data directly from the bank supervisory authorities of the 18-country dataset. References of the data source points are presented, by country, below.

Australia

Australian Prudential Regulation Authority (www.apra.gov.au)

- *Prudential Standard APS 110-Capital Adequacy, July 2003*

Austria

Oesterreichische Nationalbank (www.oenb.at)

- *The Austrian Banking Act and Austrian Financial Market Authority Act (2002)*

72   *Quantitative studies*

Belgium

Banking and Finance Commission (www.cbf.be)

- *Circulaire D1 96/1 Aux Etablissements de Credit* (2 April, 1996)
- *Lettre Circulaire D1/TB/332 Aux Etablissements de Crédit: Adaptation du règlement relatif aux fonds propres des établissements de crédit* (13 July, 2000)
- *Circulaire D1 2001/5 Aux Etablissements de Crédit* (4 July, 2001)

Canada

Office of the Superintendent of Financial Institutions (www.osfi.gc.ca)

- *Guideline: Capital Adequacy Requirements, A-Part I, January 2001*

Denmark

Financial Agency (www.finanstilsynet.dk)

- *The Commercial Banks and Savings Banks, etc. Consolidation Act (Consolidation Act No. 787)* (4 September, 2001)

Finland

Financial Supervision Authority (www.rata.bof.fi)

- *FSA Regulation 106.6 and 203.3*

France

Banque de France (www.banque-france.fr)

- *Règlement No. 99-02 (21 June, 1999), modifying Règlement No. 91-05 of 15 February, 1991*

Germany

Federal Financial Supervisory Authority (www.bakred.de)

- *Principle I Concerning the Capital of Institutions, last amended 20 July, 2000 (Federal Gazette No. 160)*

Japan

Financial Services Agency (www.fsa.go.jp)

- *Inspection Manual* (28 June, 2001)
- *Tamura* (2003b)

Luxembourg

Commission de Surveillance du Secteur Financier (www.cssf.lu/fr/index/ html)

- *Circulaire CSSF 2000/10* (October 2000)

Netherlands

De Nederlandsche Bank (www.dnb.nl)

- *Credit System Supervision Manual*

New Zealand

Reserve Bank of New Zealand (www.rbnz.govt.nz)

- *Banking Supervision Handbook* (July 1998)

Spain

Banco de España (www.bde.es)

- *Basic Regulatory Structure of the Spanish Banking System, Annex 1* (2000)

Sweden

Swedish Financial Supervisory Authority (www.fi.se)

- *Capital Adequacy and Large Exposures (Credit Institutions and Securities Companies) Act (SFS 1994:2004) Amendments up to 1 March, 2000*

Switzerland

Swiss Federal Banking Commission (www.ebk.ch)

- *Implementing Ordinance on Banks and Savings Banks, translated from Germany by KPMG Legal (*www.kpmg.ch*)*

United Kingdom

Financial Services Authority (www.fsa.gov.uk)

- *Interim Prudential Sourcebook: Banks, June 2001*

United States

Board of Governors of the Federal Reserve System (www.federalreserve. gov)

- *Bank Holding Company Supervision Manual* (December 2001)

5 Explaining implementation-quantitative tests

Introduction

This chapter takes the first cut at testing a selection of hypotheses that explain uneven degrees of compliance with the baseline rules of the 1988 Basel Accord. To this point, I have presented measures of the degrees of compliance with the provisions of the Accord and some of the variables that might be used to explain why some states adopted strict interpretations of the baseline rules while others adopted lax or non-compliant interpretations. In this chapter, I subject these explanations to a series of econometric examinations.

The measure of compliance operationalized in Chapter 4 indicated that states made asymmetrical interpretations of the Basel rules in measurable ways. The Capital Regulatory Index (CREG) indicated that convergence appeared in some of the credit risk regulations addressed by the Accord, and that some convergence emerged as the implementation period extended into the 1990s. Yet, the overall picture was one of some persistent divergence in the world's capital adequacy practices. This measure will serve as the dependent variable in this chapter.

The factors that should influence the observed levels of differentiated compliance fall along five dimensions: the severity of a state's pre-Basel Accord capital regime; the preferences of a state's commercial banks; a state's macroeconomic environment; the organization of a state's political system; and international influences. This chapter will seek to corroborate, or falsify, each of these explanatory variables. The one exception will be the exclusion of international pressure, which received little support in Chapter 4.

The next section presents the statistical results for the first implementation period of Chapter 4. These results contribute to an understanding of the influences on states' initial interpretations of the Basel rules. The results from this section suggest that path dependence and the incidence of banking crises were important contributors to implementation decisions made during this time period. The influence of private market governance is also found to have some influence.

Next, I present results for the second implementation period in order to investigate inter-temporal changes in Basel rule interpretations. Similar to the results from the first period, the path dependency argument is found to maintain some support. Yet, this section also reveals that private market governance was also important to implementation decisionmaking from about 1991 to 2000.

In all cases, these econometric results should be interpreted with caution. The sample sizes employed are extremely small; they never exceed 18 and drop down to as low as 8. I attempt to mitigate the methodological problems inherent in such small sample sizes by relying on small-N friendly statistical techniques. In particular, I rely fairly heavily on bivariate correlational associations and I follow Verdier's (2002) lead in utilizing a bootstrapping technique when conducting estimations. Yet, there are limits to drawing firm conclusions from statistical methods with sample sizes as small as those employed here. It is for these reasons that these hypotheses are also investigated qualitatively in the chapters that follow.

First period: analysis of implementation

This section will formally test competing explanations for a sample of industrialized states' initial interpretations of the 1988 Basel Accord rules. The dependent variable is the initial period (t) of the CREG discussed in Chapter 4. The independent variables are the initial period compliance hypotheses discussed in Chapter 3 and operationalized in Chapter 4. Testing these hypotheses contributes to an understanding of why the industrialized states interpreted the Basel Accord the way they did during the late 1980s. As the "soft law" provisions of the Accord provided these states with pockets of discretionary rule making within the Basel convergence framework, it is expected that this section will reveal a strong path dependence tendency for most states' initial implementation of the Accord. In other words, it is reasonable to argue that states will interpret the Basel rules in a manner consistent with their pre-Basel capital adequacy regime. Yet, there are a wide variety of political economic variables that could well condition or intervene between a state's existing rules and its interpretations of the Accord.

With a dataset of 18 states and no time series, there are too few observations to estimate (1). This is especially the case since limits in data availability for several of the explanatory variables will push the sample size down to well below 18. It is necessary to rely on bivariate correlational analyses to assess the feasibility of the hypothesis before conducting multivariate analyses. First, bivariate correlational analyses are conducted between the independent variable indicators and the CREG. Correlational results will also be presented for the CREG's component variables. These component results are presented to elaborate on the CREG results so that it is possible to judge if the independent variables are able to explain implementation decisions made in some Basel-related policy areas but not others. Second, multiple regression models will be estimated with select independent variables to discern whether the correlational associations are altered when controlling for the effects of one or more other explanatory variables.

Bivariate correlations

The correlational results are presented in Tables 5.1–5.3. Table 5.1 presents the correlation coefficients between the six independent variables. The results presented in this matrix indicate that no statistically significant results were found among these explanatory variables. Table 5.2 shows the correlations between the independent variables and the CREG. The results suggest a high level of support for the "path dependence" hypothesis. The index of states' previous Basel rules (PREBASEL) is positively correlated with the CREG and significant at the 5 percent level.

The importance of path dependence for each of our sample countries' Basel implementation policies is highlighted in the scatter graph in Figure 5.1. The

Table 5.1 Correlation coefficients: independent variables

	Pre-Basel	Stability	Private	Exposure	Capture	Gov
STABILITY	0.39 (0.26) [10]	1	0.29 (0.26) [17]	0.13 (0.60) [18]	−0.34 (0.18) [17]	0.13 (0.65) [15]
PRIVATE	0.22 (0.57) [9]	–	1	0.11 (0.69) [17]	−0.03 (0.89) [17]	−0.18 (0.54) [14]
EXPOSURE	−0.32 (0.36) [10]	–	–	1	−0.15 (0.56) [17]	0.01 (0.97) [15]
CAPTURE	0.37 (0.33) [9]	–	–	–	1	0.10 (0.74) [14]
GOV	0.08 (0.86) [8]	–	–	–	–	1

Notes
p-values in parentheses, number of cases in brackets.

Table 5.2 Correlation coefficients: CREG (t)

Correlate: CREG	Coefficient	p-value	N
PREBASEL	0.629	0.050**	10
STABILITY	0.434	0.070*	18
PRIVATE	−0.086	0.743	17
EXPOSURE	−0.009	0.972	18
GOV	0.197	0.482	15
CAPTURE	−0.064	0.808	17

Notes
* and ** indicate significance levels at 10 and 5 percent, respectively.

Explaining implementation-quantitative tests 77

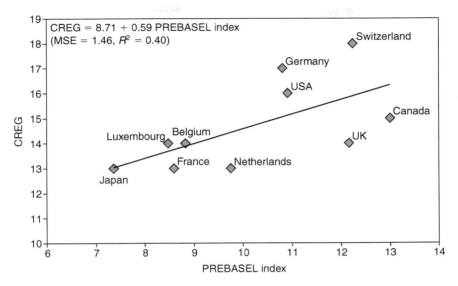

Figure 5.1 CREG and PREBASEL index comparisons.

countries with positive residuals (plotted above the regression line) are those that implemented the Accord with greater severity than the level of their pre-Basel capital regulatory stringency would have led us to predict. Here, Germany and Switzerland are especially noteworthy as their residuals exceeded one standard error in the estimated regression, while the US's score was also quite a bit higher than predicted. Looking at the negative residuals, the United Kingdom's predicted CREG score was greater than a standard error lower than predicted while Canada and the Netherlands had relatively low scores. The remainder of the sample (Belgium, France, Japan, and Luxembourg) appeared to implement the Basel Accord in a manner broadly consistent with their existing regulatory standards.

Table 5.3 illustrates further details of these relationships. This table breaks down the CREG and PREBASEL measures into their constituent variables. The results reveal that all of the statistically significant component coefficients were in the same direction as the CREG results, including the pre-Basel rule indicators. The measure of states' pre-Basel core capital definitions (PBTIER1) is positively correlated with the TIER1 indicator, though the relationship is not statistically significant. The coefficients between the pre-Basel secondary capital definition (PBTIER2) and TIER2 and pre-Basel capital levels (PBRATIO) and RATIO are both robust and significant. Interestingly, the correlation between maintaining a pre-Basel risk-weighting system and RW is negative and non-significant. On the whole, though, the pattern that emerges from the correlations is a positive relationship between the severity of states' pre-existing capital adequacy regimes and their Basel Accord interpretations.

Support was also found for the hypothesis that economic instability influenced the implementation process. The coefficient of the instability indicator

78 Quantitative studies

(STABILITY) is positive and significant at the 10 percent level. It is also interesting to observe that this variable, among the disaggregated elements of the CREG, was significantly correlated only with on-balance sheet risk-weighting frameworks. The variable is actually negatively correlated with ratio requirements, though not statistically significant.

Perhaps as interesting as the statistically significant results are the non-results that contradict prior expectations and theory. Surprisingly, no support is found for the relationship for the political institutional variables. The agglomerated measure of the ability of banks to "capture" the policymaking process (CAPTURE) yielded a very weak, though non-significant, correlation in the predicted direction ($r = -0.064$).

Also surprisingly, the measure of market governance (PRIVATE) yielded unexpected results. The bivariate relationship between this measure and CREG was weak and non-significant. Table 5.3 indicates that PRIVATE did yield two significant results, yet these were in different directions.

Also, the correlation between the definition of primary capital – TIER1 – and PRIVATE was negative ($r = -0.59$) and significant at the 5 percent level. This result is unexpected as it was hypothesized that the market might enforce a strict interpretation of the Basel rules, particularly the definition of Tier1 capital that is so critical to the safety and soundness of banks. Curiously, the private market hypothesis was supported for the risk-weighting framework as RW was positively and significantly correlated with PRIVATE ($r = 0.41$; $p = 0.10$). These divergent results are difficult to reconcile with theory and these relationships will be closely investigated in the qualitative analyses.

Multivariate analysis

The bivariate correlations are useful for discerning the statistical association between two variables, yet of course the method does not allow for the statistical control of other variables' impact. The results presented here were derived by estimating regression expressions with ordinary least squares (OLS). Generally, OLS regression models are appropriate for cardinal, rather than ordinal dependent variables. The method is employed here as there are too many values (0–24) of the CREG to use a model for categorical data.

Based on the input of the correlations, four models are estimated and the results of their fitting presented in Table 5.4. Each cell reports values of observed coefficients, and standard and bootstrapped *p*-values. The bootstrap method is employed as some researchers have found that it provides more accurate measures of statistical significance when it is carried out over at least 1000 iterations in sample sizes less than 30.[1] Though the state of knowledge about the correct applications of bootstrapping in social science is still rudimentary, it is employed here as a further measure to circumvent many of the problems introduced by small sample biases.[2] Yet, the interpretation of the bootstrapped confidence intervals must also be treated with some caution.

Turning now to the results, each of the four estimated models presented in

Table 5.3 Correlation coefficients: CREG components

	Tier1	Tier2	Deduct	RW	OBS	Ratio
PBTIER1	0.53 (0.11) [10]	0.20 (0.20) [10]	0.16 (0.66) [10]	0.06 (0.86) [10]	−0.17 (0.65) [10]	–
PBTIER2	0.05 (0.88) [10]	**0.60 (0.06)* [10]**	**0.57 (0.08)* [10]**	**0.58 (0.07)* [10]**	0.41 (0.24) [10]	–
PBRW	–	−0.53 (0.11) [10]	0.16 (0.67) [10]	−0.12 (0.74) [10]	0.33 (0.35) [10]	–
PBRATIO	−0.28 (0.27) [18]	−0.24 (0.34) [18]	0.11 (0.65) [18]	**0.39 (0.10)* [18]**	−0.03 (0.92) [18]	**0.47 (0.05)** [18]**
STABILITY	0.10 (0.68) [18]	– (0.22) [18]	0.31 (0.02)** [18]	**0.57 (0.38) [18]**	–	−0.22
PRIVATE	**−0.59 (0.02)** [17]**	0.09 (0.72) [17]	−0.04 (0.88) [17]	**0.41 (0.10)* [17]**	– (0.32) [17]	−0.26
EXPOSURE	0.02 (0.95) [18]	0.14 (0.57) [18]	0.02 (0.93) [18]	−0.07 (0.77) [18]	−0.01 (0.96) [18]	−0.26 (0.30) [18]
CAPTURE	0.20 (0.44) [17]	−0.38 (0.14) [17]	0.15 (0.56) [17]	−0.30 (0.24) [17]	0.31 (0.23) [17]	0.20 (0.44) [17]
GOV	0.30 (0.28) [15]	0.21 (0.45) [15]	−0.10 (0.73) [15]	−0.07 (0.81) [15]	0.24 (0.39) [15]	−0.15 (0.60) [15]

Notes
Statistically significant results presented in bold.
p-values in parentheses, number of cases in brackets.
– indicates that a correlation could not be determined because one of the variables' standard deviation equaled zero.
* and ** indicates significance at 10 and 5 percent levels.

Table 5.5 regresses the CREG on the PREBASEL and STABILITY indicators. These variables were found to be statistically significant in the bivariate correlational results and these models estimate these variables' importance while controlling for the effects of the other explanatory variables. The chief disadvantage of this selection of models is that the inclusion of the PREBASEL variable reduces the sample size to a maximum of ten.

Quantitative studies

Table 5.4 OLS regression results: CREG (t)

Dependent variable: CREG (t)	(1)	(2)	(3)	(4)
CONSTANT	9.117 (0.01)***	7.037 (0.40)	9.057 (0.05)**	8.915 (0.06)*
PREBASEL	0.530 (0.10)* [0.01]***	0.603 (0.26) [0.23]	0.507 (0.17) [0.04]**	0.495 (0.32) [0.04]**
STABILITY	0.562 (0.64) [0.32]	0.474 (0.77) [0.77]	−0.125 (0.92) [0.84]	0.836 (0.66) [0.52]
EXPOSURE		0.00 (0.80) [0.79]		
PRIVATE		0.150 (0.86) [0.85]		
GOV			0.072 (0.16) [0.24]	
CAPTURE				1.045 (0.84) [0.78]
R^2	0.41	0.43	0.62	0.42
Adj. R^2	0.25	0.14	0.34	0.07
Standard error	1.53	2.00	1.51	1.79
N	10	9	8	9

Notes
Ordinary least-squares with *p*-values presented in parentheses and bias-corrected *p*-values calculated on 1000 bootstraps in brackets.
*, **, and *** indicates significance levels at 10, 5, and 1 percent, respectively.

The first model includes the PREBASEL and STABILITY variables in isolation in order to control for their effects on one another's relationship with CREG. The results indicate that while the path dependency index and the economic instability indicator retain their predicted signs, only the path dependency measure remains statistically significant. The PREBASEL index is significant at the 10 percent level according to the standard *p*-value presented in parentheses and at the 1 percent level according to the bootstrapped *p*-value included in brackets.

Models 2–4 add the other explanatory variables to this regression result. Model 2 incorporates the bank preference variables while Models 3 and 4 incorporate the political institutions and government ownership indicators, respec-

Table 5.5 OLS regression results: CREG (PRE-BASEL excluded)

Dependent Variable: CREG (t)	(1)	(2)	(3)
CONSTANT	16.440	13.980	13.586
CRISIS	1.768	1.434	1.631
	(0.06)*	(0.14)	(0.09)*
	[0.00]***	[0.05]**	[0.00]***
EXPOSURE	1.060		
	(0.83)		
	[0.36]		
PRIVATE	0.322		
	(0.39)		
	[0.04]**		
GOV		0.021	
		(0.60)	
		[0.42]	
CAPTURE			0.997
			(0.71)
			[0.42]
R^2	0.23	0.20	0.19
Adj. R^2	0.05	0.06	0.08
Standard error	0.31	0.26	0.23
N	17	15	17

Notes
Ordinary least-squares with *p*-values presented in parentheses and bias-corrected *p*-values calculated on 1000 bootstraps in brackets.
*, **, and *** indicate significance levels at 10, 5, and 1 percent, respectively.

tively. Confidence may be given to the result that path dependence influences implementation as PREBASEL is in the predicted direction in all three of these models and significant in two according to the bootstrapped *p*-values. The STABILITY measure's relationship with CREG varies to some degree across the models as it takes on a negative sign in Model 3, though it remains statistically insignificant in all of the models. The other explanatory variables remain statistically insignificant.

A chief caveat of these regression results is that they do simply lower the sample size too far. Also, the weak coefficient of the instability measure in the regression studies when compared with the bivariate correlations may be the result of the steep lowering of *N* that occurs when PREBASEL is introduced. Two sample countries that experienced financial crises during the sample period (Australia and New Zealand) were excluded from the regressions due to missing pre-Basel data. Table 5.4 introduces regressions for all of our sample countries by eliminating the pre-Basel measure from the right-hand side of the estimated equation. In all three models, STABILITY is in the predicted direction and is now statistically significant according to the bootstrapped *p*-values. As before, the other explanatory variables remain statistically insignificant, with the exception of the private market governance variable (PRIVATE) which is now significant at the 5 percent level in the absence of the PREBASEL measure in Model 1. These results seem to suggest that economic crises are indeed an important predictor of capital adequacy policy during the late 1990s, at least when the "path dependency" concerns are not endogenized. Yet, also observe that R^2 for these models remain much lower than those in which PREBASEL was included in Table 5.5. This may suggest that the path dependency variable remains a critical contributor to understanding variations in implementation.

Yet, the results presented in Table 5.4 make it difficult to discern the relative importance of path dependency and economic instability on interpretations of the Accord's rules during this first time period. Ideally, it is necessary to compare the relative importance of PREBASEL and STABILITY for the full 18-country sample. Yet, the limited amounts of PREBASEL data make this comparison impossible. A second best solution is to conduct the estimation with a proxy indicator of the path dependency measure that is available for all 18 countries. Table 5.6 presents the results of such an analysis by utilizing the measure of states' pre-Basel capital-to-assets ratios (PBRATIO) in place of the PREBASEL index. This ratio variable is highly correlated with the PREBASEL index ($r = 0.84$) and available for all 18 states. Before utilizing this variable as a proxy, however, it is important to remember that in Table 5.3, PBRATIO was only significantly correlated with RATIO and RW and was actually negatively correlated with the definitions of capital indicators (TIER1 and TIER2). Hence, this variable will serve as a very rough proxy variable at best.

The regression results with this proxy are presented in Table 5.6. This table presents two estimations, with each featuring explanatory variables that were found too statistically significant in at least one model in Tables 5.4 or 5.6. The results of Model 1 indicate that while both the pre-Basel proxy (PBRATIO) and economic instability measures are in the predicted directions, only the latter is statistically significant. Model 2 indicates that this variable and the private market governance variable are in directions consistent with previous statistical findings and significant, though the PRIVATE indicator remains in an unpredicted direction. It is useful to note that R^2 for both models remain quite low relative to those obtained with the PREBASEL measure in Table 5.4. In sum, however, these results suggest the possibility that economic instabilities – and perhaps private market governance – were more important predictors of capital adequacy policy than existing rules. Yet again, such results must be taken with a great deal of caution given the rough design of the PREBASEL proxy and, again, the relatively low R^2 results in Table 5.6 when compared with those obtained with the full PREBASEL index in Table 5.5.

Table 5.6 OLS regression results: CREG (PBRATIO PROXY)

Dependent variable: CREG (t)	(1)	(2)
CONSTANT	12.466	16.230
PBRATIO	0.404	0.167
	(0.21)	(0.58)
	[0.21]	[0.55]
CRISIS	0.582	1.756
	(0.08)*	(0.07)*
	[0.00]***	[0.00]***
PRIVATE	−0.409	
	(0.30)	
	[0.05]**	
R^2	0.20	0.25
Adj. R^2	0.09	0.08
Standard error	0.19	0.28
N	18	17

Notes
Ordinary least-squares with *p*-values presented in parentheses and bias-corrected *p*-values calculated on 1000 bootstraps in brackets.
*, **, and *** indicate significance levels at 10, 5, and 1 percent, respectively.

Sensitivity exams

The findings are broadly robust to a number of sensitivity checks. First, a probit regression model was estimated with the explanatory variables outlined. To make the dependent variable amenable to a model for ordinal data, CREG was recoded into a 0–6 variable. This involved converting each of the six composite policy variables in dummies taking the value of unity if an above minimum interpretation was adopted and "0" otherwise. The conclusions reached with the OLS model remain broadly unchanged with these modifications. One key exception is that the relationship between CREG and CRISIS retains the same sign though it is not statistically significant as in the case of the estimations presented in Table 5.4. Also, the OLS regressions were run after recoding MARKET into a dummy variable. This variable is an ordinal scale measuring 0–6. The OLS procedure assumes that the exogenous variables are measured on at least the interval level and the MARKET variable is recoded to take the value of unity if a state's score is above the sample mean on this variable's score. As King (1985) predicts, incorporating an ordinal-level variable into an OLS regression seldom produces distinct results from a dummy recording, and the results do not change significantly after this modification.

Second period: analysis of implementation

This section conducts statistical tests for theoretical propositions explaining why states amended or maintained their initial interpretations of the Accord rules.

84 *Quantitative studies*

The previous section suggested that path dependency, instances of banking crisis, and perhaps private market governance influenced state's initial interpretations of the rules. As the political and economic consequences of these initial interpretations became clear, however, it is possible that states may have amended their interpretations to bolster their banks' competitiveness or solvency in reaction to changes in the financial environment that may, or may not, have been a consequence of the Accord. It is equally plausible that states would have maintained their initial interpretations throughout the 1990s in the absence of any political economic impetus for change. Studies looking at the evolution of public policy over time have concurred with Anne Krueger's observation that:

> with regulations there is not a once and for all moment ... [o]ften regulators impose regulations with a naiveté as to ramifications and then the market reacts to minimize the costs of the control ... [g]overnment actors then find the market's response unacceptable and have to alter the control.[3]

In this way, public policies travel through an iterated cycle in which regulators refine their policies in response to their actual and perceived impacts on target actors. This section will take a statistical cut at these dynamic possibilities for the implementation of the Accord.

The form of analysis will follow the same pattern as the tests in the first time period. First, the bivariate relationships between the explanatory variables with the dependent variable will be presented with a multivariate analysis to follow. As before, the objective of these statistical analyses is not only to test for the veracity of each null hypothesis, but also to set up avenues for enquiry in the qualitative studies that follow.

Bivariate correlations

First, the correlation between the indicator of economic stability and the five other independent variables is presented in Table 5.7. Only the STABILITY indicator exhibits inter-temporal variations while the others remain stationary over time. Again, the dependent variables do not exhibit a statistically significant relationship with another.

The correlation matrix for the second period of the CREG is presented in Table

Table 5.7 Correlation coefficients: STABILITY 1989–1995

Correlate: STABILITY	Coefficient	p-*value*	N
PREBASEL	0.457	0.185	10
PRIVATE	0.382	0.130	17
EXPOSURE	0.119	0.639	18
GOV	0.250	0.369	15
CAPTURE	0.332	0.194	17

5.8. The correlation matrix indicates that three variables exhibit a statistically significant relationship with the second period CREG. First, the two variables that represent lagged values of the CREG $(t + 1)$ – CREG (t) and PREBASEL – are positively correlated and significant at least to the 5 percent threshold. Interestingly, the path dependency measure utilized in the first period analysis (PREBASEL) is more robustly correlated with the second period index than the first. This suggests the possibility that some states realigned their initial interpretations of the Accord back toward their pre-Accord standards during the late 1990s. Perhaps states judged their initial interpretations too harsh or inappropriate and reverted back to their old regimes before the Accord was negotiated. This conclusion cannot be made through correlational exercises and will be an interesting topic for investigation in the qualitative investigations. Yet, the correlational results also indicate that high levels of private market governance (PRIVATE) may have also influenced implementation decisions during the late 1990s. The sign of the private governance variable is in the theorized direction and significant at the 10 percent level.

The remaining explanatory variables did not produce robust or significant associations with the second period interpretations. Most interestingly, economic stability was not associated with rule interpretations in the second period. This variable exerted a positive correlation with the first period index, yet it is weakly correlated with CREG $(t + 1)$ in a negative direction.

Table 5.9 drills down the correlational analyses by disaggregating the CREG $(t + 1)$ into its constituent variables. The matrix shows some rather surprising results. First, the private market governance variable exhibited mixed signs in a manner identical to the correlational results presented with the first period CREG in Table 5.3. The PRIVATE index is found to be negatively correlated with the TIER1 indicator though positively correlated with the risk-weights interpretation (RW); both correlations were found to be significant at the 5 percent level. There is no clear theoretical explanation for this mixed performance of the PRIVATE variable. As stated before, given the importance of Tier1 as an indicator of bank strength, it would seem likely that higher levels of private market governance might be correlated with more limited definitions of this capital class. One ex ante possibility is that regulators might have felt at

Table 5.8 Correlation coefficients: CREG $(t+1)$

Correlate: CREG $(t + 1)$	Coefficient	p-*value*	N
CREG (t)	0.553	0.017**	18
PREBASEL	0.798	0.006***	10
STABILITY	0.037	0.884	18
PRIVATE	0.393	0.090*	17
EXPOSURE	0.117	0.645	18
GOV	0.181	0.518	15
CAPTURE	0.119	0.650	17

Notes
*, **, and *** indicate significance at 10, 5, and 1 percent levels, respectively.

86 Quantitative studies

Table 5.9 Correlation coefficients: CREG ($t+1$) components

	TIER1	TIER2	DEDUCT	RW	OBS	RATIO
PBTIER1	0.37 (0.29) [10]	–	0.16 (0.67) [10]	0.30 (0.40) [10]	0.17 (0.65) [10]	**0.67** **(0.04)**** **[10]**
PBTIER2	0.15 (0.68) [10]	–	0.06 (0.86) [10]	0.49 (0.15) [10]	0.41 (0.24) [10]	0.41 (0.20) [10]
PBRW	0.19 (0.61) [10]	**0.63** **(0.05)**** **[10]**	0.16 (0.67) [10]	–	0.33 (0.35) [10]	0.33 (0.35) [10]
PBRATIO	0.00 (0.99) [18]	0.26 (0.30) [18]	0.31 (0.22) [18]	0.17 (0.50) [18]	0.03 (0.92) [18]	0.35 (0.15) [18]
STABILITY	0.16 (0.52) [18]	0.04 (0.88) [18]	0.19 (0.46) [18]	0.09 (0.72) [18]	0.34 (0.17) [18]	0.16 (0.52) [18]
PRIVATE	**0.50** **(0.04)**** **[17]**	0.23 (0.38) [17]	0.31 (0.22) [17]	**0.53** **(0.03)**** **[17]**	– (0.76)	0.08 [17]
EXPOSURE	0.29 (0.24) [18]	0.36 (0.14) [18]	0.10 (0.68) [18]	0.06 (0.82) [18]	0.01 (0.96) [18]	0.27 (0.29) [18]
CAPTURE	**0.44** **(0.08)*** **[17]**	**0.72** **(0.00)***** **[17]**	0.07 (0.78) [17]	0.05 (0.86) [17]	0.31 (0.23) [17]	0.21 (0.42) [17]
GOV	0.23 (0.41) [15]	0.17 (0.55) [15]	0.44 (0.10)* [15]	0.08 (0.77) [15]	0.24 (0.39) [15]	0.03 (0.90) [15]

Notes
Statistically significant results presented in bold.
p-values in partheneses, number of cases in brackets.
– indicates that a correlation could not be determined because one of the variable's standard deviation equalled zero.
* and ** indicates significance at 10 and 5 percent, respectively.

leisure to permit a wide range of items to qualify as Tier1 capital if they were confident that the market aided in the supervision of their domestic banks. As before, verification of this working hypothesis requires qualitative input.

Second, these bivariate results suggest that banks' potential to "capture" the policymaking process might have been of some importance. The CAPTURE indicator was significantly correlated with definitions of Tier1 and Tier2 capital, though in opposing directions. It is not necessarily clear why this variable was so robustly correlated with TIER1 in a positive direction and negatively correlated with TIER2. These relationships require further analysis through a multivariate study to ensure that a spurious effect has been observed.

Multivariate analysis

Multiple regression model estimation results for the second period are shown in Table 5.10. Five models are estimated in the first instance. All five include the two variables that produced significant results in the bivariate correlations (PREBASEL and PRIVATE). The second model includes one bank preference

Table 5.10 OLS Regression results: CREG ($t + 1$)

Dependent variable: CREG (t+1)	(1)	(2)	(3)	(4)	(5)
CONSTANT	0.523	4.837	5.346	4.534	5.549
PREBASEL	0.578 (0.00)*** [0.00]***	0.612 (0.00)*** [0.00]***	0.555 (0.01)*** [0.00]***	0.572 (0.02)** [0.00]***	0.608 (0.00)*** [0.00]***
STABILITY			0.134 (0.84) [0.76]		
EXPOSURE		1.547 (0.64) [0.62]			
PRIVATE	0.497 (0.08)* [0.07]*	0.482 (0.11) [0.10]*	0.520 (0.11) [0.11]	0.584 (0.23) [0.18]	0.450 (0.15) [0.11]
GOV				0.013 (0.65) [0.63]	
CAPTURE					0.728 (0.65) [0.61]
R^2	0.85	0.85	0.85	0.80	0.85
Adj. R^2	0.80	0.77	0.76	0.61	0.77
Standard error	0.00	0.02	0.02	0.14	0.02
F ratio	16.6	9.74	9.32	4.10	9.72
N	9	9	9	6	9

Notes
Ordinary least-squares with *p*-values presented in parentheses and bias-corrected *p*-values calculated on 1000 bootstraps in brackets.
*, **, and *** indicates significance levels at 10, 5, and 1 percent, respectively.

measure (EXPOSURE), the third includes the macroeconomic indicator (STABILITY), the fourth adds the GOV measure, and the fifth considers the political institutions variable (CAPTURE).

The most striking feature of these regression analyses is the extremely high R^2 produced by the five models. Though King (1985) warns against drawing firm conclusions from R^2 data, it is a reasonable measure of these models' "goodness-of-fit" as identical dependent variables are being utilized across the models.[4] In this regard, the high R^2 do suggest that the variables utilized in these models – particularly PREBASEL and PRIVATE – were important predictors of implementation in this second time period.

In addition, it is interesting to observe the consistently significant results produced by the path dependence and market governance variables. The coefficients of PREBASEL are in the predicted direction and statistically significant (generally at the 1 percent level) in all five models. The private market indicator retains the predicted sign in all five models and remains significant in two, falling just short of obtaining a significant result at the 10 percent level in the bootstrapped *p*-values for Models 4 and 5. Controlling for the effects of other explanatory variables does not modify the coefficients of these variables to any great degree. In particular, it is interesting to observe that the inclusion of the CAPTURE indicator in Model 5 does not reduce the relationship of the PREBASEL or PRIVATE variables with CREG, nor is this measure significantly related to CREG.

In order to further examine the contours of the relationship between the CAPTURE variable and implementation uncovered in the correlational analyses in Table 5.11, two ordered probit models were estimated. These probit regres-

Table 5.11 Ordered probit regression results: CREG (*t*+1) component results

Dependent variables	TIER1	TIER2
CONSTANT	1.561	0.504
	(0.13)	(0.55)
PBWEIGHT	1.046	
	(0.08)*	
PRIVATE	0.247	
	(0.05)**	
CAPTURE	0.473	0.563
	(0.59)	(0.81)
Log likelihood	5.67	1.12
N	17	9

Notes
p-values in parentheses.
* and ** indicate significance 5 and 10 percent, respectively.

sion models situate the TIER1 and TIER2 components of the CREG ($t + 1$) as the dependent variables as these two variables were found to have a statistically significant bivariate relationship with the CAPTURE variable. The independent variables chosen are CAPTURE and the other two variables found to be significantly correlated with CREG: PBWEIGHT and PRIVATE, respectively.

The results of the two probit models indicate the possibility that CAPTURE's bivariate relationship with the CREG components was spurious. The CAPTURE measure does not retain the same direction of relationship with the TIER1 and TIER2 measures in the probit models as those uncovered in the bivariate correlations. In fact, the directions of effect are actually reversed. Also, CAPTURE is not statistically significant in either model estimated. Conversely, the PRIVATE and PBWEIGHT measures retain the same sign in the probit model and remain statistically significant. These results provide further support for the importance of the path dependence and market governance hypotheses of implementation during this second period and raise doubts regarding the viability of the importance of banks' political power explanations.

In sum, these second period results provide a great deal of confidence in two conclusions regarding the implementation of the Accord. First, the G-10 states' capital adequacy regulations continued to be path dependent well into the 1990s. Though more than half of the original implementing states amended their initial interpretations from 1988 to 2000, these changes did not significantly depart from their original pre-Basel rules or involve recalibrating their interpretations of the Accord back to their pre-Basel shape. Second, some evidence suggests that states subject to a high degree of private market governance were more likely to strengthen their capital adequacy rule interpretations over time. This suggests that market actors may have increasingly demanded more high-quality capital adequacy procedures from banks than was required by their regulators in exchange for competitive credit ratings. This may have had the effect of leading banks to prefer or be ambivalent toward the tightening of their domestic solvency standards. This opens up the interesting possibility that markets do influence the bank policymaking process and have a hand in effecting transnational rule isomorphism as many globalization theories suggest. Yet again, the negative relationship between the definitions of Tier1 capital and private market governance indicates that this relationship is nuanced and not clear-cut.

Sensitivity analysis

As with the first period analysis, the results in this section were robust to a number of sensitivity analyses. First, the multiple regression analysis with the CREG ($t + 1$) measure (Table 5.11) was run with the explanatory variable transformations presented in the first period sensitivity examination (see Section "Sensitivity exams"). As with the first period analysis, the transformations did not produce any substantive alterations to the results presented with the original operationalizations.

90 *Quantitative studies*

Table 5.12 Correlation coefficients: ΔCREG

Correlate: ΔCREG	Coefficient	p-*value*	N
CREG (t+1)	0.596	0.009***	18
PREBASEL	0.042	0.908	10
STABILITY	0.285	0.251	18
PRIVATE	0.481	0.050**	17
EXPOSURE	0.102	0.686	18
GOV	0.424	0.115	15
CAPTURE	0.043	0.871	17

Note
** and *** indicate significance at 1 and 5 percent levels, respectively.

Second, estimations were made with the change in the value of CREG variable over time on the left-hand side. The variable ?CREG was created by differencing $CREG(t + 1)$ and $CREG(t)$. The results – presented as bivariate correlations in Table 5.12 – further support the importance of private market governance in leading to the tightening of capital adequacy policies during the late 1990s.

Summary and conclusions

The quantitative tests provided support for three of the hypotheses advanced in Chapter 3. First, an interesting mix of support was found for the path dependency hypotheses. The first, regarding the relationship between a state's initial interpretations and their pre-Basel rules, found some support. Yet, most robust support for this hypothesis was found in the second period analysis.

Second, mixed support was also found for the market supervision hypothesis. The level of private market governance was not found to be an important explanation for states' initial interpretations of the Basel rules, yet its importance increased over time. It may be the case that market actors did not have a preference toward disparate interpretations of the Accord until the political and economic ramifications of the initial interpretations became evident. Perhaps only after several years into the Accord's implementation did market actors arrive at clear preferences regarding the Accord.

Next, tests of the key macroeconomic indicator – the presence of economic stability – were also mixed. This variable was operationalized as the presence of bank crises and was found to be important during the early implementation period, but less important through the latter part of the 1990s. This may seem curious, as there were only three bank crises from 1985 to 1987, yet five from 1988 to 1996. There is no ex ante theoretical explanation for this anomaly, and it will be an interesting topic to pursue in the qualitative studies to follow.

Finally, little support was found for the remaining hypotheses. The inabilities of the regional imitation and hegemonic arguments to explain variations in implementation were discussed at some length in Chapter 4. Among the remaining hypotheses, it is most interesting that little empirical support was found for the regulatory capture argument. The comparative political power positions of commercial banks did not seem to have been a major factor in implementation decisionmaking. This is a curious result that contradicts much economic theorizing over the ability of regulated firms to sharply influence the rules that govern them. Part of the lack of quantitative support for the CAPTURE variable may be due to its crude specification. Though it has been theorized that more highly concentrated banks are capable of wielding comparatively large quantities of political power, especially in a fragmented political system, these proxies for bank power may simply be too crude. Better measures of bank power may be the level of horizontal or vertical integration in bank's associational systems or the extent to which a corporatist style system binds banking groups and regulators together in the policymaking process. Unfortunately, quantitative indicators of these phenomena are not available across a large sample of cases. Investigating this variable with the case study method will be instructive of both the influence of the political power of banks on the implementation of the Accord and of the relative strengths of quantitative and qualitative research.

Again, consideration must be given to the limits of quantitative analyses with relatively small sample sizes. As has been indicated, provisions have been taken to ensure that correct inferences were drawn from the 20 cases examined here. Yet, these results should still be approached with some caution. Thus, a key purpose of jointly employing the case method is to provide another empirical testing ground for these hypotheses in order to add confidence to the tests conducted in this chapter. More will follow in the next chapter on the combination of these quantitative tests and the system of focused, case comparison.

Part III
Case studies

Introduction

This component of the book presents a series of case studies investigating the implementation of the 1988 Basel Accord in a cross-section of four states over a 12-year time span, 1988–2000. Chapters 4 and 5 addressed what implementation looked like in a sample of 18 countries and searched for general patterns of explanation for the observed levels and types of compliance with the Basel rules at two points of time. To augment and further interpret these aggregated results, Chapters 6–8 present structured, focused comparison case studies of four of the most important players in the BCBS: the United States, France, Germany, and Japan.

Before turning to the case study analyses, this short prelude to Part III will, first, consider the goals of the cases and how, it is hoped, they will corroborate and elaborate upon the quantitative exercises of Part II. Second, this section will lay out the case study methodology to be employed.

Goals of the qualitative research

There are a large number of advantages to utilizing comparison case studies in conjunction with a quantitative approach. This is not a novel methodological tool in social science.[1] Part of the justification for this multi-method research is that while the quantitative approach is useful for building frequency distributions, making observations, and testing generalizable hypotheses across a wide range of cases, the results of such work, perhaps especially in social science, are often vague and inferences are often deduced with crude proxy indicators. As a result, case study work is indispensable in filling out the results of correlational and regression analyses.

Supporting this general point, Rossman and Wilson (1985) observed that multi-method research has three purposes: corroboration, elaboration, and initiation.[2] The first, corroboration, argues that case studies can augment and add confidence (or uncertainty) to quantitative results by providing another empirical testing ground, one based on a different data collection technique, for explanatory variables. By extending the gamut for hypothesis falsification, corroboration increases the validity of quantitative results and can potentially support the reliability of quantitative indicators. Beyond this, case studies can operate as an elaborative device by filling out the necessarily simplified modeling approach adopted for aggregated research. The rich empirical fabric of case study work can, in this instance, serve not only as a check on quantitative results but extend and further them by viewing an empirical problem from a different angle. The effects of these collaborative and elaborative mechanisms, according to Rossman and Wilson, could be the initiation of wholly new interpretations of the quantitative results and the reformulation of the initial research problem, thus opening avenues for future research.[3]

The case studies contained in Chapters 6–8 endeavor to corroborate and elaborate upon the quantitative results presented in Chapters 4 and 5. This is especially important as the parameters of the quantitative dataset were not amenable to more powerful multivariate statistical methods. Given the dataset's limited size, it was not possible to effectively control for the effects of all of the explanatory variables, and conclusions were drawn largely from bivariate correlational investigations. The qualitative analyses address this lacuna by permitting the investigation of interactive effects among the independent variables.

The case work uses the quantitative results as a form of "sign post" to help guide the cases and the search for causal influences in the morass of detail that characterizes the implementation of the Basel Accord. Each hypothesis will be put to a sort of qualitative test to determine if further detail or divergent results can be gleaned by switching the methodology through which the hypotheses are tested. It is entirely possible, for example, that a hypothesis could be confirmed or rejected for a dyad-year in the quantitative sample, yet not for any individual country in a given year when the data are disaggregated into a case study. In this sense, the case study data will be viewed as un-coded quantitative data to accomplish identical theoretical aims.[4]

Admittedly, there are some well-documented difficulties in implementing the multi-method research program to effectively achieve these corroborative goals. A critical caveat is that the results of mixing methods may measure differences in methodologies (quantitative versus qualitative) rather than differences within the data or, citing Mathison (1988), "different methods may tap different ways of knowing."[5]

To minimize this risk, I standardize the ontological assumptions made across the two parts of the research project. That is, I will adopt a deductive research strategy for the qualitative tests, just as was the case for quantitative analysis.

This deductivist approach will also be applied in the qualitative elaboration of the quantitative results. In some instances, these hypotheses represent new variables not considered in Chapter 4 and in others they test for modified or extended versions of previously considered hypotheses. For example, in the testing of the bank preferences hypotheses, the cases will consider a vector of qualitative indicators that were untestable in an aggregated format. In this way, I can unpack banks' utility functions by attempting to determine whether fiscal policies substituted or complemented bank preferences for a specific Basel rule interpretation. In addition, the casework can attempt to understand why some quantitative hypotheses produced mixed or unanticipated results across different dependent variable indicators. Were these an inconsistency introduced from a variable specification error or did banks have different preferences for Tier1 capital policies versus the capital ratios policy?

Lastly, the casework elaborates on the quantitative analysis through considering each hypothesis in a dynamic fashion by analyzing each major country case from 1988 to 2002. The cases will measure changes in banks' preferences and regulators' policies over the same 12-year time span. As each of these case countries implemented the Basel Accord in the same year, it will be possible to hold a variety of variables constant which could confound the analysis of uneven implementation over divergent periods of time. In addition, the qualitative studies are more amenable to studying the role of ideas in explaining departures from extant capital adequacy standards in the first period or changes in Basel rule interpretations over time. Chapter 3 discussed the importance of ideas about risk management and role of the state in governing bank capital, yet such variables are difficult to operationalize in a way convenient for statistical examination. Such ideas will be investigated here.

Case study methodology

The structured, focused comparison methodology will be employed. This method, prominently detailed by George (1979, 1985), requires the systematic collection of the same information (variables) across selected units. Using this method, the researcher, "defines and standardizes the data requirements of the case studies by formulating theoretically relevant general questions to guide the examination of each case."[6] This use of standardized sets of questions is necessary to assure the acquisition of comparable data for the case studies.[7]

This standardization will be assured in two prominent ways. First, the same series of questions will be addressed in each case study. These questions are represented by the hypotheses that have been detailed. Second, a standardized method will be utilized to bring empirical data to bear on each of these questions for each case study. That is, each case will follow a standard template that identifies the relevant actors to be analyzed and the order in which the empirical details will be presented.

The actors systematically analyzed in each case, as identified in the hypotheses, will include, for each country:

1   the commercial banks required to implement the Basel Accord and their industry associations;
2   the domestic banking regulator(s) responsible for implementing the Basel Accord in their domestic banking space;
3   the executive and legislative branches responsible for supervising the banking regulator(s).

The relationships between these actors will be accessed in more detail here than was possible with the quantitative format. In particular, the complex and often unobservable links between commercial banks and their regulators was crudely represented by multiplying each state's three-bank concentration ratio with a cardinal measure of political veto points. The qualitative studies will allow for the better specification of this regulatory relationship and the extent to which bank–regulator interactions over the Accord's implementation were structured by historically conditioned circumstances and political institutions. In addition, two additional actors will be scrutinized on an ad hoc basis, depending on the qualities of the case country's banking regime. In the testing of the hypothesis about bank preferences, the interests of credit ratings agencies will be analyzed and the importance of international institutions will be considered in testing the hypothesis specifically focusing on such institutions.

For each case, the empirical details will be consistently presented in a chronological time order. The body of each case study will be divided into three sections, see Table III.1.

This historical division is arbitrary, yet it does serve several heuristic functions. The first time period (1985–1988) allows us to focus specifically on the pre-Basel Accord capital adequacy regimes of each state, details of which will be critical for addressing the relationship between a state's pre-Basel rules, macroeconomic climate, and Basel Accord negotiating position. The second period (1988–1992) corresponds to the first period of the quantitative dataset and initial period hypotheses. The third (1993–2000) corresponds to the second period dataset. By dividing the qualitative analyses in this way, it will be possible to compare the qualitative case results to the quantitative results for the first and second periods.

Table III.1 Chronological ordering of comparison case studies

Years	Description
Up to 1988	**Background** Each case country's preferences and role in the negotiation of the Basel Accord. Also considered will be the nature of each case country's credit-risk regulations before the Basel negotiations.
1988–1992	**First Period Implementation** The earliest stages of the implementation of the Basel Accord, including each case country's transitional arrangements until full implementation in 1992. Also considered will be the domestic and international politics leading to the 1992 amendment to the Basel Accord.
1993–2000	**Second Period Implementation** The continued interactions between various domestic and international actors regarding the appropriateness of particular elements of implementation in light of numerous years of application of the Basel rules; also the politics of the major 1996 Basel Accord amendment for market risk.

In order to ensure that a tight comparison is drawn between the hypotheses – acting here as "sign posts" – and the rich, empirical data, each of the two implementation periods will be followed by a Hypothesis Review section. These sections endeavor to indicate if and how the theoretical statements developed in Chapter 3 can help explain implementation outcomes. Attention will also be given to highlighting any explanatory variables that are inductively uncovered for each case but were not considered in Chapter 3. Also, these sections aim to highlight the weaknesses of a qualitative versus a quantitative approach for analyzing uncovered implementation outcomes when appropriate.

Aggregate introduction to the cases

As the cases were chosen to corroborate and extend on some of the key quantitative findings contained in Chapters 3 and 4, a major criterion was to choose cases that provide variance on the explanatory and dependent variables. With regards the latter, and as illustrated in Table III.2, France and Japan implemented credit-risk standards in 1988 that approximated the minimum baseline requirements set out in the Accord and largely maintained these interpretations over time, though Japan did strengthen their standards in one respect after 1992. The United States and Germany, by contrast, initially implemented much stricter regulations than required, though each gradually relaxed their rigorous regulations in the early 1990s. Thus, by 1992, the three countries experienced risk-capital regime convergence. The variance in these states' rules – as measured by the standard deviation statistic in Table III.2 – fell from 2.06 to 0.96 between the two periods. There is thus fairly wide variation in implementation results among the four case countries.

These cases also provide variance on the explanatory variables that have been tested. First, the three had widely varying pre-Basel capital adequacy standards. Table III.3 presents the PREBASEL index broken into four component indices. Remember from Chapter 4 that the index measures definitions of primary (PREBASEL TIER1) and secondary capital (PREBASEL TIER2) with 1–4 scales with greater values indicating greater stringency. The maintenance of a risk-weighting assets' framework (PREBASEL RW) was a dummy variable scored as "1" if such a system were implemented prior to the Accord. The second pre-Basel capitalization measure (PREBASEL CARs) is these states' largest banks' CARs from 1985 to 1988. As Table III.3 suggests, Germany easily had the most limiting definitions of bank capital, scoring a maximum "4" for the pre-Basel measures of Tiers1 and Tiers2 capital. By contrast, France and Japan had the weakest definitions of capital but France was the only state to have a risk-capital weighting system in place. The US rules fall between France/Japan and Germany's for severity, yet American banks were better capitalized than their European competitors. The average capital to (non-risk weighted) assets ratio for leading American banks from 1985 to 1987 was well over 200 basis points higher than French and German banks during the period.[8] The four countries thus started from widely varying positions when implementing the Basel standard.

Table III.2 Comparison of CREG scores for case-study countries

	USA	France	Germany	Japan
CREG (t)	16	13	17	13
CREG ($t+1$)	15	13	15	14
Standard deviation (t) = 2.06				
Standard deviation ($t+1$) = 0.96				

Table III.3 Comparison of explanatory variable values for case-study countries

	USA	France	Germany	Japan
PREBASEL TIER1	2	2	4	2
PREBASEL TIER2	4	3	4	3
PREBASEL RW	0	1	0	0
PREBASEL CARs	4.9%	2.6%	2.8%	2.37%
MARKET	8	6	6	8
EXPOSURE	High	Low	High	High
INSTABILITY$_t$	Yes	No	Yes	No
INSTABILITY$_{t+1}$	Yes	Yes	No	Yes
CAPTURE	0.16	0.31	0.37	0.18
GOV	0%	n/a	42%	1%

Note
n/a = Data not available.

Similar disparities are found on the other explanatory variables for each state.

First, the dense institutional linkages between German regulators and their internationally active banks are generally believed to confer a great deal of political power to these states' banks. Table III.3 shows that German banks scored highest on the CAPTURE indicator with France not far behind in part because of the heavy concentration of the French banking system. By contrast, the highly fragmented and decentralized US and Japanese financial regimes are believed to weaken the power of banks to influence policymaking.[9]

Second, each country experienced a bout of banking market instability during the sample time periods. The United States experienced a major banking crisis during the late 1980s and a supply side credit crunch with accompanying banking market fragility during the early 1990s. Germany experienced macroeconomic problems after reunification that influenced bank profitability. France witnessed major bank insolvency in 1994 with the economic problems at Crédit Lyonnais. Finally, the Japanese economy and financial system entered a decade long downturn, beginning with the collapse of the asset bubble around 1990. A problem with the quantitative indicators for economic instability is that they fail to capture degrees of crisis by adopting a binary fashion. It will be useful to approach the influences of these bouts of economic instability with a more differentiated perspective provided in the case studies.

Finally, some variance is witnessed in indicators of financial exposure and government ownership. The latter is presented in the form of "high" or "low" in Table III.3, with these designations referring to whether the sample state scored above or below the mean financial exposure score for the 18 country dataset. According to these data, exposure was high for three of these states and low only for France. For government ownership, the German government exerts a much greater ownership stake than the United States and Japan. Unfortunately, the government ownership data in Barth *et al.* (2001a) did not cover France, as French authorities did not provide answers to these researchers questionnaire on the topic. Yet, as the case study data suggest, France plays an important ownership role in their domestic banking system.

Moreover, these cases were chosen for the ex ante importance that previous academic studies of the Accord have placed on these four countries. Apart from any variance on the explanatory and dependent variables of interest, the United States, France, Germany, and Japan are the key political economic players in the Basel regime. As is well reported, much of the research into the Accord's negotiation observed that the agreement was designed to benefit US banks at the expense of their French and Japanese competitors. Oatley and Nabors (1998) argued that the Accord was a weapon designed by the United States to redistribute wealth from the relatively undercapitalized French and Japanese banks to the Americans. Norton (1992) reported that Germany was not really involved in this redistribution as it was internationally isolated by being the one BCBS member to object to the Accord because it did not establish a strict enough international code. Thus by focusing on these four countries, it is possible to test the political and economic veracity of these well-worn claims and, indeed, it seems that by looking at the implementation of the standards doubt can be cast on elements of these arguments.

6 Implementation of the Basel Accord in the United States

Introduction

In order to corroborate and elaborate upon the hypotheses of implementation identified in previous chapters, it is necessary to study cases in which we observe strict and liberal interpretations of the Basel Accord. In studying these varying degrees of Basel compliance with the case study method, I will look not only at a static measure of implementation severity, but observe how implementation has changed over time (1988–2002) and how the explanatory variables fare in explaining such change. The selection of the cases was thus made with the aim of maximizing the variation on the dependent variables, namely the severity of the sample states' interpretation of the Basel rules, as well as variation on driver variables that may be associated with differentiated state responses to the 1988 Accord.

In looking at the United States, this chapter focuses on a sample state that initially implemented a highly strict interpretation of the baseline Basel Accord rules in 1988. In fact, the quantitative index, presented in Chapter 4, indicated that the three federal American regulators – the Federal Reserve, the Federal Deposit Insurance Corporation (FDIC), and the Office of the Comptroller of the Currency (OCC) – collectively adopted the third most limited interpretation of the Basel rules in the G-10, save for Switzerland and Germany. Yet within months, the US bank supervisors began to publicly re-examine and then amend their initial interpretations. These revisions were dramatic and brought the United States into conflict with fellow Basel Committee members who objected to the Federal Reserve Board's increasingly liberal interpretations of regulatory capital, which violated the Basel rules. This turn of events itself is instructive given the orthodox view that the Basel Accord was, in part, an American "hegemonic" effort to force fellow G-10 members to adopt stricter bank capital regulation.[1]

A key goal of this chapter will thus be to understand why the United States exhibited such volatility in its capital adequacy regulations over a relatively short period of time. This chapter will advance two key arguments. First, the United States' decision to implement a highly restrictive definition of capital and risk-weighting categories in 1988 was the result of the crippling funding crisis that engulfed much of the US financial services marketplace in the mid to late 1980s. American politicians demanded that the federal banking supervisors end years of interagency dispute over capital adequacy regulation and adopt a stricter regulatory code that ensured the soundness and stability of the country's banks. Though the large money center banks of New York, Chicago, and San Francisco argued that such regulations would threaten their internationally competitive positions, their influence over the policymaking process, never strong, was further weakened by the political perception that their reckless behavior had created the banking crisis. As a result, the United States departed from previous regulatory practice to adopt a very strict capital standard.

Second, the gradual loosening of America's rules resulted, initially, from the perceived impact of these restrictive capital standards. By the early 1990s, the United States entered a recession that some blamed on a supply-side credit crunch created by the Basel Accord. This resulted in the widening of the domestic political economy's interest in the Basel standards from the relatively narrow confines of the financial services policy network to a broad spectrum of business and consumer interests that relied on bank credits for their core funding. Politicians that had once mandated that the federal regulators negotiate the Basel Accord and adopt a strict domestic code now argued that forbearance be practiced and the rules loosened. The balance sheets of the largest commercial banks were now in a stronger position than in 1988 and they were emboldened to lobby for changes in the capital regime. These interests were successful in effecting regulatory change and these changes went largely unchallenged through 2000.

The US case study lends a great deal of empirical support to the economic stability hypothesis. Yet, the two periods of economic instability produced distinct results on the behavior of the US banking supervisors. The distinction may be explained by a feedback process in the bank regulatory regime that allowed some degree of regulatory learning about the impact of capital standards by the financial services policy network from 1988 to the early 1990s. In the initial implementation period, the bank crisis led to a departure from the existing US regulatory practice – path dependence was not a political option in 1988. Yet, the onset of a second period of financial instability led to a return to some elements of the pre-1988 capital regime.

The investigation of these events will begin, with a review of the US bank regulatory regime and a history of America's capital adequacy regulatory policy until the completion of the Basel Accord negotiations in July 1988. This historical sketch is longer than those presented in the other case studies and stretches back about 50 years. This allows for an investigation into whether the capital adequacy policy volatility witnessed from 1988 emerged only after the creation of the Accord or reflects a more general pattern of prudential regulatory policy. Only a longitudinal study with several decades of data can facilitate this investigation. The next section will then provide a detailed analysis of the shape of America's initial interpretation of the Basel rules from 1988 to 1992, what was termed the "first implementation period" in previous chapters. The section will question why the United States adopted such a strict interpretation of the Basel rules, and attempt to elaborate upon and test the implementation hypotheses introduced in Chapter 3. Next, I conduct a similar exercise for the second implementation period, 1993–2000, and seek to adopt a fuller empirical and theoretical understanding of the evolution of America's capital regime during this 12-year period of time. Each of the two sections investigating implementation will conclude with "Hypothesis Review" sections that summarize how the presented qualitative evidence supports or refutes the hypotheses discussed in previous chapters. The last section concludes.

Background

By some accounts, the United States exercised market power in order to coerce the G-10 countries' acquiescence to the Basel Accord. Such views conclude that "the US proposal for capital adequacy regulations was not motivated by concern about international financial stability, but by a need to satisfy competing [domestic] interest group and voter pressures ..." and thus "linkages between joint gains and the Basle Accord are tenuous at best."[2] Econometric research has been mixed when testing the latter point on the distributions of the Accord's wealth gains and losses, yet political economists have provided support for the former argument on the formative influence of US market power in the Accord's formation.[3]

As described in Chapter 2, this argument posits that the Federal Reserve employed the assistance of the Bank of England to coerce Japan and then the entire Basel Committee to adopt an agreement demanded by the American Congress and banking industry. The interests of the United States in shaping this international effort reflected domestic concerns over inadequate banking regulations amid the savings and loan and LDC debt crises of the early 1980s. Members of Congress required the three federal bank supervisors to adopt stricter domestic regulations to ensure electoral support from constituencies inundated with media reports of the government's bailout of reckless banks. While politicians wanted to be perceived as doing something about the crises by their constituents, the banks themselves argued that the unilateral tightening of regulations would further depress their international competitiveness. The solution to these concerns was America's determination to secure an inter-state capital adequacy standard.

History of capital adequacy regulation

The link between bank solvency crisis and the drive for regulatory reformulation is not unique in the American banking policy community. Financial services policy change, in general, tends to be sluggish given the pluralistic nature of American public policymaking and regulatory learning often seems to emerge only in response to immediate political or economic crisis. This is especially the case in banking regulation. Policymaking authority is divided between the two

104 *Case studies*

houses of the federal Congress, three federal regulators, 50 state-level legislatures and banking commissions, the judiciary, and the executive office of the President.[4] Many banks are subject to more than one regulatory regime. The commercial banking marketplace is also highly fractured between state and a wide variety of nationally licensed banks.[5] These banks do not have a common associational or peak organization and their interests are thus separately represented at the various levels of the federal policymaking structure. This state and firm-level fracturing, "produce a rather reactive, slow-moving policy process where narrow coalitions of interests and legislators can impede policy change"[6] until crisis makes change unavoidably necessary.

This can be observed through a brief history of capital adequacy regulation in the United States. Before the 1980s crises, US capital regulations were largely informal and, perhaps, minimally enforced. Though the twentieth century has been a historical period of declining capital ratios for banking institutions, as illustrated (with a very limited capital definition) in Figure 6.1. US banks have only been subjected to explicit, operational capital requirements since 1981. Norton (1992:14) notes that before the 1980s, the "decline in bank capital levels and the bank collapses endemic to the depression (and for that matter, to bank failures since then) give no indication that capital levels were critical: loss of public confidence leading to illiquidity, mismanagement and fraud have been and remain the primary culprits." Formal capital regulations were quite minimal and were static measures prescribing levels of capital necessary for bank formation.[7] Capital standards for the counterparty risks of banks already in operation were, "largely internalized in non-rule oriented exam and supervisory practices"[8] and varied a great deal across different federal and state bank regulators.[9] It is

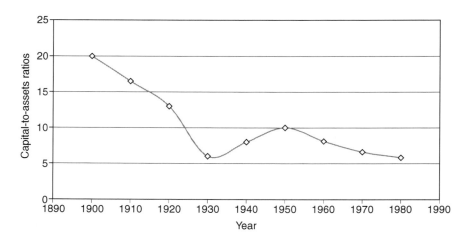

Figure 6.1 Capital-to-assets ratios for the leading ten US banks: 1900–1980 (source: comprised from data in *American Banker*, various issues).

Note
Capital defined as common stock, disclosed reserves, and retained earnings.

also possible that these informal rules were minimally enforced; prior to 1983 US federal regulators did not possess the legal authority to issue capital directives.

Yet after the Depression and before the Basel Accord, US regulators experimented with a variety of new regulatory measures of risk-based capital to address the postwar slump in ratios. The preferences that the United States took into the Basel negotiations and even into the early stages of implementation were the product of a 30-year-long debate among federal bank regulators over the concept of a risk-weighted capital regulation. The first shot of this bureaucratic debate was fired in the 1950s when the Federal Reserve Board adopted, for internal exam purposes, a simplistic capital-to-risk-adjusted-assets approach that loosely identified a broad category of risk assets through the deduction, from the total assets base, of relatively low-risk instruments (e.g. government securities).[10] Although Kapstein (1989) argues that the United States learned the RWA approach from Britain during the 1980s,[11] this 1950s regulation represented the first attempt by an American regulator to adopt a Basel Accord-style approach.

Yet, this regulatory innovation effected little actual change on banks' balance sheet management. The OCC, the leading bank regulator during the 1950s, discarded the method and adopted a non-risk sensitive capital-to-assets approach. The OCC was able to dominate the federal regulatory agenda during this period as it was charged with the oversight of all national banks not organized in a bank holding company network.[12] With this authority and with little legislative input, the OCC pushed the Fed and FDIC to adopt its non-risk-weighted capital method, culminating in the adoption of the Uniform Interagency Bank Rating System in 1978, which ostensibly created a unified federal capital standard based on the OCC system.[13] It is not clear that much real regulatory convergence actually occurred and evidence suggests that the Fed persistently adopted a stricter capital standard that led scores of banks, in the 1970s, to arbitrage the fragmented regulatory structure by exiting the Fed system to take advantage of the looser regulations of the OCC/FDIC.[14]

The most significant departure from the unified standard and the most pertinent to future Basel negotiations was the FDIC's 1981 decision to significantly tighten its capital standards and officially defect from the interagency standard. By 1981, the FDIC had grown in relative bureaucratic influence to the OCC/Fed,[15] and set out a highly original capital assessment scheme that included a threshold level of adjusted equity capital at 6 percent of total assets and emphasized a narrow, equity-centered, definition of regulatory capital that included: common stock, perpetual preferred stock, capital surplus, retained profits, contingency reserves, mandatory convertible debt instruments, and loan-loss reserves.[16] As presented in Table 6.1, this capital definition largely mirrored that adopted as Tier1 in the Basel Accord with the main exceptions being the inclusion of debt and loan–loss reserves in the FDIC definition.

The severity of this definition brought the FDIC into conflict with the OCC/Fed and a "regulatory dialectic of sorts was being joined in 1981 among the bank regulators regarding the formulation of capital adequacy standards ..."[17] In opposition

106 *Case studies*

Table 6.1 Comparison of FDIC–Basel Accord capital definitions

1981 FDIC capital regulation	1988 Basel Accord
• Common stock • Preferred stock • Capital surplus • Retained profits • Contingency reserves • Mandatory convertible debt instruments • Loan-loss reserves MINIMUM RATIO: 6 percent	• Common stock ⎫ • Preferred stock ⎪ • Disclosed reserves ⎬ **Tier1** • Retained profits ⎪ • Minority interests ⎭ • Undisclosed reserves • Revaluation reserves • General provisions • Hybrid debt capital • Subordinated debt MINIMUM RATIO: 4/8 percent

to the FDIC approach, the Fed and the OCC, after intense lobbying by their constituent banks, adopted a two-tier capital framework which portended the bifurcated Basel model and included limited-life preferred stock, subordinated notes, and a 5 percent trigger ratio, as indicated in Table 6.2.[18]

This early 1980s regulatory conflict produced two long-term consequences. First, the resulting twin-level capital structure adopted by the Fed/OCC, in opposition to the FDIC, lead to considerable capital financing innovations by banking institutions. The various qualifications applied to instruments qualifying as Tier2 capital led banks to engineer numerous innovative variations of these capital species. In fact, so much capital structure innovation was being exercised that the Fed and the Comptroller found it desirable, in 1982, to issue a joint statement providing more specific criteria as to whether particular types of bank security qualified as Tier1.[19] This early example of capital regulatory arbitrage foreshadowed the short-term nature of Basel capital standard setting as banks continually seek to engineer instruments to circumvent existing regulations requiring regulators to continually re-set the regulatory bar in order to adjust to changing market realities at a velocity seldom seen in other areas of economic regulation.[20] As a result of the arbitrage incentives established by the two-tier framework, the Fed/OCC standard may have created a preference by US banks for such a two-level structure at the international level, helping explain the content of the 1988 Accord as well as some of the dynamics of its implementation in the United States.[21]

Second, this federal regulatory battle made it increasingly clear that the United States required a clear-cut single capital standard. As Norton (1992) observed as "the more substantive or procedural differences in regulatory approaches surfaced, the argument for achieving uniformity as to definition and to application of capital adequacy standards became more compelling."[22] In the early 1980s, this became increasingly more compelling at the political level and contributed to the American push for the Basel Accord.

Table 6.2 Comparison of 1982 FDIC-Fed/OCC capital definitions

1982 FDIC	1982 Fed/OCC	1988 Basel
• Common stock • Preferred stock • Capital surplus • Retained profits • Contingency reserves • Convertible debt • Loan–loss reserves	• **Common stock** • **Preferred stock** • **Capital surplus** • **Retained profits** • **Contingency reserves** • **Convertible debt** • **Loan–loss reserves** • Limited life preferred stock • Subordinated debt	• **Common stock** • **Preferred stock** • **Disclosed reserves** • **Retained profits** • **Minority interests** • Undisclosed reserves • Revaluation reserves • General provisions • Hybrid debt capital • Subordinated debt
MINIMUM RATIO: 6 percent	MINIMUM RATIO: 5 percent	MINIMUM RATIO: 4/8 percent

Note
Bold indicates the designation of Tier 1 capital.

Negotiation of the Basel Accord

This politicization of bank capital regulation emerged in the early 1980s as Congress was forced to respond to the increasing economic weakness of America's most critical lending institutions. During the 1980s, the commercial banking and savings and loans[23] industries suffered their worst performances since the 1930s. By the middle part of the decade, macroeconomic conditions and unsound mortgage lending practices combined to render two-thirds of the nation's thrifts insolvent. The result was a US$100 billion deficit at the taxpayer-funded Federal Savings & Loan Corporation and Congress' nationalization of more than 400 thrifts, constituting US$175 billion of assets. The entire thrift regulatory regime was reorganized through the passage of the Financial Institutions Reform, Recovery, and Enforcement Act of 1989 and the lead thrift regulator, the Federal Home Loan Bank Board, was dissolved.[24] America's commercial banks fared only slightly better as more banks became insolvent (1037) in the 1980s than at any decade outside the 1930s. By the mid-1980s, aggregate bank return-on-assets hit its lowest level in 30 years; return-on-equity fell to it lowest mark in 25 years. As illustrated in Figure 6.1, bank capital-to-assets ratios fell to their lowest point in history.[25]

The commercial bank solvency crisis is generally linked to imprudent domestic and international loan decisions taken during the 1970s and early 1980s. American-led bank syndications accumulated, on a global basis, the largest exposure to LDC's debt with such loans totaling 93–199 percent of commercial banks' capitalization.[26] By 1982, Mexican debtors alone owed US banks US$23 billion or 46 percent of the top 17 American banks' capitalization.[27] Without a RWA capital standard in place, large commercial banks' incentives were to quickly build-up capital through the building of large risky, though potentially profitable, positions in the banking book. Many of these loans were channeled into the booming housing market through real-estate investment trusts

108   *Case studies*

(REITS) to disastrous results.[28] The largest money center, banks, fared the worst with bank asset size being highly correlated with the mean percentage of real-estate loan problems.

In light of these crises, Congress was forced to adopt an increasingly proactive regulatory agenda that centered on bank capital guidelines. Evidence suggests that by the mid-1980s, members of Congress were placed under enormous pressure by their domestic constituencies to ensure that taxpayer funds were not utilized in the bailout of what were perceived to be reckless commercial banks. A 1983 Reagan administration plan to "transfer ownership of a portion of developing country debt from commercial banks to the public sector"[29] by increasing America's contribution to the International Monetary Fund (IMF) by US$8.4 billion to be dispensed to heavily indebted LDCs was not well-received by Congress. Illustrative of this are comments from Ferdinand St Germain, then chairman of the House of Representatives Banking Committee that, "at a time when millions stand in unemployment lines and thousands of small businesses are filing bankruptcy petitions, the idea of an international bailout for adventurous US bankers may not be the most popular idea on the legislative agenda."[30]

The ultimate product of the banking crisis was the creation of the 1983 ILSA. This conferred capital directive enforcement powers to federal bank regulators[31] and demanded that they seek to provide a unified capital regulatory regime, both among themselves and among their international peers. Federal Reserve Chairman Paul Volcker objected to Congress' input into what had largely been an apolitical region of regulatory policymaking and supported the soundness of the 1982 Fed/OCC rules. Yet, driven by political imperatives in response to a systemic financial crisis, Congress overruled Volcker's position.[32]

The immediate result of ILSA was the intensification of the debate among the Fed, OCC, and FDIC over the form and content of capital regulations. Under the pressure of Congress and the new leadership of the Fed, however, considerable convergence was quickly achieved. By mid-1984, the three agencies separately published new capital guidelines that resembled the 1982 Fed/OCC procedures in most respects (see Table 6.2). This level of cooperation escalated after the May 1984 failure of Continental Illinois, the eighth-largest bank in the United States. In response, the Fed re-initiated its interest in a capital-to-RWA approach. Unlike the 1950s, when the Fed's RWA program was largely vetoed by the OCC, the RWA approach was the centerpiece of another joint proposal issued in January 1986.[33] The Fed was able to dominate regulatory policymaking during this period, thus supplanting the OCC, as its primary constituent banks, BHCs, exploded in size from just 53 in 1956 to roughly 5400 in 1983 and included the money center banks of New York and California.[34]

With this newly found bureaucratic strength, no doubt reinforced by Congress' demands for a strong regulatory response to 1980s crises, the Fed was able to dominate the OCC/FDIC in the negotiation of the Basel Accord and largely presented the US position in Basel. The Fed successfully initiated the US–UK capital adequacy accord in July 1986, as has been detailed in Chapter 2, and pushed its agenda to include loan–loss reserves, a critical component in holding company capital in 1987, in the bilateral accord's definition of primary capital, over the opposition of the OCC/FDIC. As Vernon *et al.* (1991) describe:

> [t]he Federal Reserve presented its position [on loan loss reserves] to the OCC as an issue on which the Bank of England would not budge. But when the OCC raised the issue with the Bank of England, the OCC discovered that the Bank supported its position, not the position of the Federal Reserve.[35]

Yet, without the political and economic imperatives generated by the 1980s bank crises, it seems likely that Congress' efforts to enforce a uniform regulatory response at the federal level would have failed as they did in the past.[36] In this instance, the Basel Accord may not have been created without a strong US effort. Yet, driven by political imperatives in response to a systemic financial crisis, Congress overruled the regulators' position, and the United States actively pursued the creation of the Basel Accord. Money center banks were resigned to the fact that Congress would need to be seen enforcing new punishing standards on them and supported the creation of the Accord so as to avoid the application of new capital rules to just the United States.[37] This convergence of legislative, regulatory, and bank action did not persist beyond the negotiation of the Accord, however, and a new policy battlefield was joined during the agreement's implementation in 1988.

First period implementation of the Basel Accord (1988–1992)

The first shot of the implementation battle originated from the three regulators' distinct interpretations of the Basel Accord's rules into their bank exam procedures. Like many of their G-10 peers, the Fed, OCC, and FDIC did not require enabling legislation from the legislature to convert the Basel standards into their own administrative guidelines.[38] Through ILSA, Congress could continue to exert pressure on the supervisors to harmonize their standards, yet it was these supervisory bodies themselves that determined the severity of the rules adopted in the first instance. The result was, initially, a strict interpretation by all three federal regulators. These interpretations were made in 1987–1990 and were due for implementation at the end of the transition period at the end of 1992.

The United States adopted a strict interpretation in each area of discretionary policy, save for one area of policy defection from the FDIC. The converging effects of ILSA were clearly still important when the implementation phase commenced as the three main federal regulators adopted nearly identically strict interpretations, despite the objections of their constituent banks. These interpretations incorporated the baselines created in the Accord in all instances and went well beyond the minima in several broad areas:

- First, the US regulators determined that the Accord would form part of the standard exam procedures for every bank domiciled in the country. Though the Accord was designed to apply only to internationally active banks, US regulators applied the agreement to all state and national banks and BHCs, regardless of their international ambitions so as to bring about a level domestic regulatory regime.[39]

- Second, banks were subjected to rigorous CAR requirements. In order to achieve the highest regulatory exam scores, banks would have to maintain CARs in excess of the 4 percent (Tier1 capital) and 8 percent (total capital) levels.[40]
- Third, a 100 percent risk-weight was assigned for mortgage loans. The US regulators had fought the European negotiators about the mortgage risk-weight in the Basel negotiations and only concurred to a 50 percent minimum weight as a concession. Back in the domestic policy arena, the US authorities imposed their original preferences for a 100 percent weighting with the justification that favoring classes of loans without economic justification was tantamount to credit allocation.[41]
- Finally, a more limited definition of regulatory capital was created. From Tier1, intangible assets (other than goodwill) were restricted and only 25 percent of a bank holding company's non-cumulative, perpetual preferred stock could qualify. From Tier2, general loan loss reserves and asset revaluation reserves were prohibited. In addition, hidden reserves (from unrealized securities capital gains) were excluded as America's Generally Accepted Accounting Principles (GAAPs) prohibited them.

In addition, the three regulators discussed the imposition of capital adequacy standards that went well beyond the policies addressed by the Accord. In particular, the regulators and some members of Congress wanted banks to put more capital aside for other business risks than the credit risks addressed by the Accord, particularly interest rate risk.[42] Negotiations on an interest rate risk standard were protracted, however, as the OCC resisted demands from the Senate Banking Committee to implement measures by claiming that such procedures were complex and took time to negotiate. As a compromise, the regulators required their banks to meet a Tier1 to non-RWA ratio of at least 3 percent.[43] This "leverage ratio" was to serve as a proxy for non-credit risk until agreement on more formal standards could be reached in Washington.[44]

For the most part, these rules were adopted as part of a united Fed–OCC–FDIC front without a great deal of bureaucratic in fighting. Yet, as in past efforts to harmonize capital standards, some elements discord did emerge between the FDIC and the national bank regulators. In particular, the FDIC refused to exclude goodwill and cumulative, perpetual preferred stock.[45] In 1988, the FDIC director informed the House Banking Committee that such forms of capital were important for many of its smaller, regional-based, constituents. In addition, the director objected to the universal applicability of the standard and claimed that the Accord provided too large a record keeping burden for small-cap, regional banks which, by money center standards, were already very well capitalized and did not have such large balance sheet exposures to lesser developed markets. It took over a year of bureaucratic debate before the FDIC, under enormous pressure from the Fed, OCC, and Congress, brought their interpretation into line.[46] Yet, it would not be the first Basel-related defection by the FDIC.

This bureaucratic discord was brief and minor relative to the objections raised by the American financial marketplace. Though the money center institutions had supported the Accord in order to avoid being asymmetrically regulated relative to their international competitors, both they and regional banks lobbied against every discretionary interpretation made by the federal supervisors as these effectively unleveled the playing field created in Basel.

The key debate centered on the 100 percent weighting assigned to home mortgage credits. The chief fear was that money center banks would need to shift their lending away from mortgage loans as the opportunity costs were increased for lending to lower-weighted activities (such as loans to OECD governments), other high-weighted activities where the rate of return was generally greater (loans to the private sector), or toward OBS instruments. In particular, the Federal Home Loan Mortgage Corporation (Freddie Mac), a congressionally chartered organization that makes secondary mortgage markets, argued that the weighting would disadvantage them relative to foreign competitors subject to a 50 percent weighting, and to securities issued by the US Government National Mortgage Association (Ginnie Mae).[47] A spokesman for Freddie Mac argued that placing their "securities at a competitive disadvantage vis-à-vis Ginnie Mae's will also have the unfortunate and unnecessary effect of increasing the cost of conventional mortgages for homebuyers."[48] This fear led to a widening of the public debate over the Accord's interpretation to include a number of non-financial institutions such as consumer organizations and home building associations who were anxious to stabilize prices in the industry after the Savings and Loan crisis of the early 1980s.[49]

In addition to risk weights, the banking industry placed severe political pressure on their supervisors to amend their regulatory capital definitions. First, many bankers observed that there was no financial logic in excluding loan–loss reserves, which formed a critical component of the capital base of most G-10 domiciled banks. The Chairman of Citicorp observed that:

> unlike pollution standards, which are supposed to be based on scientific knowledge, new and constantly changing definitions of bank capital do not rest on such solid ground ... as part of the Basle Accord, US regulators threw out loan loss reserves as parts of capital and all the sudden, US banks were under-capitalized – this massive shift of policy went unnoticed by most except those immediately affected.[50]

The American Bankers Association concurred with this view and argued that, with loan–loss reserves included, "our members continue to believe that the banking system is adequately capitalized and until the banking agencies can demonstrate that this is not the case, the implementation of any risk-based standards should be delayed."[51]

112 *Case studies*

Beyond loan–loss reserves, money center banks were joined by the FDIC in objecting to the treatment of BHCs' capital. In the first instance, America's largest banks, led by Citibank, argued that the application of the Accord at the holding company level created, yet another, competitive disadvantage for America's largest banks. The banks also argued, with the support of FDIC chairman L. William Seidman, that extending the Accord to holding companies compromised the legal firewalls built between BHCs and their subsidiaries. In letters to the Fed, the banks argued that the application of the Accord would cause the public to perceive that the holding company is covered by the same protection that the government provides the bank.[52] To exacerbate these problems, the Fed (the lead regulator of BHCs) excluded goodwill and cumulative preferred stock from the tally of allowable Tier1 capital though these instruments formed a critical component in holding companies' capital bases.

When confronted with these complaints in 1988–1999, the three federal regulators largely stood firm on their interpretations. Though, as already discussed, the FDIC made some effort to provide regulatory forbearance to their region-oriented constituents by adopting a looser capital definition, the OCC/Fed argued that the binds created by the 1988 Accord limited their scope for independent action on behalf of their banks' interests. In particular, Seidman suggested that the EC would never agree to the acceptance of goodwill. The Fed's Chairman, Alan Greenspan, observed that, "there are elements of this [the Accord] all of us would like to change, but we accept it as it is or we go back to the drawing board."[53]

The only major exception to this position was announced several months after the interpretations were issued in August 1988. The Fed yielded to the money center's demands for the inclusion of perpetual, cumulative preferred stock in Tier1 for holding companies. Though these instruments were expressly prohibited by the Accord, the BHCs had lobbied especially hard on this issue as, according to Salomon Brothers, this instrument comprised US$5.6 billion of the aggregate American BHC capital base in 1988 and its allowance would save the holding companies US$1 billion of equity in their efforts to comply with the Accord. Yet, the Fed did mandate several restrictions: only 25 percent of a BHCs' cumulative stock could qualify as capital and the stock's dividends could not be determined by auction. These were highly restrictive parameters as 40 percent of the total cumulative preferred stock base carried dividends determined by Dutch auction or were actually money market preferred stock issues.[54] The Fed thus provided some regulatory relief to its constituents, over the objections of its banks and the FDIC, though it held firm on most of its 1988 interpretations.

For about three years, US banks worked toward compliance with these comparatively rigid new capital requirements. Yet, as America's largest banks raised their capital ratios, the broader economy shifted into a recession. Growth in gross domestic product slowed from 3.5 percent in 1989 to negative in 1991. More acutely, the slowdown was accompanied by a downturn in bank lending.

American politicians, again anxious to avoid blame for economic mismanagement, accused the federal regulators of implementing unnecessarily strict capital standards.[55] Though Congress had insisted on tough capital standards in the late 1980s through ILSA and demanded that interest rate risk charges be set, now many members of Congress argued that American banks had been forced to hold too much capital relative to their international peers. As the 1992 legislative and Presidential elections neared, Washington was awash with plans to ignite bank lending to lift the macroeconomy out of its slump. In particular, the Bush administration issued a large package of proposals to reduce the solvency standards for savings and loans and commercial banks to encourage such lending.[56]

Though Greenspan objected to this political interference and claimed that the changes demanded would not ease lending practices, the Fed, the OCC, and FDIC considered the loosening of America's risk-capital regime as the Basel transitional period ended in 1992.

Hypotheses review: first period of implementation

The key goal of a theoretical analysis of the first period interpretation of the Accord in the United States is to account for a relatively strict interpretation. Though some regulatory reversion began to take hold by the early 1990s, the main theme in America from 1988 to 1991 is that bankers had behaved irresponsibly during the 1980s and needed to be dealt with in a heavy handed manner.

These events provide a high level of support for the economic instability hypothesis. Severe financial crises during the 1980s made the tightening of financial regulations a political imperative so that path dependence was not an option in America. Regulators overrode the "path dependent" interests of their constituents and implemented a narrow definition of the Accord. In this regard, economic instability is positively correlated with a strict definition of the Accord. The long historical view perspective provided by the first part of this chapter suggests that this sort of regulatory response to a major macroeconomic dislocation is not without precedent as it was the events of the Great Depression of the 1930s that led regulators to severely restrict the activities and geographical reach of large, commercial intermediaries.

Due in part to these 1930s restrictions, American banks do not wield a great deal of political power at the best of economic times. They are numerous, highly diverse by income and market segment, geographically separated, and regulated by a fragmented regulatory structure. They thus suffered from a classic collective action problem in their efforts to coordinate a common offensive against their regulators' interpretations. In addition, any influence that the banks may have ordinarily exercised on their regulator's behavior was confounded by their weak financial position in the 1980s, the very public blame received for excessive risk-taking, and the high level of policy orchestration among the Federal Reserve, OCC, and FDIC.[57] There is thus very little support for the hypotheses that bankers' preferences wielded much importance during the early years of the Accord's interpretation. In addition, there is little evidence to support the view that these preferences were influenced by a desire to "signal" to the international market or access other states' banking markets. American banks' preferences seemed to be geared toward maintaining the status quo or, at least, preventing the further tightening of their capital standards.

However, these events may lend some rather indirect support to the "capture" hypothesis: weak US banks were unable to successfully influence their regulators' interpretation of the Basel Accord. A more reliable test of this hypothesis requires a study of the impact of economic crisis on capital adequacy policy in a banking system in which banks wield greater political power. This will be investigated in the case of Germany in Chapter 7.

Little empirical support is afforded to the Regional Effects Hypothesis under scrutiny. In particular, regional influences do not seem to have played a role in producing policy outcomes.

Second period: implementation of the Basel Accord (1993–2000)

As the previous section argued, the United States implemented one of the strictest initial interpretations of the Basel Accord. This section will illustrate that by 2000, the American risk-capital rules were considerably weaker and on par with the rules adopted by other industrialized states. Curiously, as the implementation period of the Accord proceeded, America's capital regulations returned to the more informal, non-rule-oriented style that had characterized the pre-Basel era. The Fed, OCC, and the FDIC re-worked the severe risk-weighting framework, further extended the definition of allowable primary capital, and may have reduced the enforcement of capital directives. These policy reversals made the United States open to the charge that its commercial banks may have started to earn regulation-related competitive advantages. Whether they did or not, many BCBS members made such accusations and a new conflict emerged in Basel, only now it was the United States that was targeted for maintaining weak capital regulations.

This section reviews these changes in America's capital standards by examining three episodes. First, the federal regulator's acquiescence to President Bush's capital adequacy program will be discussed. This follows-on from the previous section as Bush endeavored to jump-start the ailing US economy in the run-up to the 1992 presidential elections. Second, America's controversial decision to allow tax-shielded preferred stock into its definition of Tier1 capital will be reviewed. Many BCBS members, especially Germany, considered this decision to be in violation of the spirit of the Accord and an international furore emerged. Finally, the Federal Reserve's decision to permit asset revaluation reserves in Tier2 capital will be discussed. It was the BOJ's allowance of this capital instrument that had partially led the US Congress to demand the Basel Accord be negotiated in 1987. It is thus ironic that the United States began to adopt this practice and it is instructive of the changes that occurred in regulation of banking risks during the 1990s.

As discussed in the last section, the political recriminations from the 1991 to the 1992 recession and bank credit crunch produced great political pressure on the federal regulators. Though data released in 1993 indicated that both macro-economic growth and national bank profitability had improved throughout 1992, the Federal Reserve remained pressured by politicians and banks to amend its Basel interpretations. In December 1993, this pressure resulted in the amendment of the Federal Reserve's asset risk-weighting structure.[58]

The result was a halving of the capital that commercial banks were obligated to carry for the construction of multifamily housing loans. The reduction of mortgages to the 50 percent weighting category eased the US risk-weighting standard into convergence with most other G-10 states. This was a dramatic step-down for the Fed as they had negotiated hard for the 100 percent weighting of these assets in Basel and had only allowed Germany and other committee members to assign a 50 percent weighting as part of the compromise to conclude the Accord.[59] When the Fed had decided to apply a 100 percent weight in 1988, it had argued that applying a lower weight would essentially result in a system of government credit control: the government would simply be responding to the political pressure of particularistic interests for cheaper access to bank credit. In the end, Greenspan was accurate and the purpose and intended effect of this loosening was to target voters for the presidential and congressional election campaigns in November 1992.

The Fed did manage to defend its initial 100 percent weighting for quite sometime. The announcement to reduce the risk-weight was not announced in the *Federal Reserve Bulletin* until December 1993, more than a year after President Bush called for change. Yet, it may be inferred that the broad political pressure placed on the Fed was simply too strong. As was discussed in the previous section, debate on this element of the Accord had expanded well beyond the relatively narrow confines of the banking policy network to include building and consumers organizations. In the end, the Fed conceded.

It should be observed that the Fed's acquiescence coincided with an improving macroeconomic environment and strengthening banking sector. America's recession appeared over by 1993. Economic growth increased from just over 1 percent to 3 percent from 1992 to 1993 while unemployment fell from 6.1 percent to 5.6 percent during the period.[60] The pre-tax profits of BHCs increased by 92 percent over their 1991 performance.[61] More importantly, the country's largest banks experienced a rapid acceleration in growth. As Figure 6.2 shows, unweighted Tier1 capital for the country's largest banks increased from under 5 percent in 1991 to nearly 7 percent by 1993 before leveling off. By the time that the Basel transition period ended in late 1992, US banks had total capital ratios nearly 200 basis points above the 8 percent level. This increase does not seem to, at least solely, reflect the influence of the Accord as these bank's CARs had experienced a significant drop from 1988 to 1991 before rebounding. This seems to suggest that the end of the recession, rather than the effects of the Accord, produced these solvency improvements. By the time the Fed had thus given in to political pressure, American banks were

116 *Case studies*

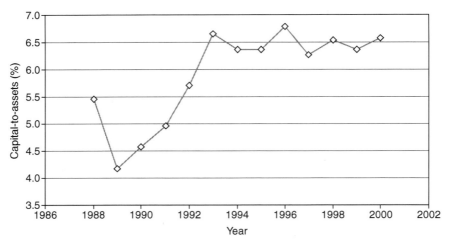

Figure 6.2 Unweighted Tier1 capital-to-assets ratios for the leading ten US banks: 1988–2000 (sources compiled from data in *The Banker*, various issues).

returning to profitability and were maintaining capital ratios well in excess of the Basel minima.

More importantly, perhaps, the Federal Reserve began to dramatically concede to bankers' demands to further widen the definition of regulatory capital throughout the 1990s. The key source of bankers' grievances with the Accord began to emerge when non-financial institutions began to issue tax-deductible preference shares in 1994. American corporations had initiated the issue of these securities in late 1993 and US investment banks followed suit soon after. These securities allow issuers to raise tax-shielded preferred stock. This form of equity was considerably cheaper than commercial banks' existing capital raising methods, yet such instruments were not permitted by the Accord.[62] They were of questionable international legality – even within the "soft law" rules of the Accord.

America's largest banks insisted that the Accord disadvantaged them vis-à-vis domestic non-bank financial institutions because of the structure of America's financial activity regulations. This situation was partly the result of then US regulations forbidding commercial banks entry into securities, insurance, and real-estate markets. Since the 1933 Glass-Steagall Act, American commercial banks' capital has been regulated distinctly from securities firms, who are regulated by the Securities and Exchange Commission. The result is that banks and securities firms are subject to distinct capital adequacy rules; a fact that commercial banks have always indicated has provided them with a competitive disadvantage both in regard to domestic securities firms and with their international commercial bank competitors. In this instance, non-bank financial institutions were not bound by the Basel Accord's exclusion of tax-deductible issues.

On this occasion, however, the Federal Reserve was receptive to commercial banks' concerns. In October 1996, the Fed approved the use of tax-deductible preferred stock as Tier1 capital. In practice, US banks could issue these securities through two methods. The first was to allow BHCs to establish operating companies similar to REITS, called special purpose vehicles (SPVs). These SPVs would essentially be assigned real-estate assets and would then be allowed to issue tax-deductible preferred stock that would qualify as a minority interest. Many banks that did not have large real-estate holding complained that they would be disadvantaged by this system. By mid-1996, these banks suggested that BHCs be allowed to issue deeply subordinated debt as tax-deductive preferred stock and then "downstream" this to individual banks. In the Basel Accord, such minority interests are acceded Tier1 capital status. The Fed agreed to recognize this status if the stock issues met a set of minimum criteria.[63]

Though rumors on Wall Street suggested that federal and state tax authorities viewed these capital instruments as little more than a tax dodge, their use rapidly proliferated in the American money centers. Between October 1996, when the Fed gave its approval, and February 1997, US banks issued over US$30 billion in Tier1 tax-deductible stock. The impact of these instruments, marketed as capital securities, was evident. This much is clear from the reaction of the market to the extensive use of these assets. As this stock qualified as Tier1 capital, there was no Basel limit on their use in banks' capital bases. Yet, the relative weaknesses of these instruments, relative to pure equity or retained profits, were recognized by credit ratings agencies who were believed to have insisted that these instruments not comprise more than 20 percent of a bank's Tier1 capital or a downgrade would be considered.

Thus by 1997, the shape and structure of a major US downgrade in its capital regulatory severity was clear. The American tax authorities did not intervene and thus US banks were allowed to issue a new kind of capital instrument that did not necessarily violate, but certainly was not in the spirit of the Basel agreement. Recognizing that such instruments were indeed economic capital but not the pure equity capital that the Basel agreement intended to establish as Tier1, the market acted in a facilitating but limiting manner.

The Federal Reserve's decision created an international furore that resulted in a new showdown in Basel. It was not only the market that recognized the relative weaknesses of this Tier1 instrument, but European and Japanese banks demanded that their regulators permit them to issue these securities so as not to be competitively disadvantaged. French banks Crédit Agricole and Crédit Lyonnais attempted to issue such securities in 1993, yet their regulators forced them to reclassify these securities as Tier2. European and Japanese regulators were initially reluctant to approve this capital structure, yet began to develop a compromise solution in several rounds of negotiation in Basel. A solution was not easy to reach, however, for while the new tax-deductible securities were "minor in the grand scheme of bank capital raising and management, [their use] was proving to be exceptionally divisive."[64]

In particular, German regulators broadened the debate over tax-deductive securities into a wider attack on the Fed's implementation of the Accord. The Germans objected to freedom given to US holding companies to issue capital securities on behalf of their member banks. This criticism struck at the Fed's 1989 decision to allow BHCs to issue cumulative preferred stock as Tier1 equity, America's first defection from at least the spirit of the Accord, as well as the tax-deductible issues. The United States retorted by objecting to Germany's policy of allowing dated securities to qualify as Tier1. The state-owned Landesbank do not have publicly listed shares, but instead issue dated debt securities called *Stille Einglagen* or silent participations. These instruments were explicitly permitted by the Basel Accord for use in Germany, yet the US regulators defended their BHC policies by indicating that the silent participations provided German banks an analogous competitive advantage. The Fed's case was boosted when Deutsche Bank issued a *Stille Einlagen* variant during the course of the negotiations.[65]

The BCBS negotiations on the American Tier1 decision were thus difficult and protracted. It was not until October 1998 when a compromise solution was reached. As might be expected, however, the solution did not amount to a detailed, point-by-point, guideline of the use of debated capital instruments, but to a short, two-page, pronouncement.[66] The pronouncement essentially emerged as another piece of Basel "soft law." The BCBS resolution did not address the source of the dispute – Germany's use of silent participations and the Fed's approval of holding company down streaming – but provided vague and tacit approval to the US and German practices. With regards to the use of tax-deductible stock as Tier1 capital, the BCBS ruled that such instruments could not exceed 15 percent of the total primary capital base. As a *Euromoney* article noted, "what the BIS has done is to legitimize the approach already taken by the rating agencies, and admit that there now exists an upper and a lower tier-one capital structure."[67] In effect, the Fed's unilateral departure from the Accord resulted in the amendment of the Accord in its favor. The beneficiaries, however, were not simply American money center banks, but those of most of the G-10. The regulators of Japan, the Netherlands, and Italy quickly allowed their internationally active banks to mimic their American counterparts, while most of the remaining Basel Committee states approved these new capital securities with time.

Shortly after this international dispute's resolution, the entire American bank regulatory community agreed to extend the definition of Tier2 capital. Soon after the BCBS decision on tax-deferred equity, the Fed, OCC, FDIC, and the Office of Thrift Supervision (OTS) agreed to allow their banks to count up to 45 percent of their unrealized, pre-tax, holding gains for the sale of equity securities.[68] Japan's use of these capital instruments had been heavily criticized during the 1987 negotiations for Japan's accession to the US–UK bilateral capital accord. In fact, one author noted that the dispute over these instruments had prevented Japan from joining the 1986 agreement for over six months.[69] Though these instruments were permitted by the GAAP, US regulators had shied from permitting their treatment as regulatory capital because the value of these instruments, and hence their ability to absorb bank losses, was dependent upon their market value. The potential volatility of such instruments, as was observed with Japan's use of them in the early 1990s, proved secondary to the US regulator's growing concerns about the international competitiveness of their banks. These concerns led to a mass approval of the use of this instrument – all the way to the Basel minimum of 45 percent – for all domestic financial intermediaries.

What can explain this rapid transformation in America's interpretation of the Accord? In the space of ten years, the United States had turned from charging other states with adopting excessively loose capital standards to being the target of such charges. Part of the answer lies in the fundamental shift in bank capital management and bank regulation that occurred in the United States during the 1990s. On an international basis, we have already seen that US banks were relatively well capitalized before the Accord. As these banks began to further increase their capital levels after the 1990s recession, the philosophy of credit risk management began to change in both America's banks and regulatory methods.

The management of credit risks is by far the most important job for a commercial bank manager.[70] Traditionally, these risks have been managed by raising and holding capital; this is obviously the regulatory position of the Accord's rules. Yet, the high levels of capital at US banks during the 1990s led to a shift in thinking about the use and purpose of bank capital by the American banking community. Capital was now being viewed as an instrument for maximizing shareholder value, rather than simply a balance sheet cushion against counterparty default.[71] Bank managers argued that the Accord has made them overcapitalized and this was producing economic inefficiencies as holding capital entailed high opportunity costs that did not apply to their non-bank financial institutional competitors. Reflecting this, Citicorp – which had famously struggled to meet the Basel ratio minima by 1992 – made a June 1995 announcement to buy back US$3 billion of its own shares over a two-year period. Other money center banks announced their intentions to follow Citicorp's example and the era of bank capital raising problems appeared over.

Such changes appear to have been partially responsible for guiding regulatory policy during this time. The loosening of capital standards was a key part of a shifting trajectory of the overall shape of bank regulatory policy. Decades of restrictive legislation were abolished during the 1990s so that, by 2000, banks were able to operate in product areas and geographical markets that had been forbidden to them since the 1930s depression legislation as Glass-Steagall was abolished.[72] By 1999, commercial banks were permitted to operate in securities, real estate, and insurance markets. Regulators responded by allowing commercial banks to hold and manage risk-capital in ways similar to the firms that operated in these markets. By the late 1990s, money center banks demanded that they be allowed to set their own credit risk capital charges with proprietary modeling tools. They demanded the right to use derivative products to manage their balance sheets.[73] The Basel Committee had permitted banks to utilize such tools to manage market risks in 1996, yet not credit risks.[74]

The Fed did not agree to such demands. Though the Fed has supported the international adoption of these new risk management techniques into the Basel Accord II, they did not unilaterally permit the use of internal modeling and derivatives methods. Yet, they did extensively water down their interpretations of the Basel rules. They allowed banks to function more like securities firms and hold tax-deductible preferred stock as primary capital. They permitted them to hold assets with an underlying market value as secondary capital. In addition, some evidence exists that US regulators reduced their level of capital enforcement. In the mid-1990s, it emerged that the FDIC may not have been enforcing many elements of the Basel agreement to its constituent banks.[75] As the FDIC regulates, the so-called "super-regional" banks had always been better capitalized than their money center peers, and the FDIC had always opposed elements of the Accord's application in their sphere of influence. Though Seidman had failed to gain extensive concessions for his banks in 1988, the FDIC may have provided regulatory relief in the enforcement stage of the policy cycle.

Hypotheses review: second period of implementation

During the second time period of study, US capital adequacy regulation made a full circle return to a policy similar to that in place prior to 1988. The increased widening of the regulatory capital definition, increasing reliance on more informal capital-to-assets ratio requirements, and perhaps discretionary enforcement of capital policies all signal a reversion in America's capital policies. What do the hypotheses generated in Chapter 3 have to say about such a reduction in the severity in the Accord's interpretation?

The relevance of the "path dependency" bank preference variable seems in some doubt. These events suggest that the path dependency hypothesis' propositions worked in reverse in the US case. Economic crises led to a new regulatory path in the early 1990s, while increased bank profitability was correlated with a return to the original shape of the pre-Basel rules or a return to the original regulatory path. Yet, it is not clear that it was longing for the original, pre-Basel regime, which guided banks, regulators, or politicians preferences during this period. Moreover, the crux of the path dependency preference was that international "soft law" would little effect domestic policy change. In this regard, to suggest that the hypothesis is relevant after such a change occurred in the (t) period seems to present a time order difficulty for this hypothesis.

In an indirect manner, the policy reversion might provide some corroboration to the quantitative finding that private market governance is related to regulatory loosening for Tier1 capital. American banks were subject to relatively high levels of market governance. The market influenced the policies of banks during this period as they placed limits on the use of tax-deductible preferred stock as Tier1 capital that even the regulators did not. It is possible that American regulators felt able to reduce their regulatory stringency in the knowledge that the market would enforce minimum standards on banks. Indeed, a key US position at the Basel II negotiations has been that the market should exercise a key function in the setting of banks' credit risk charges.[76] This suggests a refinement to the market governance hypothesis so that the preferences of regulators, not simply banks, may be driven by the market enforcement mechanism.

Less support is found for the remaining hypotheses. The economic instability view suggested that regulatory change would occur in the presence of economic difficulties during the second period. Yet, US regulatory change seemed to occur throughout the 1990s during economic difficulties and during economic prosperity. Little support was provided to this hypothesis for the second period.

A more interesting question concerns the capture hypothesis during the second implementation period. US banks did appear to extract large concessions from their regulators despite exercising relatively limited quantities of political power. Yet, the details of this chapter seem to suggest that these extractions were not so much the product of "capture" as mutual learning about the appropriateness of the Basel Accord to the banking system. Both US commercial banks and regulators recognized that the capital adequacy regulatory game had changed in the mid-1990s. New financial instruments and increasing levels of bank capital made elements of the American interpretation of the Accord less appropriate. As a result, a new consensus seemed to emerge among banks and regulators regarding a looser regulatory framework that permitted them to act more like the securities firms against which they would be engaging in direct competition.

Finally, the second period discussion suggests the importance of incorporating a number of possible explanatory variables not anticipated in Chapter 3. First, capital adequacy rule stringency may well co-vary with the elements of the electoral cycle. In Section "Background," the decision of Congress to demand their regulators pursue the Accord was clearly linked to the political need of congressmen to signal a heavy-handed approach to the "reckless" banking industry to their constituents. Second, President Bush's 1992 electoral platform prominently listed his support for a weaker capital standard as a key plank in his inflation-fighting program. The hypotheses investigated here follows Ho's (2002) advice in assuming that capital adequacy policy setting is largely an apolitical and technocratic policy area. Yet, evidence from the US case suggests that this may not always be the case.[77]

Conclusions

This chapter has detailed the implementation of the 1988 Basel Accord in the United States. It has argued that up to the early 1990s, capital adequacy policy in the United States was driven by the severity of the LDC and savings and loan crises of the late 1980s. As a consequence, the United States pushed for the adoption of the Basel Accord and implemented a severe interpretation of this agreement on their commercial banks. As the effects of this crisis receded by 1992, regulatory policy began to change. By 2000, American regulators were adopting a capital adequacy standard more similar to their pre-Basel rules and more in-line with international practice.

These events have been instructive on the applicability of a number of our hypotheses to this country case. The case did not provide unequivocal support for any hypothesis as specified. Instead, some qualified support is found in the first period for the economic stability hypothesis and the private governance hypothesis. More importantly, the chapter has suggested some important qualifications to the hypotheses. First, it has suggested that measures of bank political power should take the economic climate into account. In the United States, banks' influence seemed to vary considerably in times of recession and solvency crisis versus periods of stability. Second, this chapter suggests that the quantitative studies are incomplete as they cannot operationalize and test the concept of regulatory learning. This appeared to be a critical element in America's capital regulatory decisions over the period and it is necessary to address this possibility.

7 Implementation of the Basel Accord in Europe
The case of France and Germany

Introduction

The EU followed a very different approach to promulgating capital adequacy standards when compared to the United States. Unlike the United States, the EU quickly moved to expand the coverage of the Basel Accord to investment banks and the market risks of commercial banks. In this respect, the EU moved more quickly than the Basel Committee in expanding the scope and coverage of a transnational capital regulatory framework, though with the unique goal of forging a single continental marketplace for financial services within a single prudential regulatory framework.

Yet, recognizing the limits of bringing about immediate convergence of inter-European banking regulations, the EU permitted their member states to implement the Accord with the same "soft law" discretionary method set out in Basel. The result has been persistent divergence in Europe's risk-capital regulations. This chapter will discuss this process of implementation in Europe generally, and France and Germany in particular.

These two states provide an interesting variation on the independent and dependent variables under investigation. Germany opposed the Basel Accord because it created a regulatory framework far more lax than its domestic capital standards. Yet, over the course of the 1990s, German regulators acquiesced to domestic demands and reduced the stringency of their regulatory capital definitions to facilitate their financial institutions' international competitiveness. This loosening of regulatory stringency persisted in Germany throughout the 1990s as the economic climate of the country declined after German reunification and the banking system experienced extreme financial distress. By 2000, Germany's position on capital adequacy had turned full circle so that they opposed the Basel II Accord negotiations for creating too strict a code.

By contrast, France has been viewed as a loser in the Basel Accord process. Oatley and Nabors (1998) argued that French banks operated with comparatively lax international capital ratios and standards during the 1980s and thus had this privilege taken away at American and British insistence at Basel. There are grounds to challenge this argument. France's pre-Basel capital ratios were on-par with most of continental Europe's banks, their capital standards did not appear to be more lax than other G-10 state's standards and, unlike Germany, France had implemented a risk-weighting approach well in advance of the Basel Accord. Moreover, France's solvency standards do not appear to have altered much from the mid-1980s to 2000. France adopted an interpretation of the Accord that was roughly in-line with their existing practices and maintained this interpretation throughout the 1990s.

By examining France and Germany together, it is possible to formulate strong comparisons of two distinct reactions to the Accord. This chapter endeavors to understand why Germany's capital adequacy regime experienced extreme volatility during the 1990s while France's solvency standards remained largely constant. This chapter provides strong support for the path dependency and economic instability hypotheses. Both states' negotiating positions and initial implementations were path dependent, though the presence of a macroeconomic downturn in Germany led to a novel regulatory path by 1993 while the absence of such difficulties allowed France to retain its initial interpretations. Support may also be suggested for the "regulatory capture" view. Continental European banks traditionally wield more political power than their American counterparts and the French and German regulators' decisionmaking over the 1990s appears to have been largely congruent with the preferences of their banking industries.

The first section provides background to understanding the implementation of the Basel Accord in the EU. After the Basel negotiations were completed, Brussels set to work on implementing the Accord into EC law. This additional layer of regional governance structured the implementation process in France and Germany and it is important to set out how this may have uniquely influenced European states' implementation of the Basel Accord. Next, I present the capital adequacy background and Accord negotiating positions of France and Germany. Section three discusses implementation during the first period of analysis (1988–1992) and Section four will look at the second period (1993–2000). In order to facilitate the close comparison of France and Germany's reactions to the Accord, both states will be simultaneously analyzed in these sections. This will also allow for the succinct analysis of interactions between these two states over the Accord's implementation. The last section concludes.

Implementation in the EC

The EC negotiations for a capital adequacy agreement progressed in parallel with the work of the Basel Committee during the 1980s. Under the aegis of the BAC, the EC states set about designing a common bank capital standard as part of the broader Community objective of creating a single market in financial services. These negotiations were part of a broader program to complete a common market for financial services providers that initiated with the adoption of the First Banking Co-ordination Directive in 1977.

There is some debate about the relationship between the European and Basel capital negotiations. Some have suggested that the BACs' work was prompted largely by its objectives to complete a single-banking regulatory framework and was generally not influenced by the G-10 negotiations. As Josselin (1997:174–175) observes, this claim seems extraordinary in light of the similarity of the two capital standards and large overlapping membership of the two negotiating bodies. As the comparison between the Basel and EC rules shows, Europe created a twin-level capital structure (called own funds and additional own funds in Europe) and required banks to maintain a minimum 8 percent CAR. In addition, the definitions of capital and the specifications of risk charges for on-balance sheet and OBS assets were largely identical. It is thus seemingly inaccurate to claim that the European standard was not heavily influenced by the G-10's work on capital adequacy.

Yet there are a number of unique elements to the European capital directives. First, the definition of regulatory capital is slightly more stringent as current year profits may only be included if they are verified by auditors and latent revaluation reserves are expressly excluded. Moreover, the EU adopted a much larger list of deductions required from capital. While the Accord only requires goodwill to be deducted from primary capital before its inclusion in the list of regulatory capital, the EU requires that own shares and current year losses be subtracted.

Beyond just the stated capital adequacy guidelines, however, a key distinction emerged between the long-term objectives of the two agreements. As has been mentioned, both the Basel and EC solvency rules provided for large degrees of national discretion or home-country control. Yet, the Own Funds Directive states that, in the future, the process of "competition between jurisdictions" in Europe may produce high levels of regulatory isomorphism as convergence becomes increasingly attractive and the single financial market is completed. The opportunity costs of persistent European regulatory divergence would drive European banks to demand that their domestic solvency regime be brought in line with that of their largest EC trading partners. Moreover, the Directive required Member States to consider increased convergence with a view to a common definition of own funds and requires the European Commission to submit a report on the uniform adoption of the directive to the European Parliament and Council of Ministers by 1 January 1996.[1] Article 2(2) of the Council Directive of 17 April 1989 on the Own Funds Directive required this report be prepared "with the aim of tightening [the Directive's] provisions and thus achieving greater convergence on a common definition of own funds."[2] In this way, the European capital accords were more ambitious than the Basel standard.

Yet, did this ambition produce a higher degree of capital rule convergence? The univariate statistical analysis in Chapter 4 suggests that it did to some extent. The coefficients of standard deviation were not particularly lower in the European states than in other BCBS members in the first period (1988–1992), yet it appears that some convergence did emerge in the late 1990s. Still, some significant distinctions in capital practice remain. In its report to the European Parliament, the Commission noted that:

[s]ome national implementation measures are somewhat stricter than the minimum standards required by the [Own Funds] Directive, particularly with regard to further restrictions on eligible own funds and/or requirements of additional deductions from capital ... [t]welve Member States have implemented such stricter requirements.[3]

Nevertheless, the EC was quite successful in extending the original scope and coverage of the Own Funds and Solvency Ratio Directives. In the early 1990s, the EC moved more quickly in negotiating extensions and amendments to their capital standards than the G-10. If attention toward achieving credit risk rule convergence waned, the enthusiasm for creating a "soft law" framework for all financial institutions' risks gathered pace. Brussels concluded a market risk capital charge three years before Basel. The Capital Adequacy Directive or CAD (93/6/EEC) designed a market risk charge for all banks and investment firms operating in the Community and was soon updated with CAD2 (98/31/EC) that brought EU rules more in line with the Basel market risk amendment. European rules were also issued to address capital adequacy regulation related topics such as consolidated supervision of financial groups (92/30/EEC) and large financial exposures (92/121/EEC). In a number of areas, the BAC has thus led the Basel negotiations and it is intriguing that hegemonic explanations of the 1988 Accord's negotiation have not taken this into account.

Yet, the focus of this chapter remains fixed on the implementation of the 1988 credit risk regulations. Before turning to this, it is necessary to briefly discuss the negotiation of the Basel and Brussels solvency standards by Community members. The conclusion of the Basel Committee's work on the credit risk standard did not lead directly to the implementation of the Accord in Europe, but the initiation of a new round of European negotiations as the 1988 Accord needed to be enumerated into European law. Many of the intra-European conflicts present in Basel reappeared on this new negotiation battleground and, in particular, a Franco-German split emerged. Details of this split and some background into the pre-Basel capital adequacy regulations of France and Germany are presented in the next section.

Background

France

According to the orthodox account of the Basel Accord's origins, France was vociferously opposed to the agreement.[4] If the United States utilized the Basel process to create a wealth redistributive regime, then the French were among those countries that lost banking wealth to America's attempt to generate rents from an international capital standard. The French, with the Japanese, possessed the G-10's weakest credit regulations, the least capitalized banks, and as a result were the chief underwriters of America's efforts to unilaterally strengthen their own domestic capital regime.[5] By securing the implementation of the Accord, the United States would be able to tighten its own regulations without ceding any competitive advantages to its international competitors.

The evidence supporting this position, however, seems quite weak. The data that Oatley and Nabors provide are the illustration of France's relatively weak pre-Basel capital-to-assets ratios and the assertion that "Japanese and French regulators were the most vocal opponents of the U.S. initiative because the U.S. proposal would adversely affect French and Japanese commercial bank competitiveness."[6] First, the conclusion about France's low capital ratios is derived from data for only one French bank, Banque Nationale de Paris (BNP). Yet, as Table 7.1 indicates, BNP's capital ratios were about the lowest in France in the late 1980s. Moreover, if one takes the mean for the leading ten banks in each Basel Committee member state during this period, it is evident that French banks' average 1988 ratios were on-par with those of other industrialized countries when measured with identically narrow definitions of capital. These ratios are also especially high when considering that France had built up a large exposure to lesser developing countries debt during the 1980s.[7]

Second, France's capital adequacy regime does not seem to have necessarily conferred any special competitive advantage to their domestic banks. If the PREBASEL index is disaggregated into its constituent elements, France's pre-Basel capital adequacy rules meet the G-10 mean. A solvency regulation introduced in 1979 forced domestic banks to meet a risk assets/capital ratio target of 5 percent. The definition of regulatory capital to meet this target was more limited than the Basel provisions as only common equity, reserves, general provisions, and subordinated debt were allowed and deductions were required for investments in banking subsidiaries and affiliates. Most importantly, France was only one of five G-10 states to implement a risk-weighting assets approach. In

Table 7.1 Capital-to-assets ratios of the leading ten French banks, 1988

Bank	Ratio (%)
Compagnie Bancaire	6.5
Paribas	4.4
Crédit Agricole	4.1
SG Groupe Ecureuil	3.4
Banque Indosuez	3.2
Crédit Lyonnais	3.0
Groupe des Banques Populaires	3.0
Groupe Ecureuil	2.9
Banque Nationale de Paris	2.8
Groupe CIC	2.4
Average	3.6
G-10 1988 Average	3.9

Source: *The Banker.*

Note
Capital defined as common equity, disclosed reserves, and retained earnings.

some respects, the risk-categorization limits were more lax than the Basel/EC minima as inter-bank loans received a 5 percent (as opposed to a 20 percent) charge, yet in many areas, France's regulations resembled the pending international codes.[8]

While it is true that France did oppose American efforts to craft the Basel Accord, its opposition was not qualitatively different from that of most G-10 members. France's objection to the Accord was, ostensibly, on the basis that it was not possible to derive an objective and generalizable definition of capital and that capital adequacy depended as much upon the entire scope of a bank's activities and its management quality as it did upon its bank book portfolio.[9] In this objection, France was joined by Germany and, about 1999, the Federal Reserve changed course to argue this point of view at the Basel II Accord negotiations.[10]

Also, the French objected to the Accord when negotiations were leading to the exclusion of capital instruments that were important to their banks capital bases and were appropriate for their accounting standards. In particular, French banks (like their American counterparts) argued, in Basel and at the EC negotiations in Brussels, that loan-loss provisions must be included as, throughout the 1980s, they had built up such provisions to 40 percent of their exposure to Third World debtors.[11] Also, they demanded that the unrealized appreciation in physical assets, such as buildings, be included. Though excluded in those countries implementing GAAP standards, unrealized gains formed an important component of the French banking system's capital definition and indeed in most of the EC, except for Germany and the United Kingdom.[12] In demanding the inclusion of these items as regulatory capital (they were both included as Tier2 capital in the 1988 Accord), France was no more an opponent of the Accord than the United States, who demanded the inclusion of preferred stock as Tier1 capital, nor most members of the EC that also pressed for the inclusion of unrealized gains. Thus, it is not clear that the implementation of the Accord was necessarily any more harmful to French interests than to any other G-10 country's interests, nor that France's pre-1988 capital rules were singularly weak.

What is unique about the French case, and relevant to the enforcement of capital standards, is the high level of state involvement in the banking industry that persisted through the early years of the Accord's implementation. The French state has maintained a high level of intervention in the banking sector since well before the nineteenth century. Economic historians have explained this intervention as partly a product of the fragmented nature of the sector which has been traditionally divided between large commercial banks with a national marketing reach (such as BNP, Société Générale, Crédit Lyonnais), numerous financial cooperatives with a regional orientation, and banks organized to target particular industries with credits (Crédit Agricole for agriculture; Banques Populaire for artisans; Crédit Mutuel for agriculture and small/medium-sized enterprises). Until the 1980s, these differing credit institutions did not coordinate their policy objectives very effectively and, in the absence of a strong orientation toward local or regional governance in France, this fragmentation resulted in the national government assuming an important role in the sector.[13]

With this role, the government assumed a great deal of domestic economic control. Part of this control has been implemented through the direct ownership of banks and the design of elaborate credit allocation systems. For the former, the government has initiated two large nationalizations in the last 50 years or so. The first involved the nationalization of the largest commercial banks directly after World War II. During the most recent mass nationalization, in 1982, the government took control of 36 banks and two large financial holding companies that gave the state control of 90 percent of bank deposits and 85 percent of outstanding loans.[14] With regards to the control of credit flows, these became especially complex during the 1970/1980s as the government established a credit allocation regime that tailored restrictions for individual banks, as opposed to defining a quota for the whole banking system. The result was the creation of 70 separate interest rate regulations, covering 44 percent of the country's total bank lending by 1981.[15]

By controlling this chunk of the country's bank lending, the state exercised a sizable amount of leverage on the patterns of domestic investment. Part of the traditionally high level of state control in France is facilitated not only by the degree of state ownership in the banking industry but by the pivotal role that financial intermediation has played in funding French industry since the 1960s. Securities markets have tended to be especially weak and investment credits have originated from banks rather than corporate debt or equities markets. As Coleman observed, "[t]his is an economy where borrowers, especially non-financial enterprises, are highly dependent on the allocation of credit by institutional lenders following policy signals from the state."[16] Though efforts have been made to move away from this bank-centered model since the 1978 Loi Monory, in 1991 financial intermediation represented, on a flow-of-funds basis, close to 80 percent of aggregate financing. This continues to give the state a large vote in the allocation of domestic credit.[17]

In addition, the high level of state control has shifted a great deal of financial product innovation capacity to the public sector. A large body of regulatory research, initiated by Kane (1991), suggests that generally a regulatory dialectic persists between regulators and regulated firms. Firms will engineer new products to circumvent the effects of new regulation. In order to ensure that the original standards remain relevant in light of these efforts, regulators will respond by issuing new rules, thus initiating the dialectic anew. Yet, De Boissieu (1990) argues that the large state role in French finance alters this game so that, "[e]ven if the 'regulatory dialectic' is also valid in the French case, it appears that in France, as in Italy, *public* financial innovation predominates. Rather than a challenge, financial innovation is considered as a tool for economic policy."[18]

However, it should not be assumed that, given this high level of state control, French banks are necessarily politically weak. In fact, at the end of a paper largely devoted to explaining the role of the state in French banking, Coleman (1997) concludes by questioning: "can the state counter (contre pouvoir) the power of the banks ... [e]vidence suggests that this capability has weakened."[19] Though France's score on the quantitative indicator of banks' political power is

130 *Case studies*

well below the G-10 average (0.31 versus 0.46), this measure may not be capturing the changes emerging in state–bank relationships in France.

Part of the explanation for this apparent paradox may be that the gap between state and bank control has been narrowing since the creation of the 1984 Banking Reform Act. This Act resulted in French banks' gradual shift to a universal bank model, and the establishment of a strong corporatist banking policy network where political disagreements would be resolved rather than in the legislature. This policy network was created through the rationalization of the bank regulatory regime so that rules for different classes of intermediaries were harmonized and supervisory responsibility centered in three organizations: the Comité de la Réglementation Bancaire (CRB) which was charged with rulemaking; the Comité des Etablissements de Crédit (CEC) for licensing new banks; and the Commission Bancaire (CB) for supervising the implementation of regulations. The Act also required all banking organizations to join an industry association that was a member of a government created peak organization, the Association Française des Etablissements de Crédit (AFEC). Lastly, the largest commercial banks have begun to move out of government ownership as Société Générale, BNP, and Crédit Lyonnais were privatized in the 1980s/1990s and Crédit Agricole moved out of direct state control in 1987. These changes may have strengthened the political power of French banks.[20]

Germany

Germany entered the Basel and EC capital adequacy negotiations with the strictest standards in the G-10. Prior to the implementation of the Accord, the German Federal Banking Supervisory Authority (FBSA) permitted only paid-up share capital, disclosed reserves, and net profits to qualify as regulatory bank capital.[21] Thus, Germany's negotiating positions in Basel and Brussels were not so much geared toward ensuring the inclusion of capital elements important to their domestic banks so much as arguing that a narrow definition of capital be internationally adopted. Germany had incrementally developed its capital regime over a 40-year period and was anxious to maintain existing rules without suffering further competitive disadvantages relative to its G-10 and European peers.

Germany's strict capital regime, and thus its Basel/EC negotiating positions, originated in the country's postwar organization of the domestic financial services industry. After 1945, a West German system of "organized liberalism" emerged in which financial services policy was generated and implemented within a highly centralized and corporatist policy network. Prior to the 1960s, the MOF and Bundesbank formulated policy with the consultation of the commercial banks that were represented by a comprehensive peak association, the Bundesverbank deutscher Banken. Historically, this regime's origins may be explained by the patterns of politically disruptive financial conditions that the country endured after its unification under Bismarck. The 1873 Berlin financial crisis and the hyperinflation of the Weimar Republic contributed to a post-World

War II consensus that financial institutions need to be deeply tied in to the oversight of the state to provide for stability.[22]

Though state ownership did not emerge, banks became the centerpiece of the government's industrial policy. Tax incentives were created to facilitate copious amounts of cross-share holdings between banks and other financial service providers, and between these "universal bank" groups and industrial corporations.[23] As Story summarized (1997:252), "Banks are part of a nexus of banks, insurance companies, and industrial corporations, which own each others' shares and share each others' supervisory seats. This nexus is woven into the fabric of the German state...." The result was a highly bank-oriented financial system in which 18 percent of corporate investment between 1950 and 1990 were derived from bank credits. The ratio of bank assets/GDP was 1.21 in the 1990s, second only to Switzerland in the G-10, while the ratio of claims of deposit money banks on the private sector/GDP was 0.94, the third highest in the G-10.[24] As the key government program for economic growth after 1945 focused on building an export-oriented industrial strategy, banks were of central importance in order to extend credit to these industries directly and in funding the Hermes export insurance scheme.[25]

This central importance of banking in postwar Germany has two important consequences for understanding its bank capital regime. First, it was necessary for Germany to create a strict capital standard to ensure its massive commercial banks remained solvent. Though preventing bank failure is important in any domestic political economy, it was especially so in Germany given the key role these organizations played in funding domestic investment. The result was the incremental development of a strict regulatory portfolio that sought to increasingly limit the activities of commercial banks.

Though tough regulations were discussed during the drafting of the Basic Law in the 1940s, much banking regulation remained state-oriented until Germany adopted an especially strict, federal bank capital standard with the 1961 Banking Act. This act was created to enforce a nation-wide standard that would replace the disparate state regulations and provide the legal basis for the creation of the FBSA, a banking super-regulator. The act required that all domestic financial intermediaries maintain a capital buffer that included mostly common equity and excluded preferred equity, debt, and any sort of hybrid debt/equity instrument.

These strict regulations were tightened even further in response to Germany's banking crises of the 1970/1980s. After the collapse of Bankhaus I.D. Herstatt in 1974, the FBSA created a new Bank Structure Committee to consider reformulations of the credit rules. The result was that the ceiling for large-scale credits was reduced from 75 percent to 50 percent of equity capital, and capital adequacy standards were enforced on the consolidation of banking groups, including foreign subsidiaries. The latter was especially damaging to German banks as it closed an avenue by which they circumvented their narrow capital requirements by building up credit pyramids with their domestic and foreign subsidiaries without increasing the capital base of the parent bank.[26] The financial

132 *Case studies*

difficulties experienced by SMH-Bank in 1983 brought a similar response from the Committee as the German regulators brought pressure to bear on the level of banks' CARs.

Though German capital standards were the strictest in the BCBS on the basis of the narrow regulations adopted, the banks' capital ratios were actually among the lowest in the 1980s. In 1988, the average CARs for the leading ten German banks (by capital levels) was 59 basis points lower than their top ten French competitors and 248 basis points lower than their American peers. Even if the analysis is limited to the top three German banks (Deutsche Bank, Dresdner Bank, and Commerzbank), the Germans' ratios remain 17 and 206 basis points lower than the French and Americans, respectively. This comparison may not be surprising given the high capital standards to which German banks adhered. In fact, *The Banker* observed that Germany's ratios would be considerably higher if their regulations permitted the inclusion of the vast levels of hidden reserves that the banks had built up through their cross-holdings of German manufacturers.[27] Nevertheless, these low ratios were a source of worry for the FBSA and pressure was placed on the banks to raise their CARs.

Yet, while banks were subject to these strict requirements, it should not be deduced that they were a politically weak force in the German political economy. In fact, their role in the corporatist policy network allocated a powerful role to them in the federal public policymaking process. The FBSA regularly includes the industry in the policy creation process and, perhaps more importantly, relies on it to ensure implementation and compliance. The Bundesverbank deutscher Banken (BDB) is perhaps the most influential bank peak association among the industrialized countries. The organization's membership has funded and managed its own guarantee and settlement systems, provided emergency liquidity facilities to distressed members, and been charged with self-regulatory powers in a number of issue areas.[28] Numerous domestic interest groups, often led by the center-right Free Democratic Party, have accused the banks of exercising unjustifiable amounts of power through their equity holdings in the country's largest firms and demanded that the government clamp down.[29]

Thus, the German banks did not have strict capital standards forced on them, as in the United States, but agreed to such standards in a policy network that emphasized consensus. It follows that as Germany entered the Basel and EC capital adequacy negotiations, its regulators and banks jointly pursued the adoption of a strict international capital standard. The centralized German policy network had, over a period of 50 years, produced a capital standard that satisfied the goals of the regulators and commercial banks and suited the risk management requirements of the German financial system. In addition, German banks were highly supportive of their supervisors' efforts to create a tough international standard after their domestic regulations had been designed as tough initially and tightened further still in the aftermath of the Herstatt and SMH-Bank crises.

Despite this convergence of state and firm international goals, Germany was, of course, not ultimately successful in shaping the ultimate outcomes of the

Basel or EC negotiations. They were initially successful in forcing a set of rigid capital standards in the EC negotiations, over French objections, when the "Proposal for a Council Directive on the Own Funds of Credit Institutions" (EC/C243/06) was submitted to the European Commission in September 1986 with the exclusion of perpetual debt instruments. Germany also successfully delayed the Basel negotiations for numerous years by vetoing the inclusion of undisclosed reserves, revaluation reserves, and loan–loss provisions. Yet, the trilateral agreement orchestrated among the United States, the United Kingdom, and Japan scuppered Germany's ambitions, and the interests of the majority of G-10 states for the inclusion of their desired capital instruments defeated Germany's aim to enforce a stringent standard on the world's banking system.[30] These failures by the German bargainers in Basel and Brussels shook the consensus that had emerged in the policy network over capital standards and, for the first time, a wedge emerged between the regulatory preferences of the German regulators and those of the constituent banks.

First implementation period (1988–1992)

France

France was among the quickest EC member states to implement the Basel Accord. While Germany did not implement the agreement until 1990, the Banque de France forwarded a letter to the French Banking Association in November 1988 seeking immediate compliance among internationally active banks. A more formal guideline issued by the CRB in June 1989 went beyond the minima by applying the Accord to all French banks before the EC Own Funds Directive and Solvency Ratio Directive were implemented in February 1990 and March 1991.

The decision to quickly implement the Accord may be partly explained as a bargaining strategy that France adopted for the EC capital negotiations in December 1989. After successfully pushing for the inclusion of loan–loss reserves as part of Tier2 capital in Basel, France faced the possibility that Germany and the United Kingdom would force their exclusion from the EC definition of own funds. Germany had strongly objected to the 1988 Accord on the grounds that it allowed far too many weak forms of capital, with questionable abilities to absorb financial loss, compared with its own largely equity-centered capital rules, and both the Germans and British had announced their intentions to exclude loan–loss reserves from their own Basel interpretations. Yet when the Own Funds Directive negotiations occurred, under the French Presidency of the EC, the French MOF was able to water down the definitions preferred by Frankfurt and London to include these reserves, citing the fact that they had been implemented in France's Basel Accord interpretations for all of its domestic and internationally oriented banks, for over one year.[31]

Beyond this, however, French regulators adopted the most minimalist interpretations possible for nearly each discretionary element of the Accord. Unlike the United States where there was a minimal amount of commercial bank input into the initial implementation process, the much tighter French policy network produced a high level of regulator to bank interactions in the Basel interpretation process. The result was an initial CREG score of 13, compared to the mean of 14.5, and a credit risk regime that shadowed the bare definitional and ratios minima. The only area of strict implementation involved the exclusion of asset revaluation reserves that, before Basel, had been disallowed due to French accounting regulations. These reserves were later allowed in 1990 when France's largest banks lobbied for their inclusion after Germany added asset revaluation reserves to their definition of regulatory capital.[32]

Ostensibly, French banks did not have a great deal of difficulty complying with these Basel Accord interpretations. The Tier1 (non-risk weighted) capital adequacy of the leading ten French banks increased 53 basis points from 1988 to 1992, compared to the 25 and 32 basis point increases for the American and German banks over the same period. Focusing purely on capital ratios, one author observed that "on a global level, the French banking sector has not much to adjust in order to comply with the Cooke ratio."[33]

Yet, the exact manner in which the French increased their ratios to these levels was controversial and created some political friction within the Basel Committee. First, one may conclude that it is not difficult to imagine that the French could increase their ratios faster than their German and American counterparts as, according to the quantitative implementation index, they were permitted a larger quantity of financial instruments with which to raise capital and, most importantly, did not require the deduction of the holdings of other financial institutions' capital from Tier2. Another explanation maybe that, beyond the scope of the rules covered in Basel, French regulators allowed their banks to follow some creative efforts to raise fresh capital. One prominent example is that state-owned banks topped up their CARs by swapping shares with other state-owned companies.[34] As industrial enterprises tend to be much better capitalized than financial institutions, this provided French banks with the opportunity to dip into these rich capital reserves while providing some relief for the state who would have had to front the capital necessary for the nationalized banks.[35]

In addition, French banks, with the encouragement of the government, put considerable effort into engineering financial instruments that provided an alternative to equity financing in order to raise capital. Ultimately, banks of every nationality engaged in this sort of financial engineering with the aim of circumventing the Basel rules, yet French banks began this process early. In the early years of implementation, before 1993, numerous banks issued perpetual subordinated capital debt to qualify as Tier1.[36] Members of the Basel Committee, however, were suspicious of this regulatory treatment and, in November 1988, initiated an investigation into Crédit Lyonnais' issue of these notes. By the year's end, the committee ruled that such issues must be classified as Tier2 capital, over the objections of the French government and its banks.[37]

EC regulators raised similar objections over France's risk-weighting of securitization issues. In a likely effort to assist banks' capital raising efforts and

Paris' long-term challenge to London as Europe's premier financial center, the CB adopted a standard which would relieve French banks of having to provide any capital charge to securitization issues made through their special-purpose vehicle companies, which were designed by banks to make these issues. The result was that the banks would be able to shift loans off of their balance sheets without any capital charge penalty as would need to be paid by another Basel Committee country. Though this practice was permitted by the EC, it was given considerable review as negotiations proceeded for the CAD.[38]

Thus, while France has been generally perceived to be disadvantaged by the Basel process, it is not especially clear that this was the case. France did not depart, in any sizable measure, from its existing capital regulatory practices when implementing the Basel framework. As the French negotiators objected to the creation of the Accord in the first instance, this seems to be a sizable diplomatic victory.

Germany

By contrast to France, Germany was the last Basel Committee state to implement the 1988 Accord and the last EC member to adopt the 1991 Own Funds/Solvency Ratio Directives. Though in May 1990, the FBSA did amend the Banking Law to incorporate some of the Accord's terminology into their domestic rules, significant distinctions remained until implementation formally occurred in 1992. Until this date, Germany's regulations made no distinction between primary and supplementary capital, did not provide for any risk-weighting methodology commensurate with the Accord, and did not require their banks to meet a common capital-to-assets ratio. Though the largest German banks were required to report information on their implementation of the Basel guidelines to the Bundesaufsichtsamt from 1990, it is not clear with what exact capital standard these reports were made.[39]

This slow implementation seems extraordinary in light of Germany's tough pre-Basel capital standards. Oatley and Nabors (1998) concluded that the Accord was redistributive only for Japanese and French banks and their paper seems to suggest that the Accord was largely neutral for Germany as the country did not need to strengthen their own rules to meet the Accord and, unlike the United States, German regulators were not aiming to drastically increase their own domestic regulations in the years leading up to the Accord. Though German rules were tightened in the mid-1980s, these changes were not a wide departure from the pre-existing standards, unlike the US Congress' demands for a new American capital standard in the late 1980s. In fact, utilizing Oatley and Nabors's model, it may not seem entirely inappropriate to conclude that the Accord could be viewed as wealth distributive in favor of German banks, especially as they were in the process of completing a single European market in financial services with a selection of states which, save for Britain, held far weaker capital rules. If this model were correct, one would logically expect Germany to instantly adopt the new Accord, as the United States did, while

136 *Case studies*

France would waffle in its implementation. In fact, it seems the opposite effect emerged as France adopted the Accord a full four years in advance of Germany.

One explanation that may be posited to solve this paradox is derived from Germany's pre-Basel negotiating position. Germany may be the only Basel Committee state in which both regulators and commercial banks agreed that a strict international standard should be developed. The other two proponents of a Basel standard with a narrow definition of capital, the United States and Britain, experienced heavy criticism from their domestic banks which were not eager to follow a new rigid set of regulations if there was a chance that their international peers would be freed from such rules by their own regulators. Thus, the conclusion of the negotiation of the Accord (and directives) represented a failure for the entire German policy network. Every major Basel Committee member achieved some concession from the negotiations: Japan was permitted to include asset revaluation reserves; France won the right to include loan–loss reserves; American banks were permitted to issue non-cumulative preferred stock as primary capital. Yet, Germany did not seem to receive any concession as the adoption of Germany's position would threaten concessions made to other members.

Once the Accord moved into the implementation phase, the initial response of the FBSA was simply to alter the existing domestic regulations to comply with the regulatory language established in Basel. That is, classify some of its permissible capital elements as Tiers1 and Tiers2 and adopt the risk-weight bucket delineations on top of its pre-existing risk-weighting regulations.[40] Germany would essentially follow the status quo, though now its banks would need to adhere to a capital-to-assets standard that was 250 basis points higher.

German banks objected to this arrangement. Though the largest commercial banks, represented by the peak association, had supported their negotiatora' strict stance in Basel, they now demanded the sort of regulatory concessions that the FBSA had allowed to their Japanese, French, and American counterparts by agreeing to the Accord. While the German banks were only legally allowed to count equity and equity-like instruments in their capital base, some estimations suggest that their hidden reserve holdings were as high as those of Japanese banks in the 1980s; yet they were to be entirely excluded from Germany's Tier2 capital definition.[41] As policymaking in the German banking policy network tended to rely on consensus, the result of this FBSA-bank stand off was the total paralysis of capital adequacy rule making in the early years of the Accord's implementation.

It should be understood that German banks were not entirely unresponsive to the Accord. Some reports suggest that most German banks were complying with a form of the standard on a voluntary basis from 1988, though it is not clear what this standard may have been. The largest banks increased their capital ratios by 32 basis points from 1988 to 1992; a full 13 basis points more than the American money center banks over the same period.[42] Data from the Basel Committee indicates that, in the early 1980s, German banks were making an effort to increase their capital ratios by increasing their capital stocks and shedding assets.[43] This is quite unique as it suggests that some market pressure for compliance was exerted on German banks during this period in which there was no clear domestic commitment to implement the Basel Accord.[44]

The implementation standoff eventually ended with the economic crises of the early 1990s. The reunification of Germany exerted enormous costs for the banking system of West Germany from 1990. Banks found it increasingly difficult to maintain, much less increase, their capital ratios as the deadline for the full implementation of the Accord neared in 1992. Faced with the possibility of being the only Basel Committee state, save for Japan, to fail to meet the implementation deadline, the FBSA conceded to banks' demands and, in the first instance, permitted the inclusion of hidden securities reserves as Tier2 capital.[45] Once this concession was made, others quickly followed as, by the end of 1992, the FBSA permitted the inclusion of revaluation reserves and general loan provisions.[46] Faced with pressure from their banks and a tough economic climate, German capital regulations quickly fell into line with other members of the G-10.

Hypotheses review: first period

The analysis of France and Germany's implementation in the first period suggests that the two were initially guided by the rules of their pre-Basel standards. Though characterized as a loser in the Basel negotiations by Oatley and Nabors (1998), France successfully negotiated the inclusion of the capital elements most important to its domestic banks, particularly loan–loss reserves. While the bank political power hypothesis suggested that banks with relatively weak domestic power positions would suffer a strict interpretation of the Basel rules, this does not appear to have been the situation in France during the late 1980s. The high level of state involvement in the French system provided for a more symbiotic relationship among regulators and banks, rather than the conflicting relationship assumed by the hypothesis. If the regulators increased the capital requirements, it would be the state itself that would have to bankroll much of this increase. The high level of government ownership in the French banking market thus seems to have been influential. In addition, the regulators and firms were especially anxious to influence the EC capital adequacy negotiations to ensure that the 1986 German-led effort at a strong standard was watered down to allow for the inclusion of France's capital preferences. To accomplish this, the entire French policy network presented a united front at the Own Funds/Solvency Ratio Directive negotiations. This convergence of goals continued into the 1990s so that the regulators allowed and even suggested that banks issue capital instruments and engage in capital raising activities that drew objections from other Basel Committee states.

For France, there did not appear to be much of a distinction between the initial implementation and the evolution of implementation over time. The same regime that the country adopted in the 1970s survived largely intact until the early 1990s. Path dependence characterized the French approach to the implementation of the Accord as the agreement did not make any major demands for change upon existing practice and there were no influential domestic interests that supported change.

Likewise, Germany's initial interpretation of the Accord largely mirrored its extant practice. Distinct from France, however, this path dependency originated in the divergent, not isomorphic, interests of the German regulators and banks. As Story (1997:267) observed, "the German social market's buzz word is inclusiveness which is a feature of corporate governance among the firms and of federal and state politics." Within this framework of policymaking, the German banking regulator was reluctant to implement capital standards that the country's major banks opposed, especially as the peak association was responsible for many implementation/compliance duties on behalf of the state. Without a consensus, there was no effort to implement the Basel Accord until the early 1990s and the existing capital standards, already among the strictest, were left unchanged for numerous years.

Unlike France, however, Germany experienced a great deal of evolution in its Basel interpretations during the first three years of the Accord's implementation. Support seems to be provided for the economic instability hypothesis. In Germany, there was a massive change in regulatory content over a two-year period. Unlike the United States, however, this change did not come so much from a Kane-style regulatory dialectic process so much as a practical response to the fear that their largest banks would be among a minority of the G-10's internationally active banks who would not comply with the Accord by 1993. It seems that international and regional imitation factors were important in driving the convergence of Germany's capital regime with that of other G-10 and European states. The economic upheaval created by Germany's reunification strained their banks' resources to the point where it became clear that a change would have to be made. As the German peak association already had a list of improvements to the Credit Law prepared, which called for the inclusion of hidden reserves and loan–loss provisions, the easiest option for the Federal Bank Supervisory Office was to agree to their requests. In doing so, Germany altered a capital adequacy regime that had remained largely intact since the 1960s. The failure of the FBSO and Bundesbank to negotiate any of their positions successfully in Basel and Brussels placed Germany's banks in a position where they could no longer support their regime while the economic difficulties of the 1990s pushed the FBSO into an agreement with its banks.

Drawing together the results from the initial implementation period of France, Germany, and the United States, banking crises seem to have been the chief contributor to departures from pre-existing regulatory regimes. The political economic imperatives created by banking crises led to changes in the German and American regimes and, in the absence of such a crisis, the French maintained the status quo. The success of this hypothesis seems to augment explanations that predict that domestic interpretations of international "soft laws" will largely reflect only the state of the previous regime, since the presence or absence of an imperative such as a financial crisis may intervene in this relationship. Evidence for the capture hypothesis seems more mixed as the bank power positions in Germany remained constant over the period of time studied yet different regulations emerged over time.

Lastly, little support seems to be provided for the international pressure or hegemonic hypotheses. Other than EC objections to France's weighting of securitizations, which made little impact on French practice, there is not much evidence that the Basel members exerted pressure on one another's interpretations during this period. In the case of Germany, fear of international competitive disadvantage drove the loosening of regulations. Yet, such pressures emerged only after the onset of macroeconomic instability. This latter variable thus seems to be more important in explaining Germany's policy during this period.

Second implementation period (1993–2000)

Unlike their American counterparts, French and German regulators did not constantly adjust their capital adequacy standards through the 1990s. Germany's capital standards remained constant after 1993 and France's constant for the entire sample period. Understanding why these European states' credit risk standards were relatively stable for this seven-year period of time will be the concern of this section.

First, it should not be suggested that attention to capital adequacy regulation waned in Europe after 1993 and remained active solely in the United States. Rather, the focus of European regulators seemed to shift more toward the negotiation and implementation of substantial amendments and extensions to the Own Funds and Solvency Ratio Directives. Though the Americans discussed the formation of a unilateral interest rate risk charge and proved to be keen advocates of the Basel market risk amendment and the negotiation of the Basel II Accord, European states were involved in an endless round of negotiations on the capital adequacy of their financial institutions.

In particular, the EU rapidly negotiated a standard for the market risks of their financial institutions. The negotiation of the CAD1 agreement in advance of the 1996 Basel market risk standard seems quite natural from the point of view of their implementation of the 1988 Basel Accord. The application of this credit risk standard to all financial institutions (including local and regional banks and securities firms in addition to transnational commercial banks) made it more necessary to develop a charge for banks' market risks – a more critical business risk for investment banks than commercial banks. European states were thus more concerned with the integration of these standards into the credit risk regulations than US banks. The market risk amendment was not implemented in the United States until 1996 and then was only applicable to a sub-set of the US banks.

To understand the influence of these negotiations on France and Germany's credit risk regulations, the following sections will analyze the state of the French and German banking markets and regulatory practices from 1993 to 2000.

140 *Case studies*

Germany

Capital adequacy regulation became an increasingly important political topic in Germany after the 1988 Accord. As discussed, deep fractures emerged in the relationship between German money center banks and the FBSA during the implementation of the credit risk directives. This politicization intensified through the 1990s as the scope of regional and international capital adequacy negotiations seemed to further diverge from German interests.

Germany had become increasingly wary of multilateral efforts to regulate capital. In particular, it was extraordinarily delinquent in its implementation of CAD1 and the Investment Services Directive (ISD). These directives were implemented by nearly all EU member states by the January 1996 deadline. Yet, Germany claimed that the complexity of the directives prevented their immediate implementation for German banks and securities houses. It is not clear why these regulations were more complicated to implement in Germany than the other 14 signatories yet many believed that German banks derived a substantial competitive advantage from not implementing these directives. This was certainly the view of many EU states that also had to deal with complications arising from how to regulate German banks operating within their jurisdictions. The EU rules require the home state to regulate subsidiaries operating abroad, yet this delineation is complicated when the host state implements regulations that the home state has not.[47]

Moreover, it is possible that Germany was able to sidestep the effects of the original CAD altogether. CAD2 was negotiated in line with the 1996 Basel amendment to allow banks to set their own capital requirements for market risks with their own risk management modeling systems. Many German banks opposed any effort to implement CAD1 after the 1996 deadline expired, and moved straight to the implementation of CAD2, which would impose a smaller regulatory burden. Such behavior was not well received in many European capitals though a London-based finance industry lobbyist observed that:

> [t]he Germans have been bloody smart about this ... [o]nce CAD2 is in place they [German banks] can have one-stop implementation ... [o]ur banks [in Britain] have had to go to standard rules for two years, that has meant a big investment in systems.[48]

Germany has also been instrumental in delaying the successful negotiation of the Basel II Accord. German regulators have insisted on being provided with special derogations from the new Accord's definitions of capital and risk-weight specifications. Germany claims that these derogations are necessary to ensure the Accord matches the idiosyncrasies of its banking market, much like the 1988 Accord was molded around the particularistic interests of G-10 states in a "soft law" arrangement. Yet, on this occasion, the Basel Committee has not been so easy to convince that Germany is not simply out to preserve competitive advantages at the expense of domestic financial stability and a homogenous regulatory playing field. Many agree with *The Economist*'s conclusion that German regulators are seeking "to protect their charges by rigging international rules in their favour."[49] Alan Greenspan warned Germany to stop playing politics with a necessary amendment to the Accord in the protection of "provincial interests."[50] This rift has proven more serious than the 1998 US–German dispute and some journalists have hypothesized that it portents the end of the collegiality of the Basel Committee and may hamper future efforts to work through this committee.[51]

By mid-1999, the Basel II deadlock was broken as the United States agreed to most of Germany's objections. Looking back at the negotiation of the 1988 Accord and EC directives, it is unexpected that Germany should emerge as a threat to the Basel process. Referring back to the discussion of the Accord's negotiation in Chapter 2, Germany joined France and Japan in opposition to elements of Basel I; yet they were alone in arguing that the Accord established too lax a standard for multinational banks. Germany moved from a position of rejecting financial "soft law" that provided a wide latitude of national discretion to the loosening of their own capital standards in the early 1990s. More particularly, Germany became an opponent of multilateral capital agreements on the basis of their severity and an unambiguous non-complier with European capital directives.

France

France's capital adequacy policies provide an interesting contrast to American and German practices after 1993. Like Germany, France did not alter its Basel rule interpretations to any great extent during the 1990s, nor did it emerge at the center of international regulatory disputes like it did at the original Basel negotiations and like Germany during the late 1990s. A search of the pages of French language publications *Les Echos*, *Le Monde*, and *Europolitique* reveal eight stories concerning *fonds propres* from 1991 to 1992 and just six from 1993 to 2000. Moreover after 1993, the stories radically alter from discussions of how French regulators and banking markets are adjusting to the Basel provisions to reports on the negotiation of additional capital standards in Brussels and Basel. There are no juicy soap operatic stories of diplomatic wrangles between Paris and other capitals over banking risks. A study of the steady stream of financial code updates of the CB reveals little mention of changes to France's capital standards during the late 1990s.

The only major alteration in French policy involved the implementation of the 1998 BCBS document concerning tax-deductible Tier1 preferred stock. A number of French banks, especially Crédit Agricole and Crédit Lyonnais, had attempted to raise capital with such instruments in New York markets during the early 1990s. Preferred stock was not allowed by French regulators at this time and French banks hoped to circumvent domestic law by issuing these securities through Wall Street subsidiaries and "downstream" them to the parent firm as American banks sought to do in the mid-1990s. French regulators had ruled that such behavior was unacceptable, and relegated these issues to Tier2 status. In

142 *Case studies*

implementing the 1998 agreement, France allowed its banks to give this Tier1 status.[52]

Yet, France did not play a large role in this German–American dispute. France thus seemed to move from a position of voicing opposition to the 1988 Accord to being a more passive contributor to additional capital codes. The French moved from a position of being bullied by the United States in international capital negotiations in the late 1980s, to being a seemingly cooperative partner by 2000.

Hypotheses review: second period

A survey of the behaviors of France and Germany toward transnational capital adequacy policy from 1993 to 2000 produces some unexpected results. Given the bargaining positions of these two European states at Basel, it is surprising that Germany turned into an opponent of efforts to extend the international capital adequacy regime while France did not. The economic instability hypothesis seems to play an important role in explaining these policy changes. Looking at the capital-to-assets and bank profitability data for France and Germany during this period, it seems that German banks did not recover their profitability after German reunification (Figure 7.1). German CARs were consistently over 200 basis points below those of their French competitors during the entire 1990s, while profitability only caught up during the latter part of the decade. Traditionally, German capital ratios were not high by international standards, yet many considered Germany a tough regulator because of its restrictive definition of bank capital. After this definition had been expanded, Germany's ratios now make the country seem a poor enforcer of solvency standards. As a result, Germany has adopted the position, once held by France and Japan, of opposing international capital adequacy policy and faces the potential risk of being disadvantaged by such agreements.

Conversely, French banks seemed in relatively good shape during the period. Though the largest ten commercial banks experienced a large profitability lag in 1994–1995, this did not effect CARs to any great degree. Consequently, in the absence of economic crises to force a massive shift in capital adequacy, French regulators and banks preferred to keep the status quo.

Also, the private governance hypothesis seems to add little insight into either of these cases. In the case of the United States, private market governance seems to have been quite instrumental in shaping banks and regulators preferences. Yet, French and German banks are subject to a much lower level of market governance than the United States, and in line with the private governance hypothesis little market effect seemed to operate during the period under study.

A final question pertinent to the study of these EU states is whether much of what occurred during the sample period was the result of regional imitation effects. In a related issue area, Simmons (2000) found that states were significantly more likely to liberalize their capital accounts if their regional peers had liberalized. The root of this hypothesis was that adjacent states may share

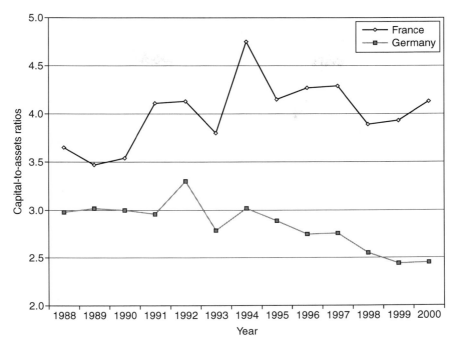

Figure 7.1 Unweighted Tier1 capital ratios for the leading ten French and German banks, 1988–2000 (source: compiled from data in *The Banker*, various issues).

Note
The following banks are excluded from the averages as they had extraordinarily high capital-to-assets ratios that were extreme outliers: Hamburgische Wohn'stalt in 1988 (61 percent), Electro Banque in 1998 (37 percent), 1999 (37 percent), and 2000 (48 percent), and Union des Banques Arabes et Française (11 percent).

similar business practices and philosophies and regional economic exchange would be facilitated through the implementation of similar policies. This sort of regional effect does not seem to have influenced French and German regulators. The "mutual recognition" framework of EC single market policies ensures that regulatory convergence is not necessary to facilitate exchange. It may perhaps be argued that regional effects drove German regulators as they reduced their standards during the first implementation period and thus moved their standards closer to the French position. Yet, the changes in German policies appeared to be driven more by concern for the financial health of German banks rather than intra-European competition. Despite the wide degrees of regulatory cooperation in Europe, little regional convergence was evident.

Conclusions

This chapter detailed the implementation of the 1988 Basel Accord into European law and then analyzed the implementation of the EC Own Funds and Solvency Ratio Directives in France and Germany. The empirical detail suggests that France adopted a path-dependent implementation position. The French "fit" their pre-Basel capital standards within the "soft law" provisions of the Accord and did not alter their interpretations to any great degree throughout the entire sample period. It was indicated that such policies lend support to the path dependence and economic instability hypotheses.

Germany started off on the same path-dependent course as France. Yet, the onset of economic instability was correlated with a loosening of Germany's standards during the early 1990s. Moreover, Germany moved from a position of opposing international capital adequacy agreements because they established weak credit standards in the late 1980s, to opposing them on the basis of their stringency during the late 1990s. The events also provided support for both variants of the path dependency hypothesis and the economic instability hypothesis.

8 Implementation of the Basel Accord in Japan

Introduction

Japan was expected to be financially disadvantaged by the 1988 Basel Accord. As previous chapters emphasized, many academics and members of the financial media believed that the Accord was designed by the United States to stem the international ambitions of Japanese banks by forcing them to adhere to the sorts of capital adequacy standards recognized by other industrial economies. This chapter commences by challenging this claim. Drawing from the political analyses of Tamura (2003b) and Sawabe (1995) and a string of econometric results by Wagster (1996), this section argues that significant amounts of Japan's input went into the final drafting of the Accord. Moreover, financial market actors regarded the Accord as a victory for Japanese banks during the late 1980s. Institutional investors and credit rating agencies believed that Japan's largest banks would easily meet the capital adequacy standards laid out in the MOF's interpretation of the Accord.

As the second and third sections explain, Japanese banks were subject to a relatively lax interpretation of the Accord's rules. This interpretation contributed to the domestic and international market optimism regarding the ability of Japanese banks to benefit from the agreement. Yet, this optimism quickly turned to pessimism as Japan's economy shifted into more than a decade of recession from 1990. The collapse of the domestic asset price bubble exerted a disastrous impact on many of Tokyo's largest banks. Generally, declining asset prices can impact any country's banking system, yet the effect was far more acute in Japan where significant portions of bank capital are directly linked with equity market values. From around 1990 to after 2000, Japanese banks operated almost exclusively in the red and many may have maintained CARs significantly below the Basel minima.

Curiously, the severity of MOFs' interpretations of the Accord varied very little during this period of economic instability. This chapter advances the argument that international market and political pressure prevented MOF from providing regulatory relief to their constituents for fear that such actions would further undermine confidence in the banking sector. Yet, it is extremely likely that Japan practiced "hidden defection" from the Accord by not penalizing banks for non-compliance with prudential codes and allowing – or indeed encouraging – banks to adhere to accounting and loan–loss provisioning policies that were of dubious prudential value. Though direct evidence for these implicit forms of defection are not easily obtained, research by Fukao (2002) attempts to quantify the impact of these policies on providing the cosmetic appearance that technically insolvent commercial banks were adhering to the Accord. In addition, significant amounts of secondary data by financial market analysts and actors support the existence of such policies.

This chapter places new demands on the hypotheses enumerated in Chapter 3. The theoretical propositions were designed to explain variations in the stated severity of capital adequacy policy after the implementation of the Accord. Yet, such an approach seems of little heuristic utility when coming to grips with Japanese capital adequacy policy through the 1990s. Initial interpretations of the Accord, just after 1988, provide support for the "path dependency" hypothesis in the predicted direction. Yet, the emerging gap between stated policy and actual bank practice alters the dependent variable of interest. It is advanced that the maintenance and increasing severity of Japan's stated capital adequacy codes resulted from international pressure from financial markets and BCBS members to hold domestic banks to a tough regulatory line. Yet, economic instability forced MOF to provide some regulatory relief while maneuvering through systemic constraints. The result was a return to the types of capital adequacy practices Japan maintained before the Accord: unenforced and of questionable prudential value.

Background

According to most political economy accounts, Japan joined France in being economically disadvantaged by the Basel Accord. Oatley and Nabors (1998) and Kapstein (1989, 1991, 1994) concluded that the Accord established a regulatory capital definition much more severe than Japan's existing practice and required a minimum capital-to-assets ratio much greater than Japan's international banks could comfortably meet. This section advances the argument that the extent of Japan's disadvantage from the Accord has been overstated. In a similar fashion to the discussion of France's pre-1988 capital regime in Chapter 7, it will be argued that Japan's extant capital practices were not necessarily much weaker to those in other industrial economies. At best, Oatley and Nabors, Kapstein, and others advanced their arguments without providing sufficient evidence to remain convincing when put to simple empirical test.

Second, this section investigates why Japan was so willing to agree to a multilateral capital adequacy accord in 1986 while EC states balked. As Chapter 2 discussed, Japan agreed to join the 1986 US–UK bilateral capital agreement fairly expediently, while Germany and France denounced the bilateral deal as a threat to achieving a truly international accord. Oatley and Nabors conclude that the fear of being shut out of international banking markets was responsible for Japan's acquiescence to the trilateral accord. Yet, by drawing on Sawabe's

(1995) discussion of the domestic politics of Japan's preferences in the Basel negotiations, this section concludes that the Accord was much more congruent with the interests of Japan's policymakers and banking institutions than is generally considered.[1]

Part of the explanation for this is that Japan's financial regulatory regime was entering a period of relatively radical change in the mid to late 1980s. The financial sector was burdened with binding regulations after World War II. As Hall (1993:86) observed, "the post-war Japanese financial system was characterized by [the] rigid compartmentalization of financial institutions, underdeveloped financial markets, and blanket regulation, reinforced by extensive administrative guidance (i.e. moral suasion) of all financial intermediaries." Under American supervision during the postwar occupation, banks and securities businesses were separated with legal firewalls.[2] The banking sector itself was further segmented into institutions specializing in the issue of long-term or short-term credits, those serving small- and medium-sized businesses and specific industries, and those based in major cities or in more rural areas.[3] The two lead regulators – the MOF and the BOJ – micromanaged commercial bank's activities by setting standards on the sources and uses of their funds, the terms on which they could borrow and lend, and their ability to establish branches or merge/acquire other intermediaries.[4] Heavy controls limited the activities of Japanese banks abroad and prevented foreign banks from operating in Japan.[5] This tight system of regulation persisted for roughly 40 years, yet began to weaken under a vector of domestic and international pressures in the mid-1980s.

Internationally, the United States worked to effect regulatory reform of the Japanese financial system in order to slow the growing international dominance of Japanese banking institutions. During the 1980s, the large Japanese "city" banks initiated an enormous global expansion program. Japan's banks had always played an important role in their domestic political economy through their cross-share holding linkages with the country's largest industrial manufacturing and high-technology firms in the zaibatsu and keiretsu networks. Yet, until the late 1980s, these banks were relatively small participants in the international marketplace. In 1980, only one Japanese bank (Dai-Ichi Kangyo Bank Ltd) ranked among the world's largest ten.[6] Under a host of domestic regulatory incentives, however, this situation quickly changed over the course of the 1980s so that by 1988 Japanese banks held 38 percent of the international banking assets and all ten of the world's leading ten banks, by capital, were Japanese.[7]

A large proportion of their expansion occurred through the acquisition of market share in the United States. By 1991, for example, US branches and subsidiaries of Japanese banks accounted for 18 percent of all US commercial and industrial (C & I) loans. This easily made Japan's banks the largest foreign banks in the United States. Moreover, Japanese banks accounted for over 60 percent of C & I loans issued by foreign banks and over 50 percent of the US banking assets held by foreign banks.[8] Part of this rapid expansion may be explained by a favorable macroeconomic environment in which Japanese banks

148 Case studies

benefited from a booming domestic equities market, low domestic interest rates, and the strong value of the Yen vis-à-vis the US dollar over the decade. Yet, banks and policymakers in the United States felt that this uncanny international expansion at least partly resulted from the favorable regulatory environment provided by Japan's banking regulators.

Members of the US banking community objected to the weak capital adequacy standards enforced on Japan's international banks. As discussed in Chapter 6, part of these objections originated with the low capitalization levels permitted by the MOF and the BOJ and the allowance of unrealized gains from investment accounts into the definition of regulatory capital.[9] More broadly, however, US regulators argued that Japan's aggressive international expansion was due to the tight reign that regulators kept on all aspects of the Japanese financial system. It was argued that controls on deposit rates permitted Japanese banks to raise capital cheaply by providing reliable access to low-cost deposits. As Figure 8.1 indicates, Japan's cost of equity has been significantly cheaper than other G-10 states. The absence of any international competition further kept capital costs down as the price of domestic bank shares on the Tokyo equity market was internationally high.[10] In response to these perceived sources of competitive inequality, the United States initiated numerous dialogues and discussion groups[11] to negotiate the liberalization of the Japanese market and the American Congress even threatened retaliation if national treatment were not adopted.[12]

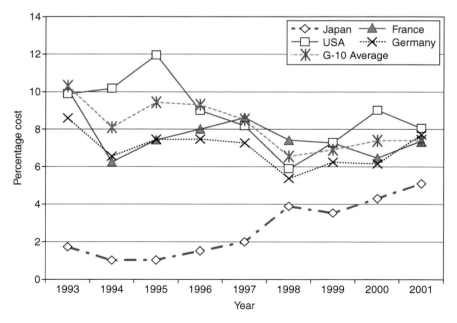

Figure 8.1 Averages for G-10 countries' major banks cost of equity, 1993–2001 (source: adapted from data presented in Maccario *et al.* (2002: 27)).

Interestingly, American demands were not inconsistent with those of Japanese bankers. As Japan's banks accumulated a larger share of the global marketplace, they lobbied for the removal of the binding regulations on their range of activities. In parallel with the American banking policy network, Japanese banks demanded the liberalization of their deposit and lending rates, the removal of narrow maturity restrictions, and the ability to issue new financial instruments in which they could offer rates as competitive as other actors in their domestic market.[13]

Japanese regulators responded to these demands, yet placed strengthening the prudential regulatory framework ahead of a "big bang" liberalization.[14] In June 1985, the MOF advisory committee issued a paper entitled "The Development of Financial Liberalization and its Environmental Arrangements," which highlighted to amend banks' capital adequacy practices in advance of plans to liberalize the domestic or international activities of banking institutions. Japanese banks had been subject to explicit minimum capital requirements since 1945, yet these were not enforced by regulators and largely ignored by banks.[15]

However, MOF officials had little reason to hope that strict capital adequacy standards could be implemented in tandem with their liberalization program. A 1979 effort by MOF to tighten capital regulations – through the implementation of a minimum 10 percent ratio requirement – was soundly defeated by the commercial banks' powerful peak organization, the Federal Bankers' Associations of Japan (FBAJ). The FBAJ successfully appealed to the governing Liberal Democratic Party (LDP) to remove MOFs' capital adequacy regulations from the legislative agenda. Bankers argued that they were more capable of monitoring their own solvency than regulators and possibly sealed their case by making contributions to influential legislators.[16] Hence, Japan's lead banking regulator needed to employ an alternative policy strategy in order to strengthen prudential standards over bankers' objections before liberalization proceeded.

Tamura (2003b) and Sawabe (1995) argue that the MOF utilized the Basel Accord as part of such a strategy. Unable to overcome domestic political opposition to the implementation of a unilateral capital adequacy standard, Japanese banking regulators used the international forum to foist a new prudential standard on their regulatees. The need for such a strategy was evident by early 1987. An effort to revisit the tightening of capital standards after the issue of the 1985 liberalization paper proved that banks remained resistant to attempts to raise their capital ratios. In May 1986, the MOF issued an administrative guidance considerably less severe than their 1979 attempt. Banks with overseas branches were required to hold 6 percent of non-RWA in capital and were permitted to count 70 percent of their unrealized capital gains as regulatory capital.[17] Moreover, the legislation did not grant any new enforcement powers to MOF or the BOJ to assign penalties for non-compliance.[18] Despite MOFs' concessions, banks were largely unresponsive. There is little evidence that banks complied with the regulatory capital limitations and eight of the main 13 city banks decreased their CARs in 1986. Tamura (2003b:7) concludes that, "[t]he new guidelines were a victory for banks, on balance."

150 *Case studies*

The result was the MOFs' acquiesce to the 1986 US–UK bilateral capital accord.[19] It should not be concluded that MOF sought to discipline their banks while subordinating the goal of representing their interests entirely in Basel. It certainly was not in MOFs' interests to stem the raising international profile and competitiveness of their constituents. Remember that American and British regulators were opposed to permitting any quantity of unrealized capital gains into regulatory capital. Such gains (which qualify as "asset revaluation reserves" in the Accord's Tier2 capital) were viewed as a highly impure form of capital that could potentially destabilize a banking system. These reserves represent banking holdings in securities and real estate and thus their value (and their ability to contribute to a "capital cushion") may be diminished by declines in the market values of these assets. British and American regulators pointed out that such reserves could decline during a market downturn, therefore creating a procyclical exacerbation of the economic cycle. This was the exact opposite of the intended effect of capital adequacy policy. Nevertheless, these reserves were an important component of Japanese banks' capital and MOF battled its international counterparts for their inclusion and was ultimately successful in securing a clause allowing 45 percent of such reserves into the US–UK accord and ultimately the 1988 standard.[20]

Nevertheless, much evidence suggests that MOFs' objective was also to pull their banks into line. Tamura (2003b:10) argues that MOF leveraged the information asymmetries created by the closed nature of the Basel (and US–UK trilateral) negotiations to force Japanese banks to raise their CARs. Banks were warned that the negotiations were not proceeding according to their interests and that banks must agree to re-capitalize and be prepared to compromise over levels of required capital and specifications of capital.[21] The result was that the FBAJ was satisfied with the ultimate results of the trilateral negotiations and willing to comply with the new standards, glad that revaluation reserves were to be permitted and the capital-to-assets ratio was no greater than that prescribed by MOF in 1986.

Thus, as the Accord moved into the implementation phase, it is not clear that the key members of Japan's banking network were dissatisfied with the results. MOF was able to at last implement a firmer prudential framework to underpin the liberalization program, while Japanese banks felt that they had achieved a victory in the international negotiations. In fact, in PriceWaterhouse's (1991) survey of bankers in the Basel and EC countries, Japanese bankers responded that they did not feel disadvantaged by the Accord nor did they have any major amendments they would aim to make to the Accord's provisions.[22]

What are the implications of this result for the redistributive explanation for the Accord's negotiation? Oatley and Nabors (1998) argue that the Accord was designed to distribute market share away from Japan in order to distribute it to its US and British competitors. This argument assumes that Japan had relatively weak capital ratios and capital standards before the Accord and that Japan's banking policy network maintained a monolithic preference.

First, as in the case of France, it is not easy to unambiguously assert that

Japan's capital adequacy practices were below the international norm. While MOF certainly thought that its banks' capital ratios were too low to sustain their level of international involvement, statistical analysis confounds the easy confirmation of this argument through cross-national comparison. The un-weighted capital ratios of Japanese banks' (see Figure 2.1 in Chapter 2) are not among the highest in the G-10, yet over a 15-year period (1970–1985) they are also not the lowest. Moreover, these data are taken from *The Banker*'s global bank rankings that compare banks on a very limited capital definition: common stock, disclosed reserves, and retained earnings. Japan maintained a relatively narrow definition of capital save for the inclusion of unrealized gains. The amount of these reserves was unknown. A 1989 Merrill Lynch Capital Markets study concluded that an approximate figure might be around US$300 billion, yet the property price bubble that emerged in the 1980s potentially made the reserves virtually "limitless."[23] In fact, when the revaluation reserves are included in the capital definition, Japan's capital ratios are nearly 200 basis points above the G-10 average.[24]

It may be asserted that including any quantity of unrealized gains constitutes a weak capital definition given the potential procyclical effect these leverage on bank's balance sheets. Yet, Japan was not the only state to maintain such reserves and, as Table 4.4 in Chapter 4 illustrated, the majority of the sample utilized here adopted some form of revaluation reserves. Finally, it is extremely difficult to argue that revaluation reserves constitute a weaker capital instrument than allowing cumulative preference shares in Tier1 as the United States maintained. As with implementation, there is probably not an either/or conclusion possible, yet a nuanced or "degrees of severity" possibility that endogenizes tax and accounting standards, costs of equity, and a number of other political economic variables. A thorough review of the capital adequacy literature in Basel Committee on Banking Supervision (1999) indicates that such an analysis has not been successfully completed.

Where Japan may have indeed been demonstrably weaker is in the enforcement of its pre-Basel standards. Though codified since 1945, neither MOF nor BOJ possessed powers of enforcements and clearly, from the discussion above, enforcement was a key problem. Yet, the Accord did not provide much guidance on the domestic enforcement of its provisions and hence it is not clear that Oatley and Nabors' (1998) argument is relevant to this concern.

Second, the redistributive argument assumes that all members of the Japanese banking policy network maintained convergent preferences at the trilateral and multilateral negotiations. By assuming that states are unitary actors, Oatley and Nabors sketch a parsimonious explanation of the Accord's economic intentions and effects. In doing so, they "black box" away the extent to which MOF leveraged upon multilateral public policy for local policy enforcement. In so doing, these authors miss Tamura's (2003b) conclusion that both Japanese regulators and bankers were satisfied with the Basel Accord for the domestic and international objectives that it helped fulfill as the agreement entered the implementation phase.

First period implementation of the Basel Accord (1988–1992)

Japanese bankers seemed especially optimistic about their prospects for further international expansion immediately after the implementation of the Basel Accord. The MOF implemented the 1988 Accord with an administrative guidance issue soon after the multilateral talks completed. The result was a new domestic capital adequacy standard that offered banks a wider selection of capital instruments to count as regulatory capital. Though bankers needed to work their balance sheets to meet the new Tier1 ratio targets and MOF had implemented a slightly stricter interpretation of the risk-weighting framework than Basel required, the growth of the domestic equities market remained unabated in the late 1980s and bank profitability continued to rise. Some academics have gone so far as to conclude that equities markets rewarded Japan's banks for emerging from the Basel regulations without incurring any disruptive compliance costs.[25] As this section narrates, however, this optimism ended as soon as equities markets began to tumble in 1990. By 1992, many city banks struggled to meet the Basel ratio minimums. Similar to the case of the United States in early 1990s, this economic turbulence led bankers to lobby for leniency in the application of the Accord's provisions and a break down in the Accord's enforcement resulted.

Yet before the burst of the Japanese "bubble economy," the Accord produced optimism in the Japanese banking markets. Bankers, regulators, and international market actors were confident that the city banks would easily clear the minimum requirements and some expected the Accord to fuel further international market expansion and profitability. The reason for such optimism seems to be the performance of the Tokyo equities market during the late 1980s. As Figure 8.2 indicates, the value of the Nikkei 225 index escalated rapidly from 1985 to 1990.

While American, French, and German bankers battled with their respective regulators over the minutia of the implementation process, Japanese banks worked to raise capital through the realization of securities profits.[26] Though only 45 percent of such profits contributed to the capital base, the value of such holdings continued to inflate as the broader macroeconomy accelerated. If there was any cause for concern, it was in the city banks' ability to raise sufficient quantities of Tier1 capital. One report concluded that these banks would need to raise 6325 billion yen of equity capital to reach the minimal standard.[27] Yet with the booming stock price performance of the city banks, it became increasingly easy for these banks to raise fresh equity. Indeed, an officer at Dai-Ichi Kangyo Bank commented that after a series of fresh equity injections, the bank would have a CAR well in excess of 8 percent and would seek to use this as a marketing tool to further their inroads into the American and European markets.[28]

Some academic studies of the microeconomic effects of the Accord concurred with this optimistic assessment. In particular, Cooper *et al.* (1991) and Wagster (1996) estimated the effects of public regulatory announcements concerning the implementation of the Accord on the stock prices of internationally active banks. They found that Japan benefited in the eyes of investors. In

Implementation of the Basel Accord in Japan 153

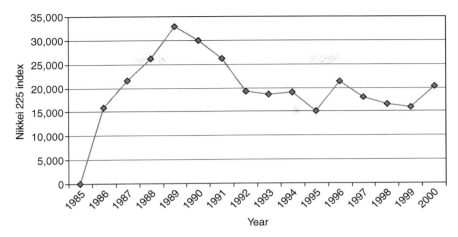

Figure 8.2 Nikkei 225 index: 1985–2000 (source: Fukao (2002)).

particular, Wagster (1996) found a statistically significant 32 percent cumulative wealth gain for Japanese banks when analyzing public announcements until 11 July 1988. The author concludes that this indicates that investors considered the Accord a "ratification by the G-10 and EC countries of the market share gains made by Japanese banks."[29] Before the Accord, Japanese banks faced the prospect of being shut out of the American and European markets through political intervention. Yet, the Accord assured access so long as these banks met the Basel standards. By allowing Japanese banks to count 45 percent of their unrealized gains, the Accord assured that compliance could be easily obtained and that compliance costs would be minimal compared with the benefits of diffusing the political controversy over Japan's regulatory system.

The MOFs' generous interpretation of the Accord seems to support this set of inferences. As Chapter 4 revealed, Japan's First Period CREG score was 13, which was about one standard deviation lower than the 18-country sample mean. Minimal interpretations were adopted in three of the six policy areas (Tier1 capital, minimum ratio requirement, and OBS risk-weights) with superequivalent interpretations being made in two (Tier2 capital and on-balance sheet risk-weights) and a below minimum interpretation in one (capital deductions). The superequivalent interpretations are the result of the exclusion of one form of asset revaluation reserve in regulatory Tier2 capital and the imposition of a 10 percent weighting on local government credits. The below minimum interpretation included the watering down of the requirement that banks deduct the value of investments in the capital in unconsolidated banking and financial subsidiaries. The latter likely reflects MOFs' desire to support the broad cross-equity holding structures of many keiretsu. Thus on balance, MOFs' interpretations were just at the minimal level. Both market and political actors seemed to regard this as an advantageous regulatory position for Japanese banks.

154 *Case studies*

As observed earlier, however, this optimism evaporated very quickly when the Japanese economy slipped into recession. Beginning in 1990, economic growth dramatically slowed and the value of traded equities tumbled. As Figure 8.2 illustrates, the Nikkei 225 index lost over 40 percent of its value from fiscal years 1989 to 1990. Banks' share prices were particularly hit as the slump in equities prices directly bit into their capital bases through the plummeting value of core capital and the stunting of banks' abilities to raise secondary capital through the realization of securities holdings. As Figure 8.3 indicates, the fall in the index of banks' share prices was particularly brutal from a high of 97.1 in 1989 to 56.4 in 1992.

As the extent of the burst of the asset bubble became clear, many worried that Japanese banks would be unable to meet the Basel minima by 1992. While declining equities prices can produce deleterious consequences for any publicly traded banks' capital adequacy, it is especially the case for Japanese banks due to their strong reliance on unrealized securities values. As mentioned, these instruments can contribute a procyclical effect on bank stability as their values decline in a general market downturn, just when intermediaries require them most urgently. Yet, it was their key importance to the Japanese banking industry's capital practice that makes this a more acute difficulty than in other G-10 and European economies. *The Banker* produced a rough estimate (see Table 8.1) that the further the Nikkei 225 fell below 22,000 the greater the number of Tokyo city banks would fall below the minimum Basel ratio requirements. Though *The Banker*'s data can only be regarded as an estimation, if these data are plausible then all but one of Japan's city banks would have total capital-to-risk-assets ratios below 8 percent by 1992.[30] It is impossible to empirically verify whether such an event occurred as Japanese banks' disclosures of their full Basel ratios was sketchy at best. Yet, looking at the un-weighted primary capital data employed in other case studies, it is clear that Japan's ratios were declining in absolute and relative terms. Moreover, the poor disclosure record of the total risk-weighted ratios is suggestive of a possible breach of the Basel

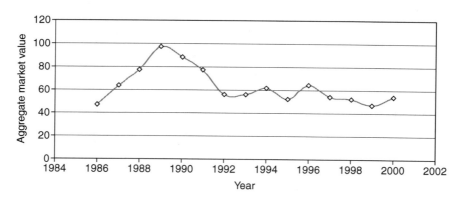

Figure 8.3 Aggregate market value of Japanese bank shares: 1985–2000 (source: Fukao (2002)).

Implementation of the Basel Accord in Japan 155

minima, particularly in consideration of Dai-Ichi's earlier comments that the publication of such ratios would be employed as a marketing tool.

Moreover, the declining equity market was not the only difficulty hitting Japanese banks' balance sheets. The collapse in the Tokyo market raised suspicions about the stability of Japan's banks in the international financial markets so that raising other forms of supplementary capital was stymied. Though again the unwillingness of Japan's bankers to publicly discuss their funding positions makes primary data sources difficult to obtain, market data suggest that after 1990, Japanese banks were forced to offer 14 basis points more on CD issues in the Eurodollar inter-bank market than their North American and European competitors. Despite the economic difficulties of many American, French, and German banks during this period, they were able to issue CDs at around 7 basis points below the London inter-bank bid rate (LIBID) while Japan's banks paid 7 basis points over LIBID, up from 3 basis points at year-end 1989.[31] Efforts at raising supplementary funding were also hit on the domestic market as demand for Japanese banks' freshly issued subordinated debt was not sufficient to allow this instrument to make up for the decline in unrealized securities gains' values.[32] Also, Hall (1993:17) observed that the initiation of the MOFs' liberalization program hurt bank funding. While emboldened to pursue deregulatory policies now that a formal capital policy was in place, MOFs' decision to lift official deposit rate ceilings from 1990 impaired city banks' margins further thus hurting these banks' abilities to add retained earnings to regulatory capital.

In short, what emerges by the end of the Basel transition period is a full 180-degree turnaround in the fortunes of Japan's largest banks. The economic response by the city banks was a growing retrenchment from their expansive growth in both international and domestic positions that had evolved steadily since 1945. Peek and Rosengren (1999) suggest that the macroeconomic contraction led city banks to reduce their asset holdings after 1990, the first such decline since the end of World War II. Japan's banks may have sought to shift

Table 8.1 Estimated effects of the Nikkei 225 on city banks' capital ratios (%)

Nikkei 225 Level	18,500	19,500	20,500	21,500
Dai-Ichi Kangyo	7.21	7.41	7.61	7.80
Mitsui Taiyo Kobe	7.06	7.30	7.35	7.35
Sumitomo	7.61	7.79	7.96	8.14
Fuji	7.51	7.70	7.90	8.09
Mitsubishi	7.39	7.59	7.80	8.01
Sanwa	6.99	7.19	7.39	7.59
Tokai	7.50	7.73	7.96	8.05
Daiwa	7.42	7.71	8.00	8.29
Hokkaido Takushoku	8.25	8.46	8.67	8.74
Bank of Tokyo	6.85	7.01	7.17	7.33
Kyowa Saitama	7.56	7.79	8.01	8.24
Average	7.40	7.61	7.80	7.97

Source: *The Banker*, 1 January 1992.

lending away from the low-margin but high-volume businesses that had bolstered their international position in the 1980s into low risk lending in domestic housing loans, government bonds, and guaranteed loans to domestic small- and medium-sized enterprises (SMEs). Though unpublished, the market decline may have caused the level of NPLs to explode, possibly to a level of 7 percent of total outstanding credits during this time.[33] Moreover, Japanese banks began to withdraw from their international exposures. Though more of this will be discussed later, the withdrawal of Japanese banks from the American market may have exacerbated the supply-side credit crunch that emerged throughout the United States during the early 1990s (see Chapter 6).[34]

The city banks' political response was to demand forbearance of the Basel Accord's application. Like their American peers, Japanese banks demanded that MOF provide regulatory relief to banks in light of the changing economic environment. The composite of data collected on Japan's implementation of the Accord suggests that banks were only partly successful in this effort. Relying on Japanese language documents, Tamura (2003b) argues that MOF resisted efforts to change their interpretation of the Accord. Noishimura Yoshimasa, the director of MOFs' Fiscal and Monetary Research Institute, argued that this was necessary as a lenient or postponed interpretation of the Accord would only exacerbate the growing international confidence crisis in the Japanese financial system.[35] In fact, rather than water down their interpretation of the Accord, MOF further codified their post-Basel capital regulations by supporting a 1992 revision to the Banking Law that provided a statutory – rather than administrative guidance – basis for formal, domestic capital requirements patterned on their interpretation of the 1988 agreement.

Other evidence, however, suggests that banks were not so overruled as a literal reading of their statutory requirements might suggest. European and American bankers, academics, and regulators seem fairly unanimous in believing that Japan's capital adequacy regulations were poorly enforced.[36] Though further evidence of this came to light in the mid to late 1990s, by 1992 it was clear that MOF was not likely to punish banks that did not meet the required Basel minima. No prompt corrective mechanism was in place to automatically sanction banks for failing to meet the trigger ratios laid out in the Accord and there is no evidence that MOF took any discretionary action to sanction city banks that were clearly in breach of the Accord. By 2000, evidence suggests that this "enforcement gap" increased to the point that it may be argued that MOF intentionally circumvented the spirit of the Accord through lax enforcement guidelines. This will be further discussed in Section "Second period implementation of the Basel Accord (1993–2000)."

Hypotheses review: first period implementation

The first several years of the Accord's implementation in Japan lends some support to a number of the hypotheses. First, elements of the broader "bank preferences" hypotheses received some support. Banks' preferences seemed conditioned by a desire to include elements of the pre-Basel capital regime – or rather non-regime – into the 1988 Accord and its domestic interpretation. As part of a broader effort to support their continued international expansion, Japanese bankers resisted efforts to implement an international standard that excluded unrealized securities, the key idiosyncratic instrument of their capital base. The inclusion of these instruments in the bilateral and multilateral Accords might reflect a negotiation victory for Japanese regulators and banks and it minimized the gap between Japanese banks existing practice and new demands placed on them by a Basel Committee agreement.

However, contrary to the predicted direction of effect, the involvement of Japanese banks in international markets did not prompt them to pursue the implementation of a stricter standard than the international norm. Yet, given the positive signals given by international equity markets to Japan's implementation of the Accord, this does not seem to have been necessary. If anything, supporting the implementation of any international standard that included some portion of unrealized securities by the city banks was enough to placate international markets that might have feared far worse when the US–UK bilateral deal was announced without such reserves in regulatory capital.

The macroeconomic variables also seem to receive some measured support. Principally, economic instability from 1990 clearly had an adverse impact on the Japanese banking industry. Yet, the collapse of the asset bubble did not contribute to a change in the published capital policy. In fact, some evidence suggests that the level of international governance might have interacted with the macroeconomic crisis to produce this "no change" as MOF officials worried about the influence of lax capital adequacy regulations on international markets. Yet, banks were not without some regulatory relief as evidence suggests that MOF did act to forbear the bite of the Accord through lax enforcement. In this regard, some support may be provided to "bank power" hypothesis in conjunction with the macroeconomic instability hypothesis, as Japanese banks were indeed able to acquire some regulatory relief.

The failure to endogenize enforcement is clearly a weakness of the quantitative study conducted in Chapter 5. Though numerous academics and practitioners have observed enforcement's importance in looking at the impact of capital regulations, most opinions on this topic have identified Japan as the particular culprit. The United States, France, and Germany case studies did not suggest that enforcement was of particular concern. Also, it is difficult to design an ex ante measure of rule enforcement. Given that rule enforcement involves a vector of unobservable – or at least difficult to observe – policy variables, it is difficult to capture this phenomenon with one variable. More will be said of this topic in the next section.

Second period implementation of the Basel Accord (1993–2000)

During the period of time analyzed in this section, the Japanese banking industry moved from one major crisis to the next. By some estimates, Japan's city banks

158 *Case studies*

were in the red for eight consecutive years from 1993 to 2001. As one commentator put it, "[i]t may seem strange, but banking has turned into an unprofitable, structurally depressed industry."[37] During this period of acute distress, the vagaries of allowing particular forms of capital instruments or requiring certain ratios became subordinate to constructing a package of lax enforcement and accounting standards that would permit many technically insolvent Japanese banks to remain afloat and ostensibly remain in compliance with the Basel Accord. With one exception, there was very little change in the broad contours of the interpretation of the 1988 Accord, yet policy areas touched on by the Accord were of central attention to Japanese banks, regulators, and policymakers.

The asset price bubble collapse of 1990 strangled macroeconomic growth for the remainder of the decade. Economic growth remained stagnant and even dipped into negative over the 1990s. The average real growth rate from 1991 to 2000 was 0.8 percent per annum. By the late 1990s, deflation gripped the economy despite the BOJs' adoption of a zero interest rate policy from February 1999. The GDP deflator fell 7 percent from 1994 to 2001.[38]

Microeconomically, the banking sector suffered during this time. Declining asset quality produced 72 billion yen in bad loans from March 1992 to March 2001 according to a conservative estimate. To give the idea of magnitude, this figure represents 14 percent of Japan's GDP in 2000.[39] Public funds were necessary to buy these under-performing loans and ensure a systemic banking collapse did not ensue.[40] As Figures 8.2 and 8.3 indicate, neither bank shares nor the broader Nikkei index experienced a sustained rebound. As a consequence, bank capital ratios were depressed well below the G-10 average. The risk-weighted ratios presented in Figure 8.4 suggest that, on average, the city banks' CARs varied from 8 to 9 percent from 1991 to 2000. Though these ratios were

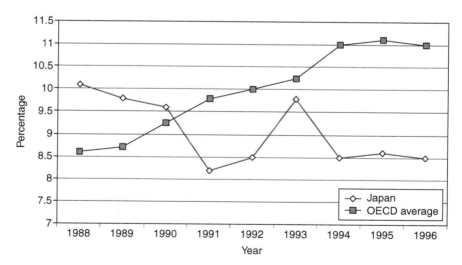

Figure 8.4 Capital adequacy ratios: 1988–1996 (source: estimated from calculations by De Nederlandsche Bank in Basel Committee (1999)).

Implementation of the Basel Accord in Japan 159

ostensibly in compliance with the Accord, they were generally 100 basis points below the average G-10 bank for the period.

Further, most academics and financial practitioners agree that Japanese banks were not even performing as well as these official data suggest. While the official capital adequacy standards and ratios were at about the Basel minimum, overwhelming evidence suggests that Japanese regulators and policymakers produced "hidden defection" of the Accord through the implementation of weak accounting requirements and continued lax enforcement. Fukao (2002) and others identified at least three key areas in which Japanese authorities manipulated the domestic capital adequacy regime during the 1990s to provide regulatory relief:

1   First, regulators may have permitted banks to operate with a financially inappropriate NPL provisioning policy. Regulatory forbearance may have been granted by MOF through permitting banks to adopt weak loan classification standards. The IMF criticized Japan for allowing banks to resist classifying as "non-performing" dubious or underwater credits. In addition, banks were not required to set aside sufficient loan–loss reserves against these NPLs.[41]
2   Second, MOF permitted city banks to hold deferred tax assets on their balance sheets inappropriately. Banks kept deferred tax assets though they had been losing money for the whole of the 1990s and loss carry forward is limited up to five years under Japanese tax codes. As there was little chance of getting the deferred tax asset through the creation of profits, MOF should not have permitted these assets as regulatory capital.
3   Third, most subordinated loans of banks are held by friendly life insurance companies. Banks, in turn, held subordinated loans and surplus notes of life-insurance companies. This practice of double-gearing and the cross-held quasi-capital should not be treated as genuine capital of banks or life insurance companies.

The expected effect of these policies was to overstate Japanese banks' capital assets ratios and water down the application of the Accord. Though poor Japanese disclosure practice during the 1990s again makes the empirical verification of the effects of these forbearance rules difficult to ascertain, Table 8.2 presents the results of the work of the Japan Center for Economic Research to estimate Japanese city banks' CARs with capital defined as primary capital, estimates of unrealized capital gains, and loan–loss reserves less standardized estimated loan losses from disclosed NPLs, and tax deferred assets for the period March 1998 to September 2000. Though the loan–loss calculations likely understated their actual levels, the figures suggest that Japan's major banks were well below the minimum ratio requirements. These figures do not reflect true "Basel ratios" as they measure capital to un-weighted assets, yet they clearly indicate a fairly low capitalization level.

When comparing these data to the officially published ratios in Figure 8.4, they suggest that city banks may have received a sizable "regulatory rent" from

160   *Case studies*

Table 8.2 Reformulated capital-to-assets ratios of major Japanese banks, March 1998–September 2000

Date	Average capital ratio (%)	Nikkei 225 level
March 1998	0.93	16,527
March 1999	2.07	15,837
March 2000	3.48	20,337
September 2000	2.36	15,747

Source: Japan Center for Economic Research (2001).

Notes
Capital defined as core capital, unrealized capital gains, and loan–loss reserves less estimated loan losses, and deferred tax assets. Sample size varies by year but includes all major banks for which data are available.

MOFs' forbearance and were not in compliance with the Accord. Though data are incomplete to support this position, the consensus of academic and practitioner opinion is that Japanese banks' CARs were highly overstated.[42]

Further support for this conclusion is provided by the reactions of international market actors and Basel Committee members to Japan's capital adequacy policies during this period. In particular, MOFs' peers in the BCBS and the IMF voiced concern over the weak provisioning and reserve policies permitted in Japan.[43] Though these standards were technically not a violation of international regulatory policy, they obscured the true solvency position of Japan's major banks.[44] The US Federal Reserve's criticisms of these policies became intense in 1995 when it emerged that Daiwa Bank's Wall Street subsidiary failed to disclose more than US$1 billion in trading losses to US regulators.[45] American regulators and credit rating agencies partly blamed MOFs' poor prudential oversight capabilities and, in particular, centered on the tangible issue of provisioning and reserve requirements for criticism.[46] A representative from Fitch IBCA commented that many Japanese banks actually had negative capital and that the 8 percent minimum was only being met through "unconventional bookkeeping practices."[47]

MOF responded to these criticisms by amending its provisioning requirements, though by only minor degrees. After 1995, MOF twice extended the NPL definition so that more doubtful credits would qualify as "non-performing" and hence require that greater loan losses be set aside.[48] Yet, it is not clear that these amendments produced much substantial change in the efficacy of these provisioning requirements as US regulators continued to demand that further action be taken to tighten loan standards in late 2002.[49] Moreover, in Barth *et al.* (2001a) survey of over 100 states' banking regulations in the late 1990s, MOF left the authors' open-ended survey questions on provisioning regulations blank. Hence, it seems that international political pressure produced only moderate changes in provisioning standards in the first instance.

More obvious international success was exhibited in efforts to force Japan to adopt a compliant interpretation of required Tier1 deduction standards. BCBS regulators had long been critical of MOFs' decision not to implement the "double gearing" deduction set out in the Accord. As discussed in Section "First period implementation of the Basel Accord (1988–1992)," Japanese banks were not required to deduct the value of cross-shareholding between financial institutions from primary capital as stipulated in the 1988 Accord. As the weakness of Japan's banks became evident in the mid-1990s, however, BCBS and market actors demanded that the full scale of these banks losses be disclosed against an internationally accepted definition of capital. MOF yielded to this international pressure in 1998 and brought Japan's required deductions in line with international standards.[50]

Yet, it is curious that the public input of Japanese banks appears to have been negligible in determining MOFs' reactions to these international criticisms. Tamura highlights the paradox that while

> [t]he fact that many lenient policies were carried out intensively in the midst of the 1997–8 banking crisis suggests that such policies were deliberately used to pump up the capital bases banks ... the Japanese Bankers Association did not publicly seek any type of capital injection to clean up [non-performing loans] or to boost capital ratios, since acceptance of public assistance would signal the banks' weak financial position and invite political interference in bank management and lending decisions.[51]

Moreover, in order to dissociate the government from claims that they simply represented the interests of insolvent banks, in October 1998 the LDP refused to accept political contributions from city banks that had received any public funds to reduce NPLs.[52] Tamura (2003a) attributes MOFs' lax policy program to LDP politicians' central concerns of ensuring re-election through stimulating the macroeconomy and ensuring that bank credits continued to flow to key members of the LDP support base such as SMEs.[53]

This suggests that Japanese city banks lost a great deal of political leverage during this period. By the late 1990s, these intermediaries were no longer the international standard bearers they had been a decade earlier. Japanese banks' combined share of international lending dropped from 38 percent in 1988 to 16 percent by year-end 1996. More dramatically, their lending share in Asia declined from a high of 50 percent to 28 percent in 1996. An analyst at ING Barings suggested that this decline represented the end of the Japanese banks' international competitiveness.[54] In addition, Prime Minister Ryutaro Hashimoto's 1997 program to liberalize wide swaths of the Japanese financial sector with a non-graduated or "big bang" measure by 2001 was partly designed to discipline Japanese banks through exposure to greater market discipline.[55]

Thus, in the lead up to the Basel II Accord discussions in the late 1990s, Japanese regulators occupy a very different negotiating position than in 1987. Rather than representing the interests of the world's largest banks in an effort to ensure continued international market access, the MOF is now seeking to ensure that a new standard will not push their domestic banks into full insolvency. In fact, in November 2002, Prime Minister Koizumi's government worked to

162 *Case studies*

implement an NPLs policy that was more in line with international practice, yet would not force city banks to declare capital assets ratios well below the Basel minimum.[56] Market actors believed Japanese banks to be well prepared for the implementation of the 1988 Accord. Twelve years later, BCBS and market actors have doubts that this Accord was ever truly implemented in Japan.[57]

Hypotheses review: second period implementation

The period of time analyzed in this section provides a strong level of support for the international influence, market governance, and macroeconomic instability hypotheses. The variation in Basel rules to be explained by these variables is explicitly only the reinterpretation of the capital deductions requirements in 1998. Yet, these hypotheses also shed light on the "hidden defection" elements highlighted throughout the section. It was illustrated that international political pressure exerted by members of the BCBS (particularly the United States after the 1995 Daiwa collapse) and international markets were critical in provoking MOF and members of the LDP to alter their "double gearing" policy and alter the scope of their NPL classification rules. Though not ultimately successful in effecting a convergence in the latter, external political economic pressure was clearly linked to even modest efforts by MOF to reorganize these standards.

Moreover, external pressure could well be considered a driver of MOFs' decisions to pursue "hidden defection" in the first place. As Fukao (2002) suggested, a key goal of the lax accounting and enforcement policies was to give the impression that banks were better capitalized than they were. Tamura (2003a:7) points out that part of MOFs' objective was to hide the true level of banks' loan losses and low capitalization levels from the Diet. While this is a plausible suggestion grounded in the broader argument that regulatory agencies seek to maximize power through the leveraging of information asymmetries, it is clear that legislators were well aware of a major problem in the banking industry from the early 1990s. It was necessary for the Diet to be involved in the formulation of public institutions to purchase bad credits from Japanese banks from early 1993.[58] Therefore, it is possible to advance that regulators and policy-makers utilized "hidden defection" policies in order to protect themselves and their domestic banks from further international criticism and further losses of market confidence. As the market governance and international influence hypotheses suggest, the Accord acted as a seal of prudential good housekeeping and all members of Japan's banking policy network were anxious to avoid poor marks.

It is also clear that domestic and international preferences were conditioned by the deleterious macroeconomic environment that emerged after 1990. In fact, the depth and extraordinary length of Japan's economic malaise during the 1990s and early 2000s may be the key causal variable of the events discussed in this section. Of all of the variables analyzed, it is the only one that varies from the first to second implementation periods. Before the economic crisis, Japanese banks were expected to benefit from the 1988 Accord; afterward a complex menagerie of accounting practices needed to be manipulated to give the cosmetic appearance of compliance. Like in the US case, the instance of macroeconomic shock produced a general loosening rather than tightening of capital adequacy standards after the initial interpretations of the Accord were made.

It is less certain what effect bankers' preferences made on the policy process. Tamura (2003a) argued that the city banks lost political influence as their funding positions deteriorated. Though in a bank-centered financial regime like Japan's, it is reasonable to assume that large banking institutions will always have some political power, it is not clear that the agenda was driven by the FBAJ to the same degree as it had been prior to the implementation of the Accord. Though the adoption of lax accounting and enforcement policies was likely agreeable to city bankers, the initiation of these policies was from the policy machine more than banks.

Finally, some note should again be made of the insights this section provided on the appropriateness of the quantitative methodology adopted in Part II. To a greater degree than even Section "First period implementation of the Basel Accord (1988–1992)," this section highlighted that analyzing capital adequacy policy in Japan without reference to accounting and enforcement policies produces incorrect inferences. According to the quantitative data, Japanese capital adequacy practice increased in stringency from the first to second periods through the adoption of a stricter deductions policy. Clearly, this result is incorrect when the broader capital adequacy environment is considered. If possible, future studies should endeavor to quantify the strictness of these financial policy variables that influence the strictness of capital adequacy. In lieu of such quantitative variables, it will be constantly necessary to complement the quantitative studies of capital adequacy that are of such importance in financial economics, with in-depth qualitative counterparts.

Conclusion

This chapter has detailed the implementation of the 1988 Basel Accord in Japan. It has argued that Japan was not as politically nor economically disadvantaged by the Accord as many academics and financial market commentators initially believed. Japan's regulators and international banks were successful in ensuring the inclusion of unrealized security gains into the Basel Accord, over the opposition of most G-10 states. Market actors interpreted this as a Japanese negotiation success during the late 1980s as measured by marginal stock returns to announcements on the conclusion of the multilateral accord and Japan's interpretation of the agreement. Regulators made an interpretation of the Accord that was in line with Japanese practice in many ways and support was found for the "path dependence" hypothesis.

The situation radically changed after the collapse of the Japanese asset bubble during the 1990s. The dramatic decline in the value of the Tokyo equities market exerted a disastrous impact on Japan's banks whose capital base was linked to stock prices through unrealized security holdings. The profitability of Japanese banks plummeted through the decade as the value of NPLs accumulated and the value of collateral dropped.

Yet, during this period there was little alteration in Japan's stated capital adequacy policies. It was argued that international political and market pressures convinced MOF and Japanese banks that reducing the severity of capital adequacy standards would further undermine confidence in the banking sector. Yet, substantial direct and indirect evidence suggests that the economic instability led MOF to promote a package of "hidden defection" policies that allowed banks to understate their loan–loss reserves, improperly hold tax deferred assets as capital, and avoid penalties for breaches of compliance with prudential capital codes. The goal of these policies was to provide the cosmetic appearance of compliance with the 1988 Accord by banks whose real capital ratios were well below the international minima.

These events were instructive on the applicability of a number of the theoretical propositions enumerated in Chapter 3. First, the First Period provided some support for "path dependency." Second, the extended Second Period provided support for the effects of international market and political pressures and economic instability. Yet, the impact of these variables was unanticipated as a divergence emerged between Japan's stated capital policy and actual bank and regulatory enforcement practice that were exogenous to the hypotheses' expectations. This suggests that explicit attention needs to be given to incorporating a broad array of tax, accounting, and enforcement policies in conjunction with stated capital adequacy rules when considering the implementation of the Accord. This suggests that the quantitative studies in Chapters 4 and 5 did not provide a full picture of the measurement of severity and laxity of capital adequacy policies after the negotiation of the Basel Accord. Yet, it also suggests the necessity of pairing a qualitative analysis alongside aggregate study in the understanding of compliance with the Accord.

9 Conclusions and extensions

Introduction

This study sought to contribute to a fuller empirical understanding of the impact of the 1988 Basel Accord on the regulatory behavior of the industrialized world. It endeavored to understand if an international financial "soft law" regime could produce any impact on state behavior in the absence of a political or judicial enforcement mechanism. The Accord did not produce a legally binding constraint nor did it prescribe a homogeneous selection of rules. Counterparty states agreed to adhere to a set of minimum best practices and were given wide latitudes for exercising discretionary policies and remain "in compliance" with the Accord.

Though the Basel Accord has been subject to extensive academic study, political economists have generally failed to address its "soft law" characteristics directly. Students of international law and financial economics have succeeded in identifying the legal ramifications of the Accord's "soft law" provisions and identified the microeconomic impacts of distinct national interpretations of these provisions.[1] Yet, the majority of political economists writing on the topic have adopted the assumption that the Accord ex ante enforced a uniform prudential standard. It is generally common to agree with Oatley and Nabors' (1998:49) erroneous declaration that the agreement "eliminated the regulatory status quo from G-10 policy-makers' choice sets."

The goal of this study was to conduct the first large-scale investigation of the impact of the Accord from the political economy perspective. It has been assumed that industrialized states' capital adequacy policies after 1988 reflected the interactions of domestic and international political economic variables, just as they had prior to the Accord's negotiation. By releasing political economists' assumption of the homogenizing effects of the Accord, we are free to investigate patterns of national convergence or divergence around the 1988 agreement's informal rules and understand what variables are correlated with these patterns.

This concluding chapter reviews the substantial empirical and theoretical results. The next section provides a summary of the findings. The four research questions enumerated in Chapter 1 are addressed. Next, I consider some of the implications of these findings for the political study of the impact of the Basel

Accord and, more generally, for the international and comparative political economic study of international financial cooperation. Next, I review some of the key methodological problems of this study. These provide caveats to the research findings. Particular concerns are raised by omitted variable biases and quantitative variable mis-specification. It is hoped that combining quantitative and qualitative research methodologies resolved some of these concerns, yet the difficulties of comparing results in triangulated studies creates its own problems that must be explicitly detailed. The final section suggests future avenues of academic research indicated by the findings.

Summary of findings

This book addressed four questions concerning the way the Accord was implemented. These questions were detailed in Chapter 1. Two questions touched on *how* the Accord was implemented. These questions concerned the role of the Accord in eliciting change in states' pre-Basel capital adequacy practices and in producing transnational regulatory convergence. The final two questions addressed *why* states adopted the interpretations they did and thus why we observe patterns of convergence and divergence. These questions are addressed in light of the findings of the quantitative and qualitative analyses presented in Chapters 2–8.

Question 1. Did the Accord produce or contribute to transnational convergence or divergence in industrialized states' capital adequacy policies shortly after the Accord's negotiation?

The best data with which to address this question are the descriptive statistics for the CREG in Chapter 3. These data indicate that the 18 sampled states adopted remarkably convergent capital adequacy practices over and above the minimum requirements. First, there was convergence in the overall strength of these states' capital adequacy rules as 17 of the 18 states had CREG scores over the minimum level established by the Accord. Only four of the 18 states adopted some form of non-compliant interpretation while 17 states adopted a superequivalent interpretation in at least one area of capital policy. Thus, residual distinctions involved divergence in the severity of interpretation over the minimum levels. There was little evidence that a regulatory "race to the bottom" emerged as the Accord established an effective floor that few states failed to observe.

Among the remaining distinctions, the majority centered in four of the six separate policy areas addressed by the Accord. High levels of convergence emerged in the level of minimum capital ratio levels and risk-weight charges for OBS assets. Much greater diversity emerged in the definitions of capital, required capital deductions, and on-balance sheet risk weights. These results should not seem surprising ex post. The capital definitions set out in the Accord were designed to be broad enough that the wide diversity of the BCBS states' pre-Basel capital adequacy regulations might be included within the international framework. Similarly, the on-balance sheet risk-weighting scheme was designed with a number of discretionary elements. Given the importance of primary capital to ensuring bank stability and soundness, it may be concerning that the Tier1 capital rules did not produce a higher level of convergence. Yet again, remember that distinctions here are policy divergences over and above the minimum established in the Accord.

Question 2. Did the Accord produce or contribute to transnational convergence or divergence in industrialized states' capital adequacy policies during a 12-year period (1988–2000) after the Accord's negotiation. Put differently, did initial levels of convergence or divergence alter over time?

Higher levels of capital adequacy rule convergence did emerge over the 1990s. Measures of dispersion indicated that differences in the states' interpretations narrowed over time, while the sample's average CREG score remained unchanged. As 12 of the 18 sample states altered their capital adequacy policies over time, the unchanged sample mean indicated that a fairly equal amount strengthened as weakened their interpretations of the Accord. In 2000, the number of states having adopted a non-compliant interpretation fell from four to three. The three policy areas courting the largest residual distinctions directly after the Accord's negotiation retained these positions, yet the diversity of interpretations of Tier1 capital narrowed significantly over time. While this may be positive for those prescribing international policy convergence, it is of some prudential concern as this convergence was achieved through an overall weakening of the interpretation. Yet again, diversity remains grounded in generally above minimum distinctions and, among these, a high level of convergence emerged from the Accord. Perhaps most importantly, however, no regulatory race to the bottom or series of tit-for-tat regulatory competition emerged in a way measured by the quantitative indicators.

Question 3. Why did states adopt loose or strict interpretations of the broad, "soft law" provisions of the Accord?

Providing evidence for the *why* questions is not as straightforward as for the *what* questions as data are derived from the quantitative analyses presented in Chapter 5 as well as the qualitative case studies of the United States, France, Germany, and Japan. The difficulties of deriving convergent results from triangulative methods are discussed below, but at this stage there are a number of common explanatory themes that emerge from the quantitative and qualitative data as a whole.

The quantitative and qualitative research suggests that "path dependence" considerations were important contributors to capital regulatory policy after the implementation of the Accord. In Chapter 3, the hypothesis was advanced that the Accord may have affected little independent impact on the industrialized

168   Conclusions and extensions

economies' existing capital adequacy practices. Drawing from Ho's (2002) research and that of disparate political economy and economic explanations of public policy implementation, this hypothesis suggests that any inter-state agreement's effect on state policy is influenced by the distance between the requirements of the agreement and existing state practice. As Downs *et al.* (1996) found, international agreements requiring "deep" changes to existing state practices produce less compliance than those solving inter-state coordination problems or those requiring little change. Though "path dependence" was presented in the context of a broader network of hypotheses on the impacts of domestic bank preferences, it is clear from the qualitative study that political and market actors other than banks maintained a high-powered path-dependent preference.

Though this hypothesis is intuitive to a full class of international agreements, it seems most pertinent to "soft law" agreements in general and the Basel Accord in particular. Like all "soft law", the Basel Accord was not enforceable through international law; a political or judicial authority could not sanction states for non-compliance. Moreover, the Accord might be distinguished as one of a class of international financial regulatory codes or "best practices" that are a "softer" version of "soft law". The Accord (and similar agreements) did not promulgate a set of hard and fast rules with which states must comply to be "in compliance." Rather it set out a minimum baseline of standards and then permitted domestic policymaking authorities a wide discretionary role.

The quantitative and qualitative tests found that the Accord may not have impacted state behavior as much as believed. The argument detailed in Chapter 2 is that political economists have overstated the importance of the Accord on state behavior and thus advanced erroneous arguments about the Accord's political motivations and intended effects. Previous state behaviors were found to be a key determinant of state behavior after the implementation of the Accord. In other words, the quantitative measures of pre-Basel practice – crude as they were – were found to be statistically associated with the quantitative measures of types of compliance with the Accord. Stated another way, states "fit" their pre-Basel capital adequacy practices into their interpretations of the Accord in many instances.

The qualitative research provided some specific support to this general argument. Though the quantitative results found that the United States implemented an overall stringent interpretation of the Accord just after 1988, American regulators allowed cumulative preferred stock to qualify as Tier1 capital. This was an important element of American banks' capital bases prior to the Accord and, despite a desire to push ahead with a punishing interpretation of the Accord after the LDC debt crisis and Savings and Loan fiasco, American authorities permitted this old practice to carry over to their implementation of the Accord, though such instruments were expressly forbidden in Tier1 by the agreement. Similarly, Japan's MOF was successful in negotiating and then implementing a version of the Accord that permitted their money center banks to include unrealized securities holdings in their regulatory capital. Though regulatory authorities and market actors generally regarded such instruments to be a volatile financial instrument that might exacerbate, rather than alleviate, bank instability, this practice carried over from the pre- to post-Basel stages in Japan's capital adequacy codes. Similar evidence was found for France and its regulators' inclusion of loan–loss reserves in the Basel and European capital adequacy frameworks.

Yet, neither the quantitative nor qualitative examinations suggested that the "path dependence" forces were the only determinant of the Accord's impact on the sample states' interpretations. The quantitative results suggest that the presence of a banking crisis might lead to departures from existing practice during the early years of the Accord's implementation. These results suggest that a domestic, systemic banking insolvency crisis would lead states to tighten their domestic capital adequacy practices and thus adopt strict interpretations of the Accord. As Chapter 3 enumerates, this essentially economic argument is also embedded with a political argument. States experiencing an economic dislocation would tighten their regulations as policymakers would need to intervene to protect the electorate's deposit base. The qualitative studies supported the causal importance of instability on policy. One case study country – the United States – experienced a banking crisis in the years directly before the implementation of the Accord, with the result being the adoption of a uniquely strict capital adequacy regime in that country. Path dependence was not a policy option in the United States directly after 1988 as Congress needed to assign blame for the fire storm of banking and savings and loan insolvencies to reckless bank behavior and unresponsive regulatory oversight. As has been well documented, this Congressional pressure was one of the key factors behind the negotiation of the Basel Accord over the G-10 states' apathy in the late 1980s and was linked with an initially tough interpretation of the Accord by American regulators.

As interesting as the two hypotheses receiving support, are those that did not receive strong support or those that received mixed support. First, the hypotheses that banks' preferences would be driven by market governance or their international ambitions seemed to receive some, though not robust, support. In the quantitative tests, these hypotheses were not strongly associated with compliance in a consistent direction. Among the four case studies, it was predicted that United States and Japanese compliance might be influenced by these two variables. Support was found in the United States for the impact of market governance. Japanese authorities did not come under sustained pressure from their domestic banks to provide regulatory relief when the economy entered recession in 1990 and the banking sector first came under pressure. In fact, an MOF official explicitly indicated that regulatory relief would undermine stability in Japanese banks. Interestingly, such market pressure may have contributed to the beginning of "hidden defection" from the capital accord through the lax enforcement of prudential capital regulations as regulatory relief may have been provided in a way neither easily verifiable nor quantifiable by financial markets. It is interesting that little evidence was found for these "bank preference" variables

170   Conclusions and extensions

in the US case. Previous econometric research found little evidence that the market reacted negatively or positively to the American regulators interpretation of the Accord as they did with Japan – whose implementation was initially greeted positively.[2] Thus, the market may have been rather indifferent to the details of America's interpretations relative to Japan. Wagster (1996) concluded that the rise in Japanese banks' stock prices after the implementation of the Accord reflected the market's relief that Japan's banks might not be as competitively disadvantaged by the Accord as was feared as unrealized securities holdings were permitted as regulatory capital. There is little evidence that the market ever maintained such fears about the US case and we may infer that less market attention was given to the Fed's interpretations.

Mixed support is also provided for the argument that implementation would vary according to the fragmentation of domestic political institutions. Again, little support was provided in the aggregate studies. Yet, some support was found in the three case countries with fragmented systems – the United States, Germany, and Japan. The crux of this hypothesis was that in fragmented political systems, capital adequacy policy might be influenced by a wide range of economic actors – perhaps banks, consumers' organizations, industrial manufacturing concerns, labor interests, minority political parties – able to leverage the multiple veto access points of the domestic political regime. In the United States, a wide range of economic actors such as mortgage lenders and consumers' organizations were able to exert pressure for the loosening of capital adequacy regulation by pressuring Congress. In Germany, we witness both national and state banks guiding the drastic loosening of Germany's capital policies during the first three years of the Accord's implementation period. Finally, Japanese peak organizations representing SMEs influenced the creation of capital adequacy policy through pressuring the governing LDP.

Finally, little qualitative or quantitative evidence supports the International Influences hypotheses. The first of these suggested that types of compliance would be similar within regions. The means tests in Chapter 4 provided fairly weak evidence for a regional clustering effect. More telling, the Europe case study indicated France and Germany's policymaking to be guided more by internal than regional dynamics. Though EU directives did guide and extend the Accord's capital adequacy guidelines, these were grounded in the same "soft law" or subsidiarity-type approach as the Accord. Finally, no support was found for the hegemonic argument in the qualitative or quantitative tests.

In addition to the results of those hypotheses presented in Chapter 3, this research indicates that some support may be provided to hypotheses on the influence of electoral cycles on prudential banking policy. The book did not explicitly consider the possibility that the timing of democratic elections might influence capital adequacy policy. The involvement of political actors was embedded in the macroeconomic instability hypothesis, yet for the most part, the assumption that capital adequacy policy was a largely "non-political" policy area dominated more by technical experts than election rhetoric was adopted. As a result, no quantitative exam was conducted of this hypothesis or of similar

Conclusions and extensions 171

hypotheses that types of democratic institutions influenced interpretations of the Basel Accord.[3] Yet, the United States and Japanese case studies provide support for an electoral timing hypothesis. Both the tightening of US capital policy in the late 1980s and its loosening in the early 1990s was a key electoral campaign issue in legislative and Presidential elections. Also, the LDP policy on bank capital was driven by the need to secure the electoral support of SME interests during the early 1990s. In both instances, the critical explanatory variable met macroeconomic instability, yet further exploration of elections and electoral cycles seems warranted in the future.

Question 4. What led states to increase or reduce the stringency of their initial interpretations of the Accord over a 12-year period of time (1988–2000)?

The evaluation of the evolution of the industrialized states' capital adequacy regulations after the creation of the initial interpretations faced some unexpected difficulties. These difficulties came to light only during the qualitative analyses. The quantitative results were straightforward. The modest escalation of transnational capital policy convergence was explained by the effect of private market governance leading states to tighten their initial interpretations. This was interpreted to mean that states subject to international market governance increased the stringency of their regulations in relation to the market's demands. Yet, the quantitative studies provided little indication of what prompted states to reduce the stringency of their policies over time.

Of the four case study countries reviewed, two reduced their capital adequacy stringency over time while one increased their interpretation. The United States and Germany watered down their initial definitions of regulatory capital and the United States amended its risk-weighting framework in support of economic interests disadvantaged by the allocating of mortgage loans to the 100 percent risk category. As the previous section explained, a combination of macroeconomic dislocation and political pressure effected these transitions. However, the quantitative evidence in Chapter 4 suggested that Japan increased the stringency of their initial interpretations by bringing their capital deductions policy in line with the Accord's stipulations on cross-share holdings among financial institutions. The latter case supports the quantitative findings as MOF yielded to pressure from credit ratings agencies to amend their deductions policies.

Yet, the qualitative studies uncovered a number of unanticipated variations in capital adequacy policy in these three case countries. Specifically, the United States, German, and Japanese cases exhibited variations in policies related to interpretations of the Basel Accord that were not addressed in the theoretical predictions in Chapter 3 nor the aggregate analyses in Chapters 4 and 5. These policy changes were not reflected in the quantitative CREG.

As Chapter 6 saw, regulators' attitudes toward capital adequacy policy changed dramatically in the late 1990s. The increase in the American money centers' CARs after the Accord prompted the Fed, FDIC, and OCC to alter their regulatory focus away from requiring particular ratios and limited definitions of

172 *Conclusions and extensions*

capital toward allowing banks to effectively manage shareholder value through the implementation of tailor-molded credit scoring models. As the United States removed decades of restrictive ownership and marketing regulations from commercial banks – allowing them to operate as, and own, securities firms and insurance corporations – the trajectory and focus of capital adequacy policy changed in tandem. Much of these changes – particularly credit scoring models – are exogenous to the concerns of this research. Yet, as they are of central concern to the Basel II Accord, they must be addressed in future research.

Second, capital adequacy policy did not shift quite so dramatically in Germany during the late 1990s. In fact, by battling the Fed over the inclusion of many new capital instruments at the Basel Committee, Germany seemed to fight against such sea changes in capital adequacy policy. Yet, by the 1990s, Germany had reversed course on its role in the international political economy of capital adequacy policy setting. In 1988, Germany was a central figure in the Basel negotiations. The Bundesbank was widely regarded as the hawk for adopting a stringent international capital accord and objected to efforts to design an inter-state standard that could be tailor made for all states' various capital instruments. Yet, by the late 1990s, Germany supported the watering down of the risk-weighting framework adopted as part of the first round of the Basel II negotiations. They refused to implement new European capital adequacy standards that disadvantaged Germany's commercial banks.

Perhaps most importantly, Japan's lax enforcement and accounting policies are not fully endogenized in this study. By looking only at stated capital adequacy policy, the aggregate analysis obscures the true nature of Japan's interpretation of the Accord. While the CREG records a strengthening of Japan's interpretations over time, the case study revealed an almost entire breakdown in the application of these prudential policies by the late 1990s. While it is difficult to directly observe – much less quantitatively measure – the severity of all the enforcement and accounting policies that bear on the stringency of stated capital adequacy standards, further efforts need to be made along these lines for a wide group of states.[4]

Implications of the findings

This study contributes a number of methodological and empirical findings to the international and comparative political economic study of economic cooperation. A number of the book' specific contributions to the state of knowledge of the Basel Accord were outlined in the previous section. Yet, it is also necessary to identify the place of these Basel-centered findings within the wider spectrum of the study of international economic relations. Specifically, the research suggests the importance of adopting a new, more differentiated approach to the study of the implementation of international regimes than is generally employed. Second, the implementation of the Accord contributes to research concerning the importance of international regimes to state behavior. Finally, insight is given to the process of transnational regulatory convergence in the area of banking regulation. As this section explains, these broader contributions of the book overlap in a number of important ways. For this reason, the three will be discussed in concert.

First, all points of the study suggest that existing theoretical approaches tend to be insufficiently calibrated to endogenize the sort of empirical question addressed here. Following the lead of Botcheva and Martin (2001), Chapter 3 explained that the binary conceptualization adopted by the vast majority of studies of international regime implementation obscures critical points of detail. By measuring implementation as a "yes" or "no" phenomenon, these studies are incapable of explaining elements of compliance with international legal arrangements that are soft in obligating compliance or imprecise in enumerating rules that implementing states must adhere with to be "in compliance."[5] This methodological approach is parsimonious to implement and congruent with the testing of reasonably tractable hypotheses, yet can be a liability when understanding compliance with some forms of international cooperation.

The impact of many of the international financial regulatory standards issued in the past ten years by organizations such as the IMF, IOSCO, and the Basel Committee is not amenable to dichotomization. Many of the international standards issued by these organizations are confederations of best practices or suggested codes of conduct that are not enforceable by a political or judicial authority or, more particularly, are fairly ill defined. A cursory glance at the titles of many of these agreements supports this: the majority bear labels such as "minimum standards," "codes of practice," or "principles of memoranda." Though these agreements generally enumerate a minimum regulatory level or floor that implementing states are requested to stay above, the example of the Basel Accord demonstrated that such floors can be fairly modest and quite possibly below the level of many states' existing practices. In such circumstances, binary implementation variables are difficult to design as the minimum requirements may be too vague to establish reliable trigger levels at which to code states' practices as "non-compliant." In addition, such variables may not satisfy content validity requirements as they fail to endogenize situations in which states adhere to certain elements of international agreements (perhaps well above the minimum floor) but fail to satisfy other requirements. This could lead to a situation in which a state is erroneously classified as compliant or non-compliant. An easy remedy might be to utilize an iteration of dummy indicators for various policy areas. Yet, even this approach is seldom utilized and this research suggests that if "soft law" rules are fairly complex – as in the example of many banking regulations – a more differentiated indicator may better capture compliance with the vagaries of "soft law" arrangements.

In the study of the Basel Accord, such a differentiated approach was a minimum requirement for fruitfully addressing the impact of the 1988 agreement on state behavior. The methodology and results of Daniel Ho's (2002) study of the implementation of the Accord are indicative. Following the methodological pattern of the majority of international political economy studies of regime implementation, Ho investigated correlates of the successful implementation of the Accord through a Large-N survey. He fitted a number of logistical regression models that situated a dummy variable on the left-hand side that took the value of unity if states complied with the Basel Accord. As over 90 percent of the sample was coded unity, Ho was left with the task of explaining non-compliance in about ten states, the majority of which were extremely low-income economies. Though few studies of regime compliance have such skewed datasets as this, Ho's study indicates the importance of adopting a more differentiated measure of compliance. It is intuitive that the empirical problems posed by the implementation of the Basel Accord are, why did so many states claim to be in compliance with the Accord and how compliant were they really? These questions cannot be addressed with binary measures of compliance. It is likely that studies of the implementation of other financial "soft law" agreements require the same differentiated treatment as Basel.

In addition, Ho's study does not permit researchers to conclude if the Accord influenced state behavior. As Chapter 3 observed, much of the concern of international cooperation students has centered on the independent impact of international agreements on state's practices. Distinct answers – even interpretations – of this question have divided International Relations studies into two broad camps. The first approach has been characterized as the Enforcement School.[6] This broad-church school includes Realist and rationalist Institutionalist approaches that collectively suggest that the probability of states' compliance with an international agreement increases if they are subject to an exogenous enforcement mechanism. This may be an international political or judicial institution trigger mechanism or the threat of retaliation by a hegemonic state or group of states. The opposing school of thought suggests that such measures are almost universally unnecessary as, "almost all nations observe all principles of international law and almost all of their obligations almost all of the time."[7] This catch phrase of the Management School implies that international agreements independently influence state behavior in absence of a punishment mechanism. For both schools, however, a binary conception of compliance with the Accord fails to provide enough observations for an effective test of hypotheses on the importance of punishment mechanisms. With the vast majority of nation-states claiming compliance with the Accord, there is not enough variation in the dependent variable to draw any firm conclusions regarding compliance or non-compliance.

However, the differentiated compliance variable permits a more accurate testing ground for these competing predictions. The utilization of a more nuanced measure of compliance seems to support the Management School at first glance. The descriptive statistical inferences drawn from the operationalization of the CREG variable in Chapter 4 indicated a high level of compliance with the Accord by nearly every country in the sample. Though the Basel Committee explicitly labels their regulatory recommendations as "voluntary" and does not sanction states for non-compliance, very few states failed to meet the minimum criteria in all of the policy areas addressed in the Accord.

Further support for the Management School might be obtained from the US and Japan case studies. These two states failed to meet the Basel minima in some respects. The American regulators permitted their domestic BHCs to count cumulative preferred stock as Tier1 capital, while the Japanese MOF did not require their international banks to deduct cross-share holdings with other financial institutions from total capital. In both instances, however, domestic actors within these two states argued that these breeches were necessary defections given the idiosyncratic structure of their banking systems. The dominance of cross-share holding industrial and financial complexes was an important component of Japan's industrial structure while American banks were globally unique in maintaining large cumulative preferred equity holdings before the negotiation of the Accord. In these instances, Management School theorists might suggest that these instances of non-compliance were expected as the United States and Japan could not implement the Accord due to the technical difficulties involved rather than from a desire to defect from the agreement in order to free ride on the commitments of other Committee members for material advantage.

Yet, the results of the quantitative and qualitative hypotheses tests make support for the Managerialist position less obvious. In particular, the strong performance of the "path dependence" hypothesis suggests that compliance with the Accord may not have been an arduous process for many states. Many may not have needed to amend their existing capital adequacy rules to a great degree to comply with the 1988 standards. To the extent that this is a valid conclusion, it is possible that the Management School's correlation of regime rules and subsequent state behavior is spurious in this instance. This point supports Downs *et al.*'s (1996) observation that studies of implementation must begin by assessing the extent to which an international agreement requires states to depart from their existing policy practice. Failure to specify this as a starting point creates exposure to the risk of drawing false empirical inferences as the possibility that an inter-state agreement merely ratified extant practice or solved a simple coordination problem is precluded.

It thus appears that both the Management and Enforcement schools' predictions maintain some validity here. Clearly, the Basel Accord did produce some alteration of state behavior. The statistical and qualitative evidence indicated that departures from the regulatory status quo did emerge after the implementation of the Accord. Such departures may be partially attributed to domestic political economic considerations, such as domestic banking crises, that may or may not have been related to the effects of the Accord. Yet, the Accord did constrain the discretionary behavior of regulators in some instances. In particular, Japanese regulators went to great lengths to give the impression that their domestic banks were in compliance with the Basel minima while the United States, France, and Germany each limited their definitions of regulatory capital because of the input of other Basel Committee members. There is no question that much of the Accord's effects – particularly in Japan – were related to the pressure that market actors exerted on banks and policymakers. Yet, the expectations of these actors were clearly shaped by the Accord in ways measured by financial economists.[8] Yet, at the same time, the wide discretionary bands permitted by the agreement meant that states whose pre-1988 behavior departed from the Accord's provisions to a greater degree were able to meet the standards without a great deal of domestic political or economic dislocation. The Accord thus appears to have had an impact on state behavior, though its impact may not have been as great as most political economy accounts suggest.

This mixed conclusion also applies to insights this study poses to hypotheses that financial services regulations will converge under pressure from economic globalization. A number of studies have either assumed or hypothesized that the internationalization of banking and financial services firms would produce a common regulatory status quo among distinct national regulatory practices.[9] This prediction is grounded in the view that market actors, such as institutional investors and credit ratings agencies, will punish state and firm behaviors incongruent with market preferences, resulting in high opportunity costs for non-market friendly policies and an international convergence around a common, often neoliberal, model.[10] Financial services may represent the greatest likelihood test of such predictions for as Gilpin (2001:261) observed, "[i]nternational finance is the one area to which the term 'economic globalization' clearly applies."

Yet, this study agrees with previous empirical tests of this argument in concluding that convergence has been present yet incomplete. Moran (1991) and Coleman's (1994) research of convergence in securities and banking regulations and firm practices, respectively, found that convergence emerged in some areas yet was ultimately spotty. They found that through transnational regulatory learning, market constraints, and US pressure, some levels of convergence were found. However, national policymakers and domestic financial markets retained maneuvering space in which to maintain distinct forms of policy and market behavior. With regards to the Accord, some convergence did emerge after 1988 and more was produced from 1988 to 2000. Again, much of the convergence involved the adoption of a common language for classifying and regulating bank capital and the creation of a minimum regulatory floor that seemed to constrain state behavior to some degree. Yet, the Accord explicitly permitted space for discretionary maneuverability and this seems to have been exploited.

Review of methodology

The review of the book's empirical and theoretical findings highlighted many of the strengths and weaknesses of the adopted methodology. Yet, in order to be realistic about the reliability and generalizability of the findings, it is necessary to make these qualities explicit.

First, combining qualitative and quantitative research designs presented opportunities and problems. In terms of opportunities, the three case study chapters certainly permitted the chance to corroborate and elaborate the quantitative results.[11] The aggregate studies were useful in evaluating the Accord's effect on the capital adequacy policies of a wide sample of states. In particular, the descriptive statistics for the CREG indicator in Chapter 4 allowed for the first rigorous cross-sectional and time series comparison of capital adequacy policies. Yet, the weaknesses of the quantitative tests in Chapter 5 required a qualitative companion study to ensure reliability. The extremely small sample size employed may have violated the assumptions of the central limitations theorem, despite efforts made to ensure reliability. It was thus necessary to further explore the quantitative results through detailed inspections of the observable implications of the hypotheses with an "on the ground" inspection. Though the quantitative studies examined 18 countries, only two periods of time were analyzed. Yet, the case studies allowed an examination of 12 years of study (1988–2000) of the post-Basel implementation plus a number of years of pre-Basel capital adequacy policy. In this way, the qualitative analyses extended the degrees of freedom and descriptive inferences of the research.

Yet, the combination of these two research designs is not without some caveat. It can be difficult to resolve distinctions in the results of the two methodologies. For instance, the market governance indicator was found to be positively correlated with increases in capital adequacy rule stringency in the aggregate tests for the Second Period. Yet, in the US case, high levels of market governance were correlated with a weakening of regulatory standards. This illustrates the tensions that can emerge in comparing quantitative and qualitative results. What can create a correlation among a larger sample of states may not be the case for any given state, which may be an outlier to the general trend. Though this certainly opens up the opportunity to explain deviations in the two results, which can provide further descriptive inference, it does not contribute to the drawing of parsimonious conclusions.

Implications for future research

As far as I am aware, this is the first study to systematically investigate the implementation of the Basel Accord across a large sample of states over a period of time. Inevitably, research of this nature tends to raise as many questions about an event or a theory as it answers given space, data, and human limitations. First, future work could endeavor to increase the number of observations on the dependent variable. This could be done through increasing the number of sample states and increasing the number of years observed. In particular, comparing this book's results with an empirical analysis of lesser-developed and emerging market economies seems necessary. A key finding of this study is that the Accord was implemented with various degrees of stringency by industrialized economies, yet these interpretations were generally always above the minimum levels prescribed by the Accord. It seems logical that this condition would not hold in an investigation of implementation among a broader spectrum of income levels in which a much more differentiated quantity of compliance would likely prevail.[12] Second, a similar study could be conducted into degrees of compliance with the major 1996 amendment to the 1988 Accord that extended this agreement's reach to banks' market exposure risks. Though one study suggested that the 1996 amendment did not pose as large a challenge to existing regulatory and bank practice as the 1988 agreement, this statement remains to be put to systematic empirical test.[13]

In addition, the quantitative CREG could be inputted into studies of the Accord's economic impact. Previous research has not found regulatory and political variables to be strong predictors of bank capital ratio levels compared to purely macroeconomic models.[14] Yet, the CREG variable could be shifted to the right-hand side as a predictor of ratio levels. Alternative exogenous variables might include bank stability, bank's funding positions, or costs of capital.

Moreover, a more systematic effort should be made to compare capital adequacy stringency with related policy practices. The Japanese case indicated that tax, accounting, and provisioning policies as well as enforcement quality need to be studied in conjunction with the stated capital adequacy rules. At present, existing data do not support an aggregate study of these related policy practices.

Finally, future studies of international regime implementation might consider employing differentiated indicators of compliance. As Chapter 3 argued that empirical detail can be lost for many types of international agreements by considering if states comply rather than how. Though binary compliance indicators are sufficiently calibrated to measure compliance with some types of international agreements, international financial regulatory pacts seem ill captured by such variables. As over 100 countries claim to be in compliance with the Basel Accord, clearly the interesting study is about how these countries complied. The same will be increasingly true of other inter-state financial agreements struck through international organizations like the BCBS, IMF, IOSCO, World Bank, the International Accounting Standards Board, and others.[15]

Notes

1 Introduction

1. See Basel Committee on Banking Supervision (1988), at §3. Throughout the book, the German spelling "Basel" will be employed. Early documents related to the G-10's discussions on bank cooperation bore the anglicized spelling "Basle" yet the G-10 adopted the Germanic spelling in the mid-1990s and this book will follow their example, though the anglicized spelling has crept back into usage from the late 1990s. See Marshall (1999).
2. The Basel Committee has been alternatively known as the Cooke Committee (after its first chairman and then head of the Bank of England, Peter Cooke) and the Basel Committee on Banking Regulation and Supervisory Practice. The committee is often, inaccurately, simply termed the BIS and viewed as synonymous with the BIS. Though the Basel Committee utilizes the BIS facilities in Basel, Switzerland for its secretariat, the committee it is not a component of the BIS.
3. See Basel Committee on Banking Supervision (1988), at §2.
4. This list of states is derived from Murray-Jones and Gamble (1991) and data from various national bank regulatory authorities.
5. This is confirmed by the Basel Committee on Banking Supervision (1999) and in a World Bank sponsored study, see Barth et al. (2001a).
6. Information concerning many of these economics studies of the Basel Accord's effects is conveniently aggregated in Basle Committee (1999).
7. See Kapstein (1989, 1991, 1994), Murray-Jones and Gamble (1991), Tobin (1991), Scott and Iwahara (1994), Scott (1995), Oatley and Nabors (1998), Reinicke (1998), Alexander (2000a), Lutz (2000), Simmons (2001), Ho (2002), Singer (2002), and Tamura (2003b).
8. Though not of chief concern here, for further information on the Basel II Accord see Basel Committee on Banking Supervision (2001).
9. Alexander (2000) and Ho (2002).
10. This point is well established in Scott (1995) and Scott and Iwahara (1994).
11. The key study investigating this issue was commissioned by Price Waterhouse (1991).
12. See Wagster et al. (1996); Wagster (1996).
13. Such an argument is employed extensively in Oatley and Nabors (1998) in their discussion of the Basel Accord.
14. Ho (2002).
15. The soft law characteristics of the Accord have been investigated in studies by Alexander (2000b) and Ho (2002).
16. Dahl and Shrieves (1990).
17. For a review of many of these studies, see Basel Committee on Banking Supervision (1999).

18 For more on the 1996 amendment, see Basel Committee on Banking Supervision (1996), Lutz (2000), and Matten (2000).
19 Bank of England (2002).
20 *Euromoney*, May 1998.

2 The political economy of the negotiation of the 1988 Basel Accord as a soft law agreement

1 This statistic is cited in Basel Committee (1999).
2 To a certain degree, a systematic political effort to encourage the Accord's negotiation emerged when the Basel rules were adopted as part of the BIS's Core Principles for Banking Supervision. Though these rules have been recommended to developed economies and developing economies, the latter through the advice of the IMF and World Bank as well as the BIS, most of the world's economies had adopted the 1988 Basel rules well before the Core Principles' negotiation. See Basel Committee (1999).
3 Ward (2002) observed that the Basel Accord was heavily criticized by its supporters as by its critics in 1988. Supporters recognized many of the agreement's limitations, yet found it a better solution than no international capital adequacy agreement at all.
4 Kapstein (1989, 1991, 1994) and Singer (2002).
5 Oatley and Nabors (1998).
6 Alexander (2000b) and Ho (2002).
7 Basel Committee on Banking Supervision (1988), at §3.
8 Dale (1984:11–12).
9 Vernon *et al.* (1991:130–136).
10 Ibid.
11 Quoted in Matten (2000:1).
12 Oatley and Nabors (1998:46).
13 Pecchioli (1987:106).
14 Basel Committee (1983:8–15).
15 Vernon *et al.* (1991:131).
16 Cooke (1981:238) in Dale (1984:172).
17 Euromoney (1998), Oatley and Nabors (1998), and Reinicke (1995).
18 Dale (1984).
19 Basel Committee on Banking Supervision (1981:7) in Norton (1992:35).
20 Basel Committee on Banking Supervision (1986:10–27) in Norton (1992:35).
21 Basel Committee on Banking Supervision (1986:19) in Vernon *et al.* (1991:140), emphasis added.
22 A RWA regulatory approach requires capital adequacy standards to vary with the contents of a bank's asset structure. Banks with lending portfolios concentrated in higher risk lending are required to retain more capital as insurance against counterparty default. See Matten (2000) and Dahl and Shrieves (1990).
23 See Kapstein (1989:338) and Norton (1992:37). In particular, Kapstein argues that the United States "learned" the risk-weighting approach from the United Kingdom, indicating a knowledge transfer occurred between the two states. This may not be the case, however, as US regulators had experimented with risk-weighting approaches since the 1950s. See Federal Reserve System (1956).
24 Vernon *et al.* (1991:144–146).
25 Ibid.
26 The fears of these EC states may not have been unfounded. Kapstein (1991:266) reports that Britain may have utilized its regulatory alliance with the United States to head off a "cockeyed" European effort at capital regulation spearheaded by the French and Germans.
27 Federal Reserve Board of New York (1988), Reinicke (1995), and Oatley and Nabors (1998).

28 Norton (1992:39).
29 Sawabe (1995).
30 The risk-weights have generated a great deal of criticism from regulators and banks. The 100 percent weighting in this example would apply to any private corporation, regardless of their size, prestige, or access to capital resources. This means that a local, corner store and a FTSE-100 firm would earn identical risk-weightings. Criticisms of this broad treatment of asset classes have been a key argument behind the negotiation of the Basel Accord 2. See *The Economist*, 3–9 May 2003.
31 Matten (2000:88) indicates that practitioners would be more likely to formulate the capital requirement in this way.
32 Kapstein (1989, 1991, 1994) and Singer (2002).
33 This argument has been advanced by Kapstein (1989, 1991, 1994), Reinicke (1995), and Singer (2002).
34 Peccioli (1987:115).
35 Kapstein (1989:331).
36 Mueller (1989:88) in Oatley and Nabors (1998:41).
37 Oatley and Nabors (1998:48).
38 Pattison (2006).
39 Oatley and Nabors (1998:49).
40 Shelton (2000:10).
41 Ho (2001:648).
42 This discussion draws exclusively from Alexander (2000b:6–8).
43 Cally and Majnoni (2002:13).
44 Woolcock (1996:290).
45 Ho (2002:648).
46 Woolcock (1996:296).
47 A review of these studies is provided in Basel Committee on Banking Supervision (1999:41–44). The studies covered include Eyssell and Arshadi (1990), Madura and Zarruk (1993), Cornett and Tehranian (1994), Laderman (1994), Cooper *et al.* (1991), and Wagster (1996).
48 Cooper *et al.* (1991) and Wagster (1996).

3 Theorizing degrees of compliance with the Basel Accord

1 This book treats international institutions and regimes as interchangeable terms. There are distinctions between the two as institutions refer to formal organizations such as the BIS, World Bank, and IMF while regimes refer to the implicit and explicit rules, norms, and decisionmaking procedures that guide state behaviors. Gilpin (2001:83) argues that these two terms may be justifiably treated interchangeably as it is the regimes produced by institutions that are important for shaping international outcomes. See Krasner (1982:186) for the classic definition of a regime.
2 See Mitchell (1994) for a review of the Realist position on regime enforcement.
3 See Keohane (1982, 1984), Stein (1983), Martin (1992), and Fearon (1998) for a representative sample of this vast Institutionalist literature.
4 Chayes and Chayes (1993:177).
5 For example, see Duffy (1988), Chayes and Chayes (1993, 1995), Arora and Cason (1995), and Young (1999).
6 See John (1998) for an attempt at summary.
7 Simmons (2000).
8 Baron (1995) and Krueger (1996).
9 Botcheva and Martin (2001:3).
10 Botcheva and Martin (2001:3) identify that empirical studies have identified instances of over-compliance with regime rules by states, though they did not cite any examples.

182 *Notes*

11 Chayes and Chayes (1993:176, 198).
12 See Coleman (1994) and Walter (2000) for examples of the vast convergence literature applied to banking and foreign direct investment issue areas, respectively.
13 A summary of many of these regimes is provided by the Financial Stability Forum at: www.fsforum.org/compendium/key_standards_for_sound_financial_system.html.
14 Botcheva and Martin (2001:4).
15 See Alexander (2000b) and Ho (2002) for a discussion of the ways in which the Basel Accord is an example of a soft law regime and Shelton (2000) for a collection of papers discussing the nature and ramifications of soft law.
16 See Basel Committee on Banking Supervision (1988), at §7.
17 Barth *et al.* (2001a).
18 Ho (2002:668).
19 Charney (2000:117).
20 This research was initiated by Stigler (1971) and developed by Peltzman (1976), Posner (1974), and Becker (1983).
21 Verdier (2002:134).
22 See De Bondt and Prast (2000) in Ho (2002:648).
23 See Baron (2000) for a textbook discussion of the definitions, sources, and consequences of non-market-based firm competition.
24 See Basel Committee on Banking Supervision (1999) for a summary of much of this research.
25 *Financial Times* (1987:1) in Tobin (1991:187).
26 Morgan and Knight (1997:233).
27 See Van Meter and Van Horn (1975), Sabatier and Mazmanian (1981), Cerych and Sabatier (1986), Downs *et al.* (1996).
28 Underhill (1992).
29 Baron (1997:41).
30 Vernon *et al.* (1991:150) and Story (1997:258).
31 Scott and Iwahara (1994), Scott (1995), and Barth *et al.* (2000:201) suggest this point.
32 Ho (2002:654).
33 See Simmons (2001) for a discussion of the signaling effects of international regime implementation from an international relations perspective.
34 Research has been conducted on the differential effects of degrees of deposit insurance coverage and bank competitiveness and financial system fragility and have found that degrees can matter. See Demirgüç-Kunt and Detragiache (2000), Demirgüç-Kunt and Huizinga (2000), and Kane (2000).
35 Walter (2002:9).
36 Basel Committee on Banking Supervision (1990) in Kapstein (1991:30).
37 Misback (1993) in Ho (2002:656).
38 Ho (2002:674).
39 Walter (2002:7).
40 This argument is grounded in the neo-classical economics assumption that regulators are analogous to firms and seek to maximize profits. As regulators pay may be performance related and contingent on repulsing hostile takeover bids (from politicians) then regulators, as bureaucratic actors, will seek autonomy. See Niskanen (1973) in Dunleavy (1991:154).
41 Ho (2002:659–664).
42 Compare the results of models (1) and (2) in Ho (2002:673).
43 For Ho's sample of over 100 states, a comparative measure of democracy is appropriate. The standard deviation of his sample, for the Polity III scale, is 3.841, thus indicating a great deal more variation in the democratic standards of his sample than the one collected here.
44 There are numerous variants of the theory that political fragmentation influences

Notes 183

commitment with international regimes. Some have argued, especially in the context of developing states, that insulated political decisionmaking processes are correlated with higher growth rates, see Haggard (1990) and Evans (1995). Others have argued that maintaining a separation of powers and a republican constitution increase the likelihood that a state will credibly commit to international standards, see North and Weingast (1989). These two arguments clearly address distinct empirical problems and Ho's (2002) application of the fragmentation theory should be seen as contributing to this larger network of theory.
45 Ho (2002:660).
46 Ho (2002:665).
47 Simmons (2001:15).

4 Measuring implementation and explanatory variables

1 Basel Committee on Banking Supervision (1988), at §3.
2 Oatley and Nabors (1998).
3 See Hall (1993), Scott and Iwahara (1994), and Scott (1995) for studies in comparative financial law and Basel Committee on Banking Supervision (1999) for a review of financial economic studies of implementation with the Accord.
4 Murray-Jones and Gamble (1991) and PriceWaterhouse (1991).
5 I thank an official at the United Kingdom's Financial Services Authority for impressing this on me.
6 Frankfort-Nachmias and Nachmias (2000:149–150) define content validity as meaning that a "measuring instrument covers all the attributes of the concept you are trying to measure – that nothing relevant to the phenomenon under investigation is left out."
7 See Murray-Jones and Gamble (1991), PriceWaterhouse (1991), and Hall (1993).
8 Reliability concerns the degree with which a measuring instrument contains variable errors or, in other words, the consistency of the instrument when measuring different observations of the same empirical phenomenon. Frankfort-Nachmias and Nachmias (2000:154) cite that an example of an unreliable measurement instrument would be of a ruler that yields different measurements of a desk each time its length is taken. In social science, it is notoriously more difficult to achieve reliability than in the physical sciences. Given the absence of a single repository for capital adequacy regulations, the need to establish the reliability of the CREG measure is thus especially important.
9 To ensure that an ordinal scale's coding categories are mutually exclusive, they must be engineered so that each case or unit of analysis can be coded (or classified) into one and only one category. It should be explicitly clear under what circumstances, for example, a sample state's TIER1 regulations qualify for a "2" or a "3" ranking.
10 See Frankfort-Nachmias and Nachmias (2000) for information on how to construct and interpret Cronbach alpha exams.
11 This, of course, does not necessarily imply that no alterations were made in the credit risk rules of these ten states, but that none of these alterations were sufficiently severe so as to alter the state's CREG score.
12 Ho (2002) focuses almost exclusively on the capital-to-assets ratio requirement in his determination of whether a state has or has not implemented the 1988 Accord.

5 Explaining implementation-quantitative tests

1 The bootstrap method involves generating pseudoreplicate datasets by randomly sampling the original dataset a specified number of iterations. The method permits the estimation of confidence intervals without the distributional assumptions of parametric methods. See Efron and Tibshirani (1993), Mooney and Duval (1993), and Mooney (1996). See Verdier (2002) for an example of a study that applies a

184 *Notes*

   bootstrapping method to derive standard errors in a comparative political economy study.
2 Some researchers have expressed reservations about the way that the bootstrapping method has been applied in social science. Some have suggested that it is still not clear whether the technique should be utilized to generate measures of association (for example, Pearson's r) or confidence intervals. Some researchers have also suggested that the method is ill suited for application to small samples. See Davison and Hinkley (1997).
3 Krueger (1996:172). See Sabatier and Mazmanian (1981) and Baron (1995) for further examples of dynamic theories of regulation.
4 King (1985:10–11).

Case studies

1 See George (1979) and King *et al.* (1994).
2 Rossman and Wilson (1985) in Blaikie (1998:267).
3 This paragraph paraphrases the general points covered by Blaikie (1998:267).
4 This observation is made by Blaikie (1998:268).
5 Mathison (1988:14) cited in Blaikie (1998:267).
6 George (1985:41).
7 George (1979:62).
8 The term "basis points" will be utilized extensively to describe bank CARs. A basis point equals one-hundredth of a percentage point and its utility is the easier and more meaningful comparison of smaller percentages.
9 See Coleman (1996) for an account of the power position of banks in France, Germany, and the United States and Hall (1993) for a discussion of Japan.

6 Implementation of the Basel Accord in the United States

1 Most accounts of the Basel Accord's negotiations adopt this position either explicitly or implicitly. The most rigorous elaboration of these arguments is advanced in Oatley and Nabors (1998).
2 Oatley and Nabors (1998:36), bracketed comment added to original text.
3 For an extensive review of the economics research into the effects of the Basel Accord on bank profitability, see Basel Committee on Banking Supervision (1999).
4 Coleman (1996:154–155).
5 National banks can be further sub-divided into money center banks, super-regional banks, and trust and custody banks. See "26 Big Banks Need to Raise Equity," *American Banker*, 11 December 1987.
6 Coleman (1996:154).
7 Calomiris (2000:54) provides evidence suggesting that capital requirements may have also been utilized in the nineteenth century for a variety of other aims. One example was to encourage the opening of banks in underserved rural areas where there was little incentive for banks to operate. In such areas, capital requirements were lowered, especially by state regulators, to encourage bank expansion to these areas. Thus, there may have been a variety of uses for capital adequacy regulation in the nineteenth and, perhaps, early twentieth centuries which had little to do with managing banking risks.
8 Norton (1992:14).
9 Mayne (1972) and Calomiris (2000:44).
10 See Federal Reserve Board Form FR 363 (1956).
11 See Kapstein (1989:338). I would not necessarily disagree that US regulators, especially the Fed, consulted with the Bank of England about RWA regulation in the 1980s, yet Kapstein argues that the RWA nature of the US–UK bilateral accord and the Basel Accord demonstrate a tempering of US power with knowledge. He argues

Notes 185

that if the United States had wanted to impose its standard on the world in 1988 it would have been through a non-RWA approach that had characterized US regulations prior to the Accord. Yet, the exchange of learning between the United States and the United Kingdom during the 1980s led the United States to adopt another country's capital regulation system – thus, he argues, demonstrating the limits of a power-centered explanation for the Accord. This does not seem to be exactly the case as the Fed experimented with the RWA procedure from 1950 until the Accord. Although an RWA approach was not consistently applied by the Fed, Norton (1992) argues that it was well considered by the Fed, OCC, and FDIC before the 1980s.

12 Responsibility for BHCs was given to the Federal Reserve Board after the Bank Holding Company Act of 1956.
13 Ibid.
14 Mayne (1972).
15 This can be most easily operationalized by looking at the number and size of banks regulated by the FDIC. By December 1982, the FDIC supervised 8632 commercial banks (60 percent of the US total) representing 22 percent of total bank assets. See Norton (1992:20).
16 See FDIC, "Statement of policy on capital adequacy," *Federal Register*, 46, 62 (28 December).
17 Norton (1992:20).
18 Kelly (1983).
19 Norton (1992:21).
20 Kane (1991) discusses this concept in terms of a Hegelian dialectic between regulators and banks. New forms of regulation (synbook) lead to attempts by banks to circumvent the rules (antibook) requiring regulators to adjust in order to produce another regulation (re-synbook) in an infinitely iterated game. Reinicke (1995) applies this logic to the understanding of capital adequacy regulation in the United States during the 1980s and 1990s.
21 Kelley (1983).
22 Norton (1992:20).
23 Savings and Loan Institutions are also commonly referred to as S & Ls and thrifts in the United States or building societies in the United Kingdom.
24 Kaufman (1992:95).
25 Rogers (1993:14).
26 Data presented in DeCamoy (1990) though obtained in Oatley and Nabors (1998). This figure compares to 27–82 percent for the United Kingdom and less than 55 percent for Japan at the same period of time.
27 Oatley and Nabors (1998:42).
28 Rogers (1993:13).
29 Oatley and Nabors (1998:43).
30 US House 1982, 2, from Oatley and Nabors (1998:43).
31 This was important in light of the *OCC* v. *Federal National Bank of Bellaire, Texas* (1983) decision in which the New Orleans Court of Appeals ruled that Bank of Bellaire was not required to comply with an OCC capital guideline, thus bringing into question the legal ability of federal regulators to issue enforceable capital regulations. Congress aimed to address this issue by specifically providing the legal basis by which enforceable capital directive could be issued.
32 Oatley and Nabors (1998:44).
33 Vernon *et al.* (1991:141).
34 Norton (1992:15).
35 Vernon *et al.* (1991:144).
36 Norton (1992) covers this history in extensive detail.
37 Oatley and Nabors (1998:44).

38 The relevant rules are set out in 1 and 12 of the Code of Federal Regulations, Part 3 (relating to the OCC), Part 325 (FDIC), and Parts 208 (relating to the Fed).
39 Rehm (1988).
40 Garsson (1990).
41 *American Banker*, 12 July 1988.
42 Blanden (1998:17).
43 The minimum ratio was 3 percent for banks that received the highest possible regulator exam ratings. Other banks would have to maintain a 4–7 percent ratio. See Hall (1993:65).
44 Many bankers and financial economists observed that the leverage ratio may have created a heavier regulatory burden than the Basel Accord. Martin Feldstein (1992), former Chairman of the Council of Economic Advisors and economics professor, argued that the non-risk weighted nature of the requirement punished banks far more than the risk-sensitive Basel approach.
45 The 1988 Basel Accord prohibited the inclusion of both these items as allowable Tier1 or Tier2 capital.
46 Rehm (1988).
47 Freddie Mac and Ginnie Mae perform largely the same function, yet the latter carries an explicit government guarantee and receive a 0 percent weighting.
48 Rehm (1988).
49 *Wall Street Journal*, 24 December 1991.
50 *Wall Street Journal*, 7 February 1991.
51 Rehm (1988).
52 Ibid.
53 Ibid.
54 Some adjustable rate cumulative preferred stock was permitted if the dividends were tied to interest-sensitive benchmarks such as the London Inter-Bank Offer Rate. See *American Banker*, 23 August 1988.
55 Much economic research has explored whether the US regulator's interpretation of the Basel rules did actually cause or exacerbate the credit shortage that emerged during the US recession of this period. Research has produced quite mixed results and little consensus appears to have emerged. For a review of much of this literature, see Basel Committee on Banking Supervision (1999).
56 See *National Mortgage News*, 24 February 1992.
57 Reinicke (1995) comes to the conclusion that the financial crisis of the 1980s forced a high level of regulatory convergence among America's three main federal bank regulators.
58 *American Banker*, March 1993.
59 *Federal Reserve Bulletin*, 20 December 1993.
60 World Development Indicators (2001).
61 *The Banker*, March 1993.
62 This discussion will draw heavily from *Euromoney*, March 1998; *M2 Presswire*, 29 October 1998; *The Economist*, 17 April 1999.
63 *Federal Reserve Bulletin*, 26 October 1996.
64 *Euromoney*, March 1998.
65 I thank an anonymous official at the US Federal Reserve for this information.
66 *The Banker*, December 1998.
67 "Banking Capital Raising," *Euromoney*, 1998.
68 *Federal Reserve Bulletin*, October 1998.
69 Norton (1992).
70 *Euromoney*, May 1997.
71 *The Banker*, 1 September 1995.
72 *The Banker*, December 1999.
73 *Financial Times*, 6 April 1998.

74 See Basel Committee on Banking Supervision (1996).
75 *American Banker*, June 1995.
76 *The Economist*, 3 May 2003.
77 Rosenbluth and Schaap (2001) also suggest that political variables – particularly electoral rules – are correlated with types of prudential financial policy.

7 Implementation of the Basel Accord in Europe: the case of France and Germany

1 Murray-Jones and Gamble (1991:56).
2 Commission of the European Communities (2000:3).
3 Ibid. Bracketed comments added to the original text by author.
4 Kapstein (1989), Vernon et al. (1991), Reinicke (1995), and Oatley and Nabors (1998).
5 This "strong version" of the hegemonic explanation for the Accord is argued primarily by Oatley and Nabors (1998).
6 Oatley and Nabors (1998:47).
7 Reinicke (1995:174). Curiously, Oatley and Nabors (1998:46–47) do not observe France's large exposure to Third World debt. In arguing that the Accord was not pareto-improving on an international basis, the authors lay out the level of LDC debt exposure for the United States, the United Kingdom, and Japan and illustrate that the former two had a much larger exposure and thus the Accord did not help stabilize the Japanese banking system. In addition to providing a rather simplistic conclusion given the large array of variables associated with financial stability (see Matten 2000), the authors do not provide any data for France's exposure to LDC debt.
8 Dale (1984:105) and Beduc et al. (1992:269).
9 Kapstein (1989:341).
10 *Federal Reserve Bulletin*, 2 August 1999.
11 Reinicke (1995:174) and Story (1997:258).
12 Vernon et al. (1991:150).
13 Gueslin (1992:85–87).
14 Walker-Leight (1983).
15 Coleman (1997:279).
16 Coleman (1997:275).
17 De Boissieu (1990:184).
18 De Boissieu (1990:185).
19 Coleman (1997:290).
20 Coleman (1997:281–291).
21 Murray-Jones and Gamble (1991:138–140).
22 Story (1997:246).
23 Esser (1990).
24 Demirgüç-Kunt and Levine (2001b).
25 Story (1997:248).
26 See Rudolph (1990:360–361).
27 Evans (1989:3).
28 Story (1997:247).
29 Coleman (1996:124).
30 For a description of Germany's negotiating positions and tactics at the Basel and EC negotiations, see Sawabe (1995).
31 The Germans' acquiescence to France's inclusion of loan–loss reserves in Own Funds may have also been in an effort to secure Paris' support in their attempt to reject London's push for a pan-European stock exchange. In EU single financial market negotiations, France had often found it could find more common ground with Britain than with Germany and Frankfurt was anxious to shore up France's support in further rounds of these talks. See PriceWaterhouse (1991:27) and Story (1997:258).

188 *Notes*

32 PriceWaterhouse (1991:27) and Maccario *et al.* (2002:26).
33 De Boissieu (1990:223).
34 *The Economist*, 2 May 1992.
35 One prominent example of this was organized by the government, between Crédit Lyonnais and iron/steel firm Usinor Sacilor. See Caroline Monnot and Yves Mamou, "L'augmentation de capital d'Usinor sera entièrement souscrite par le Crédit Lyonnais," *Le Monde*, 16 July 1991.
36 PriceWaterhouse (1991:15).
37 De Boissieu (1990:223).
38 Wilson (1989).
39 PriceWaterhouse (1991:29) and Murray-Jones and Gamble (1991:138).
40 Rudolph (1990:365–366).
41 Sawabe (1995).
42 Murray-Jones and Gamble (1991:138).
43 Basel Committee (1999:8).
44 The role of the market in eliciting compliance has been widely discussed, yet little direct evidence of this has been found in the academic literature, which has generally focused on compliance in the United States, the United Kingdom, and Japan. For a review of this literature, see Basel Committee (1999).
45 *American Banker*, 31 December 1991; *The Economist*, 26 October 1991.
46 For a review of Germany's present capital standards, see Maccario *et al.* (2002).
47 *Euromoney*, April 1997.
48 Ibid.
49 *The Economist*, 22 May 1999
50 *American Banker*, 7 May 1999
51 *Financial Times*, 13 May 1999.
52 *Euromoney*, March 1998

8 Implementation of the Basel Accord in Japan

1 This argument is also advanced in Tamura (2003a, 2003b).
2 For a discussion of the American influence on the postwar Japanese financial system, see Rosenbluth (1989:41).
3 Interestingly, the Japanese banking system's emulation of the American system dates further back than the World War II reconstruction era. The present day financial system can be traced back to that established after the Meiji Restoration in 1868, which was then based on the US model. See Hall (1993:13–14).
4 Ibid.
5 Verdier (2002:160–161).
6 *The Banker* (1980) produces an annual list of the world's largest banks by capital.
7 *Financial Regulation Report*, 1 June 1994.
8 Peek and Rosengren (1999:30–31).
9 Scott (1995:894).
10 Hall (1993:144).
11 Especially, the Joint Japan–US Ad Hoc Group on Yen–Dollar Exchange Rate, Financial, and Capital Market Issues.
12 This threat was included as part of the Riegle–Garn Bill. The original draft of this bill was aborted in October 1990. See Hall (1993:98).
13 Hall (1993:97).
14 Tamura (2003b) claims that the restrictive financial environment was partly the product of the weak capital adequacy regulatory requirements.
15 It is possible that regulators had made efforts to make capital standards more actionable, yet failed. Hall (1993:145) notes that MOFs 1985 paper on the topic followed a

failed attempt to implement a 10 percent target ratio over the objections of the banking lobby.
16 Tamura (2003b) suggests that banks paid as much as 500 million yen to influential LDP politicians to ensure the capital adequacy legislation's defeat.
17 Unrealized capital gains are considered to be a very weak form of capital and some have observed that their inclusion in regulatory capital can increase bank stability. More will be said of these reserves later in this chapter, yet also see Section "First period of implementation" in Chapter 4. "Bank preferences" in Chapter 3 and Rabobank International (1999) and Matten (2000).
18 Tamura (2003b:7).
19 For a further discussion of these negotiations, see Section "Negotiation of the 1988 Basel Accord" in Chapter 2.
20 Interestingly, Tamura (2003b) argues that the Japanese success in securing the inclusion of revaluation reserves was due, in part, to the importance of Japanese banks to the international banking market. Oatley and Nabors (1998) argued that it was US market power that allowed it to dominate the Accord's negotiation process on its terms. Yet, Tamura argues that the large international market share and high-quality credit ratings of Japan's banks made Japan a fully necessary part of any multilateral regulatory standard and a necessary ally for further discussions in Basel.
21 Interview with Nakahira K. Suke, Director General of the MOF Banking Bureau, September 1999 in Tamura (2003b:11).
22 PriceWaterhouse (1991:32).
23 *American Banker*, 29 September 1989.
24 Data taken from calculations made by De Nederlandsche Bank, presented in Basel Committee on Banking Supervision (1999:7).
25 Wagster (1996).
26 *The Banker*, 1 January 1989.
27 *Financial Regulation Report*, 1 June 1988.
28 *Euromoney*, July 1988.
29 Wagster (1996:1342).
30 The data cannot be assumed to be fully accurate, as they are estimates relying on possibly unreliable assumptions about the composition of banks' balance sheets (i.e. their level of risk assets) and the banks' abilities to raise capital through the issue of other instruments, such as subordinated debt.
31 *The Banker*, 16 October 1990.
32 *The Banker*, 1 January 1991.
33 Huh and Kim (1994).
34 Hall (1993:157).
35 *Sh_kant_y_Keizai*, 5 September 1992 in Tamura (2003b:13).
36 *American Banker* (20 April 1992), *Financial Regulation Report* (1 June 1994), Scott and Iwahara (1994), Scott (1995), Ward (2002), and Tamura (2003a).
37 Fukao (2002:7).
38 Fukao (2002:2).
39 Ibid.
40 *The Banker* (1 January 1994).
41 International Monetary Fund (1995).
42 Other works supporting this conclusion with empirical evidence include the following: *The Banker* (1 January 1994), Scott (1995), *The Banker* (1 January 1996), *The Economist* (22 September 2001), *The Banker* (1 November 2002), and Tamura (2003a).
43 International Monetary Fund (1995).
44 *The Banker*, 1 January 1994.
45 Federal Reserve Board (2003).
46 Tamura (2003b:7).

47 *Global Risk Regulator*, January 2003.
48 Fukao (2002:3).
49 *The Banker*, 1 November 2002.
50 *Kin-yu Yaisei Jijzo*, 22 June 1998 in Tamura (2003b:13).
51 Tamura (2003a:10, 13).
52 *The Japan Times*, 10 October 1998.
53 Tamura (2003a:11).
54 *Retail Banker International*, 18 June 1999.
55 *The Banker*, 1 June 1997.
56 *The Banker*, November 2002.
57 *Global Risk Regulator*, February 2003.
58 In 1993, the Diet authorized the creation of the Cooperative Credit Purchasing Company to utilize public funds to purchase Japanese bank's NPLs. See *The Banker*, 1 January 1994.

9 Conclusions and extensions

1 Eyssell and Arshadi (1990), Cooper *et al.* (1991), Madura and Zarruk (1993), Cornett and Tehranian (1994), Laderman (1994), Wagster (1996), Wagster *et al.* (1996), and Alexander (2000a, 2000b).
2 Wagster (1996).
3 Rosenbluth and Schaap (2001) find evidence that electoral regime types (first past the post versus proportional representation) influence types of prudential bank regulatory policy. Economic studies of the influence of a wide range of constitutional rules on economic policy outcomes have also found that such rules matter in many instances. A good review is presented in Persson and Tabellini (2003).
4 The only systematic effort to analyze the impact of tax, accounting, and enforcement policies in conjunction with capital adequacy standards looks only at Japan and the United States. See Scott and Iwahara (1994).
5 Abbott and Snidal (2000:421) identify these as characteristics of international "soft law".
6 See Mitchell (1994) for a review of these literatures.
7 Chayes and Chayes (1993:177).
8 See Basel Committee on Banking Supervision (1999) for a review of this research.
9 Moran (1991), Coleman (1994), and Gilpin (2001:261).
10 See Friedman and Rogowski (1996).
11 These goals of multi-method research were found in Rossman and Wilson (1985).
12 Evidence for this statement is found in Walter (2002).
13 Bank of England (2002).
14 DeBondt and Prast (2000).
15 A review of many of these standards is available on the Financial Stability Forum: www.fsforum.org.

Bibliography

Abbott, K.W. and Snidal, D. (2000) "Hard and Soft Law in International Governance," *International Organization*, 54, 3, 421–456.

Aldrich, J. and Cnudde, C.F. (1975) "Probing the Bounds of Conventional Wisdom: A Comparison of Regression, Probit, and Discriminant Analysis," *American Journal of Political Science*, 19, 3, 571–608.

Alexander, K. (2000a) *The Role of the Basle Standards in International Banking Supervision*, ESRC Centre for Business Research Working Paper 153, Cambridge: University of Cambridge.

Alexander, K. (2000b) *The Role of Soft Law in the Legalization of International Banking Supervision: A Conceptual Approach*, ESRC Centre for Business Research Working Paper 168, Cambridge: University of Cambridge.

Arora, S. and Cason, T.N. (1995) "An Experiment in Voluntary Environmental Regulation: Participation in EPA's 3350 Program," *Journal of Environmental Economics and Management*, 28, 271–286.

Axelrod, R. (1984) *The Evolution of Co-operation*, New York: Basic Books.

Bank of England (2002) "Fallacies About the Effects of Market Risk Management Systems," *Financial Stability Review*, December.

Banking Federation of the European Union (1998) *Implementation of the Capital Adequacy Directive*, Brussels: Banking Federation of the European Union, April.

Baron, D.P. (1993) *The Economics and Politics of Regulation: Perspectives, Agenda, and Approaches*, Stanford Business School Research Paper No. 1247, March.

Baron, D.P. (1995) "The Economics and Politics of Regulation: Perspectives, Agenda, and Approaches," in J.S. Banks and E.A. Hanushek, eds, *Modern Political Economy: Old Topics, New Directions*, Cambridge: Cambridge University Press.

Baron, D.P. (2000) *Business and its Environment*, 3rd Ed., London: Prentice Hall International.

Barth, J.R., Nolle, D.E., and Rice, T.N. (2000) "Commerical Banking Structure, Regulation, and Performance: An International Comparison," in D.B. Papadimitriou, ed., *Modernizing Financial Systems*, London: Macmillan Press.

Barth, J.R., Caprio Jr, G., and Levine, R. (2001a) *The Regulation and Supervision of Banks Around the World: A New Database*, World Bank Working Paper 2588, Washington, DC: World Bank.

Barth, J.R., Caprio Jr, G., and Levine, R. (2001b) *The Regulation and Supervision of Banks Around the World*, World Bank Working Paper 2725, Washington, DC: World Bank.

Barth, J.R., Caprio Jr, G., and Levine, R. (2001c) "Banking Systems Around the Globe: Do Regulations and Ownership Affect Performance and Stability?" in F.S. Mishkin,

ed., *Prudential Supervision: What Works Best and What Doesn't?* Chicago, IL: University of Chicago Press.
Basel Committee on Banking Supervision (1981) *Report on International Developments in Banking Supervision*, Basel.
Basel Committee on Banking Supervision (1983) *Report on International Developments in Banking Supervision*, Basel.
Basel Committee on Banking Supervision (1986) *International Developments in Banking Supervision*, Basel, p. 5.
Basel Committee on Banking Supervision (1988) *International Convergence of Capital Measurement and Capital Standards*, Basel.
Basel Committee on Banking Supervision (1990) *Annual Report*, Basel.
Basel Committee on Banking Supervision (1996) *Amendment to the Capital Accord to Incorporate Market Risks*, Basel.
Basel Committee on Banking Supervision (1997) *Core Principles for Effective Banking Supervision*, Basel.
Basel Committee on Banking Supervision (1999) *Capital Requirements and Bank Behaviour: The Impact of the Basle Accord*, Basel.
Basel Committee on Banking Supervision (2001) *The New Basel Capital Accord, Consultative Document*, Basel.
Beck, T., Demirgüç-Kunt, A., Levine, R., and Maksimovic, V. (2001) "Financial Structure and Economic Development: Firm, Industry, and Country Evidence," in *Finance Structure and Economic Growth*, London: The MIT Press.
Becker, G. (1983) "A Theory of Competition Among Pressure Groups for Political Influence," *Quarterly Journal of Economics*, 98, 371–400.
Beduc, L., Ducruezet, F., and Papadacci, P. (1992) "The French Financial System," in G.G. Kaufman, ed., *Banking Structures in Major Countries*, Dordrecht, the Netherlands: Kluwer Academic Publishers Group.
Blaikie, N. (1998) *Designing Social Research*, Cambridge: Polity.
Blanden, M. (1994) "US Merger Mania," *American Banker*, March, 38–43.
Blanden, M. (1995) "The Walls Come Down," *The Banker*, June, 22–27.
Blanden, M. (1998) "Post-Merger Prospects," *The Banker*, October, 65–66.
Bollen, K.A. and Jackson, R.W. (1990) "Regression Diagnostics: An Expository Treatment of Outliers and Influential Cases," in J. Fox and J.S. Long, eds, *Modern Methods of Data Analysis*, London: Sage Publications.
Botcheva, L. and Martin, L.L. (2001) "Institutional Effects on State Behavior: Convergence and Divergence," *International Studies Quarterly*, 45, 1, 1–26.
Boyd, J.H. and Gertler, M. (1993) *U.S. Commercial Banking: Trends, Cycles, and Policy*, Economic Research Report 93–19, C.V. Starr Center for Applied Economics, New York University.
Brawley, M.R. (1998) *Turning Points: Decisions Shaping the Evolution of the International Political Economy*, New York: Broadview Press.
Brawley, M.R. (1999) *Afterglow of Adjustment? Domestic Institutions and Responses to Overstretch*, Chichester: Columbia University Press.
Buchanan, W. (1974) "Nominal and Ordinal Bivariate Statistics: The Practitioner's View," *American Journal of Political Science*, 18, 3, 625–646.
Cally, J. and Majnoni, G. (2002) *Financial Regulatory Harmonization and the Globalization of Finance*, World Bank Policy Research Working Paper 2919.
Calomiris, C.W. (2000) *U.S. Bank Deregulation in Historical Perspective*, Cambridge: Cambridge University Press.

Cantor, R. and Johnson, R. (1992) "Bank Capital Ratios, Asset Growth, and the Stock Market," *Federal Reserve Bank of New York Quarterly Review*, Autumn.

Caprio, Jr G. and Honohan, P. (1999) "Restoring Bank Stability: Beyond Supervised Capital Requirements," *Journal of Economic Perspectives*, 13, 4, 43–64.

Caprio, Jr G. and Klingebiel, D. (1996) *Bank Insolvencies: Cross-Country Experience*, Washington, DC: The World Bank.

Cerny, P.G. (1993) "Plurilateralism: Structural Differentiation and Functional Conflict in the Post-Cold War World Order," *Millennium: Journal of International Studies*, 22, 27–51.

Cerych, L. and Sabatier, P. (1986) *Great Expectations and Mixed Performance: The Implementation of European Higher Education Reforms*, Stoke-on-Trent: Trentham Books.

Chant, J.F. (1997) "Canada's Economy and Financial System: Recent and Prospective Developments and the Policy Issues They Pose," in G.M. von Furstenberg, ed., *The Banking and Financial Structure in the NAFTA Countries*, Dordrecht, the Netherlands: Kluwer Academic Publishers Group.

Charney, J.L. (2000) "Compliance with International Soft Law: Commentary," in D. Shelton, ed., *Commitment and Compliance: The Role of Non-Binding Norms in the International Legal System*, Oxford: Oxford University Press.

Chayes, A. and Handler Chayes, A. (1993) "On Compliance," *International Organization*, 47, 2, 175–205.

Chayes, A. and Handler Chayes, A. (1995) *The New Sovereignty: Compliance with International Regulatory Agreements*, London: Harvard University Press.

Chiuri, M.C., Ferri, G., and Majnoni, G. (2001) *The Macroeconomic Impact of Bank Capital Requirements in Emerging Economies – Past Evidence to Assess the Future*, World Bank Policy Research Working Paper 2605.

Claessens, S. and Glaessner, T. (1998) *The Internationalization of Financial Services in Asia*, World Bank Working Paper 1911.

Coleman, W.D. (1994) "Policy Convergence in Banking: A Comparative Study," *Political Studies*, 32, 274–292.

Coleman, W.D. (1996) *Financial Services, Globalization and Domestic Policy Change*, London: Macmillan Press Ltd.

Coleman, W.D. (1997) "The French State, *Dirigisme*, and the Changing Global Financial Environment," in G.R.D. Underhill, ed., *The New World Order in International Finance*, London: Macmillan Press Ltd.

Commission of the European Communities (2000) *First Commission Report to the European Parliament and the Council on the Implementation of the Own Funds Directive (89/299/EEC)*, Brussels: European Commission.

Cooke, P. (1981) "Developments in Co-operation Among Bank Supervisory Authorities," *Bank of England Quarterly Bulletin*, June.

Cooper, K., Kolari, J., and Wagster, J. (1991) "A Note on the Stock Market Effects of the Adoption of the Risk-based Capital Requirements on International Banks in Different Countries," *Journal of Banking and Finance*, 15, 367–381.

Cornett, M.M. and Tehranian, H. (1994) "An Examination of Voluntary Versus Involuntary Security Issuance by Commercial Banks," *Journal of Financial Economics*, 35, 99–122.

Cox, G.W. and McCubbins, M.D. (2001) "The Institutional Determinants of Economic Policy Outcomes," in S. Haggard and D. McCubbins, eds, *Presidents, Parliaments, and Policy*, Cambridge: Cambridge University Press.

194 Bibliography

Dahl, D. and Shrieves, R.E. (1990) "The Impact of Regulation on Bank Equity Infusions," *Journal of Banking and Finance*, 14, 1209–1228.

Dale, R. (1984) *The Regulation of International Banking*, Cambridge: Woodhead-Faulkner.

Dale, R. and Wolf, S. (1996) "EU Capital Requirements and the Level Playing Field," working paper, University of Southampton.

Davis, J.A. (1985) *The Logic of Causal Order*, Sage University Paper No. 55, London: Sage Publications.

Davison, A.C. and Hinkley, D.V. (1997) *Boostrap Method and their Applications*, Cambridge: Cambridge University Press.

De Boissieu, C. (1990) "The French Banking Sector in the Light of European Financial Integration," in Jean Dermine, ed., *European Banking in the 1990s*, Oxford: Basil Blackwell Ltd.

De Bondt, G.J. and Prast, H.M. (2000) "Bank Capital Ratios in the 1990s: Cross-Country Evidence," *BNL Quarterly Review*, 212, March, 71–97.

DeCarmoy, H. (1990) *Global Banking Strategy: Financial Markets and Industrial Decay*, Cambridge: Basil Blackwell.

Demirgüç-Kunt, A. and Detragiache, E. (1997) *The Determinants of Banking Crises: Evidence from Developed and Developing Countries*, Washington, DC: The World Bank.

Demirgüç-Kunt, A. and Detragiache, E. (2000) "Does Deposit Insurance Increase Banking System Stability? An Empirical Investigation," mimeo, The World Bank.

Demirgüç-Kunt, A. and Huizinga, H. (2000) *Market Discipline and Financial Safety Net Design*, Paper Presented to World Bank Deposit Insurance Conference, 8–9 June.

Demirgüç-Kunt, A. and Huizinga, H. (2001) "Financial Structure and Bank Profitability," in A. Demirgüç-Kunt and R. Levine, eds, *Financial Structure and Economic Growth*, London: The MIT Press.

Demirgüç-Kunt, A. and Levine, R., eds (2001a) *Financial Structure and Economic Growth*, London: The MIT Press.

Demirgüç-Kunt, A. and Levine, R. (2001b) "Bank-Based and Market-Based Financial Systems: Cross-Country Comparisons," in A. Demirgüç-Kunt and R. Levine, eds, *Financial Structure and Economic Growth*, London: The MIT Press.

Downs, G.W., Rocke, D.M., and Barsoon, P.N. (1996) "Is the Good News About Compliance Good News About Cooperation?," *International Organization*, 50, 3, 379–406.

Duffy, G. (1988) "Conditions that Affect Arms Control Compliance," in A. George, P.J. Farley, and A. Dallin, eds, *U.S.–Soviet Security Cooperation*, Oxford: Oxford University Press.

Dunleavy, P. (1991) *Democracy, Bureaucracy, and Public Choice*, London: Harvester-Wheatsheaf.

Efron, B. and Tibshirani, R.J. (1993) *An Introduction to the Bootstrap*, New York: Champman & Hall.

Esser, J. (1990) "Bank Power in West Germany Revised," *West European Politics*, 13, 4, 17–32.

Evans, J. (1989) "Merrill Finds $300 Million 'Hidden' at Japan's Banks; Reserves Found in Undervalued Property and Securities Could Fuel Global Expansion," *American Banker*, September 29.

Evans, P.B. (1995) *Embedded Autonomy: States and Industrial Transformation*, Princeton, NJ: Princeton University Press.

Evans, P.B., Jacobson, H.K., and Putnam, R.D., eds (1993) *Double-Edged Diplomacy,*

International Bargaining and Domestic Politics, London: University of California Press.

Eyssell, T. and Arshadi, N. (1990) "The Wealth Effects of the Risk-Based Capital Requirement in Banking: The Evidence from the Capital Markets," *Journal of Banking and Finance*, 14, 179–197.

Fearon, J.D. (1998) "Bargaining, Enforcement, and International Cooperation," *International Organization*, 52, 2, 269–306.

Federal Reserve Bank of Kansas City (1994) *Banking Regulation: Its Purposes, Implementation, and Effects*, Kansas City: Federal Reserve Bank of Kansas City.

Federal Reserve Board (2003) *Regulators Announce Termination of Enforcement Orders Against Daiwa Bank*, press release.

Federal Reserve Board of New York (1988) "The Risk-Based Capital Agreement: A Further Step Towards Policy Convergence," *Federal Reserve Board of New York Quarterly Review*, 26.

Federal Reserve System (1956) *Form FR*, 363.

Federal Reserve System (1987) *Capital Maintenance, Revision to Capital Adequacy Guidelines*, Mimeo, 88.

Feldstein, M. (1992) "Revise Bank Capital Standards Now," *Wall Street Journal*, 6 March.

Ferry, J. (2003) "Basel II: A Continental Rift," *Risk*, 16, 5.

Frankfort-Nachmias, C. and Nachmias, D. (2000) *Research Methods in the Social Sciences*, New York: Worth Publishers.

Friedman, J.A. and Rogowski, R. (1996) "The Impact of the International Economy on National Policies," in R.O. Keohane and H.V. Milner, eds, *Internationalization and Domestic Politics*, Cambridge: Cambridge University Press, pp. 25–47.

Fukao, M. (2002) *Barriers to Financial Restructuring: Japanese Banking and Life-Insurance Industries*, presented to the NBER conference on "Structural Impediments to Growth in Japan," 18–19 March, Tokyo.

Gardener, E.P.M. (1992) *Capital Adequacy After 1992: The Banking Challenge*, Research Papers in Banking Finance 11, Bangor: University of Wales.

Genetay, N. and Molyneux, P. (1998) *Bancassurance*, London: Macmillan.

George, A. (1979) "Case Studies and Theory Development: The Method of Structured, Focused Comparison," in Paul Gordon, ed., *Diplomacy: New Approaches in History, Theory, and Policy*, London: Macmillan.

Gerschenkron, A. (1962) *Economic Backwardness in Historical Perspective: A Book of Essays*, Cambridge, MA: Belknap Press of Harvard University Press.

Gilpin, R. (1981) *War and Change in International Politics*, Cambridge: Cambridge University Press.

Gilpin, R. (2001) *Global Political Economy: Understanding the International Economic Order*, Princeton, NJ: Princeton University Press.

Goggin, M.L. and Lester, J.P. (1998) "Back to the Future: The Rediscovery of Implementation Studies," *Policy Currents*, 8, 3, 1–9.

Greenspan, A. (1998) "The Role of Capital in Optimal Banking Supervision and Regulation," in Federal Reserve Bank of New York, "Financial Services at the Crossroads: Capital Regulation in the Twenty-First Century, Proceedings of a Conference," *FRBNY Economic Policy Review*, 4, 3, October.

Gueslin, A. (1992) "Banks and State in France from the 1880s to the 1930s: The Impossible Advance of the Banks," in Y. Cassis, ed., *Finance and Financiers in European History, 1880–1960*, Cambridge: Cambridge University Press.

Haas, P.M. (1992) "Introduction: Epistemic Communities and International Policy Coordination," *International Organization*, 46, 1, 1–135.
Haggard, S. (1990) *Pathways from the Periphery*, London: Cornell University Press.
Hall, M.J.B. (1993) *Banking Regulation and Supervision: A Comparative Study of the UK, USA, and Japan*, Aldershot: Edward Elgar.
Hanf, K. and Underdal, A. (1995) "Domesticating International Commitments: Linking National and International Decision-Making," in A. Underdal, ed., *The International Politics of Environmental Management*, Dordrecht, the Netherlands: Kluwer Academic Publishers.
Heller, W.B. and McCubbins, M.D. (2001) "Political Institutions and Economic Development: The Case of Electric Utility Regulation in Argentina and Chile," in S. Haggard and D. McCubbins, eds, *Presidents, Parliaments, and Policy*, Cambridge: Cambridge University Press.
Henisz, W.J. (2000) "The Institutional Environment for Economic Growth," *Economics and Politics*, 12, 1, 1–31.
Ho, D.E. (2002) "Compliance and International Soft Law: Why Do Countries Implement the Basle Accord?," *Journal of International Economic Law*, 5, 3, 647–688.
Huh, C. and Sun Bae Kim (1994) "How Bad Is the 'Bad Loan Problem' in Japan?," *Federal Reserve Bank of San Francisco Weekly Letter*, 23 September.
International Monetary Fund (1995) *International Capital Markets: Developments, Prospects, and Policy Issues*, Washington, DC: IMF.
Japan Center for Economic Research (2001) "Monetary Policy Under Deflation," in M. Fukao, ed., *Barriers to Financial Restructuring: Japanese Banking and Life-Insurance Industries*, presented to the NBER conference on "Structural Impediments to Growth in Japan," 18–19 March, Tokyo.
John, P. (1998) *Analysing Public Policy*, London: Pinter.
Jonsson, C. and Tallbert, J. (1998) "Compliance and Post-Agreement Bargaining," *European Journal of International Relations*, 4, 4, 371–408.
Jordan, C. and Majnoni, G. (2002) *Financial Regulatory Harmonization and the Globalization of Finance*, World Bank Policy Research Working Paper 2919.
Josselin, D. (1997) *Money Politics in the New Europe: Britain, France, and the Single Financial Market*, London: Macmillan Press Ltd.
Kaminsky, G. and Reinhart, C. (1996) *The Twin Crises: The Causes of Banking and Balance of Payments Problems*, mimeo, The World Bank, September.
Kane, E.J. (1991) "Incentive Conflict in the International Regulatory Agreement on Risk-Based Capital," in S.G. Rhee and R.P. Chang, eds, *Pacific-Basin Capital Markets Research, Volume II*, Oxford: North-Holland.
Kane, E.J. (2000) *Designing Financial Safety Nets to Fit Country Circumstances*, Paper Presented to World Bank Deposit Insurance Conference, 8–9 June.
Kapstein, E. (1989) "Resolving the Regulator's Dilemma: International Coordination of Banking Regulations," *International Organization*, 43, 2, Spring, 323–347.
Kapstein, E. (1991) "Supervising International Banks: Origins and Implications of the Basle Accord," in *Essays in International Finance*, 185, Princeton, NJ: Princeton University Press.
Kapstein, E. (1994) *Governing the Global Economy: International Finance and the State*, Cambridge, MA: Harvard University Press.
Katzenstein, P.J. (1978) *Between Power and Plenty: Foreign Economic Policies of Advanced Industrial States*, Madison, WI: University of Wisconsin Press.
Kaufman, G.G. (1992) "Banking and Financial Intermediary Markets in the United

States: Where from, Where to?" in F.R. Edwards and H.T. Patrick, eds, *Regulating International Financial Markets: Issues and Policies*, Boston, MA: Kluwer Academic Publishers.

Kaufman, R.R. and Zuckerman, L. (1998) "Attitudes Toward Reform in Mexico: The Role of Political Orientation," *American Political Science Review*, 92, 2.

Keohane, R.O. (1982) "The Demand for International Regimes," *International Organization*, 36, 2.

Keohane, R.O. (1984) *After Hegemony*, Princeton, NJ: Princeton University Press.

Khademian, A.M. (1992) *The SEC and Capital Market Regulation: The Politics of Expertise*, Pittsburgh, PA: University of Pittsburgh Press.

King, G. (1985) *How Not to Lie with Statistics: Avoiding Common Mistakes in Quantitative Political Science*, unpublished working paper.

King, M. (2000) *Preferences of Institutional Investors for Macroeconomic Policy*, presented to the Conference on Financial Globalisation, London School of Economics.

King, G., Keohane, R.O., and Verba, S. (1994) *Designing Social Inquiry: Scientific Inference in Qualitative Research*, Chichester: Princeton University Press.

King, G., Tomz, M., and Wittenberg, J. (2000) "Making the Most of Statistical Analyses: Improving Interpretation and Presentation," *American Journal of Political Science*, 40, 2, 570–602.

Krasner, S. (1978) *Defending the National Interest*, Princeton, NJ: Princeton University Press.

Krasner, S. (1982) "Structural Causes and Regime Consequences: Regimes as Intervening Variables," *International Organization*, 36, 2.

Krueger, A.O. (1996) "The Political Economy of Controls: American Sugar," in T.E. Alston and D.C. North, eds, *Empirical Studies in Institutional Change*, Cambridge: Cambridge University Press.

Laderman, E.S. (1994) "Wealth Effects of Regulation of Bank Holding Company Securities Issuance and Loan Growth Under the Risk-Based Capital Requirements," *Federal Reserve Bank of San Francisco Economic Review*, 2, 30–41.

Lantis, J.S. (1997) *Domestic Constraints and the Breakdown of International Agreements*, London: Praeger.

LaPorta, R., Lopez-de-Silanes, F., Shleifer, A., and Vishny, R.W. (1997) "Legal Determinants of External Finance," *Journal of Finance*, 52, 3, 1131–1150.

LaPorta, R., Lopez-de-Silanes, F., Shleifer, A., and Vishny, R.W. (1998) "Law and Finance," *Journal of Political Economy*, 106, 6, 1113–1155.

Lewis, A. (1950) *The Principles of Economic Planning*, London: G. Allen & Unwin.

Lindgren, C.-J., Garcia, G., and Saal, M. (1996) *Bank Soundness and Macroeconomic Policy*, Washington, DC: The International Monetary Fund.

Lipson, C. (1991) "Why Are Some International Agreements Informal?," *International Organization*, 45, 4.

Lu, C., Shen, Y., and So, R.W. (1999) "Wealth Effects of the Basle Accord on Small Banks," *Journal of Economics and Finance*, 23, 3, 246–254.

Lutz, S. (2000) *Beyond the Basle Accord: Banking Regulation in a System of Multilevel Governance*, Paper Presented to the International Studies Association Conference, 14–18 March.

Maccario, A., Sironi, A., and Zazzara, C. (2002) *Is Banks' Cost of Equity Capital Different Across Countries? Evidence from the G10 Countries Major Banks*, Paper Presented to the "Risk and Stability in the Financial System: What Role for Regulators, Management, and Market Discipline?" Conference, Bocconi University, 13–14 June.

Madura, J. and Zarruk, E.R. (1993) "Market Reaction to Uniform Capital Adequacy

Guidelines in the Banking Industry," *Journal of Economics and Finance*, Spring, 59–72.

Marshall, J. (1999) "Vive la France!" *U.S. Banker*, March.

Martin, L. (1992) *Coercive Cooperation: Explaining Multilateral Economic Sanctions*, Princeton, NJ: Princeton University Press.

Matten, C. (2000) *Managing Bank Capital: Capital Allocation and Performance Measurement*, Chichester: John Wiley & Sons Ltd.

Mattli, W. and Slaughter, A.-M. (1998) "Revisiting the European Court of Justice," *International Organization*, 52, 1.

Mayne, L.S. (1972) "Supervisory Influence on Bank Capital," *Journal of Finance*, 27, 3, 637–651.

Merton, R.K. (1968) *Social Theory and Social Structure*, Glencoe, IL: Free Press.

Milner, H.V. (1997) *Interests, Institutions, and Information: Domestic Politics and International Relations*, Princeton, NJ: Princeton University Press.

Minsky, H. (1982) *Can "It" Happen Again?: Essays on Instability and Finance*, Armonk, NY: M.E. Sharpe.

Misback, A.E. (1993) "The Foreign Bank Supervision Enhancement Act of 1991," *Federal Reserve Bulletin*.

Mitchell, R.B. (1994) "Regime Design Matters, International Oil Pollution and Treaty Compliance," *International Organization*, 42.

Mooney, C.Z. (1996) "Bootstrap Statistical Inference: Examples and Evaluations for Political Science," *American Journal of Political Science*, 40, 2, 570–602.

Mooney, C.Z. and Duval, R.D. (1993) *Boostrapping: A Nonparametric Approach to Statistical Inference*, London: Sage.

Moran, M. (1991) *The Politics of the Financial Services Revolution: The USA, UK, and Japan*, New York: St. Martin's Press.

Moravscik, A. (1993) "Introduction," in P.B. Evans, H.K. Jacobson and R.D. Putnam, eds, *Double-Edged Diplomacy, International Bargaining and Domestic Politics*, London: University of California Press.

Morgan, G. and Knights, D. (1997) *Regulation and Deregulation in European Financial Services*, London: Macmillan.

Morgenthau, H.J. (1978) *Politics Among Nations: The Struggle for Power and Peace*, New York: Alfred A. Knopf.

Mosley, L. (2003) *Global Capital and National Governments*, Cambridge: Cambridge University Press.

Murray-Jones, A. and Gamble, A. (1991) *Managing Capital Adequacy: A Handbook of International Regulations*, London: Woodhead-Faulkner.

Myrdal, G. (1968) *Asian Drama*, New York: Pantheon.

Neufeld, E.P. and Hassanwalia, H. (1997) "Challenges for the Further Restructuring of the Financial Services Industry in Canada," in G.M. von Furstenberg, ed., *The Banking and Financial Structure in the NAFTA Countries and Chile*, Dordrecht, the Netherlands: Kluwer Academic Publishers Group.

North, D. and Weingast, B. (1989) "Constitutions and Commitment: The Evolution of Institutions Governing Public Choice in Seventeenth-Century England," *Journal of Economic History*, 49, 4, 803–832.

Norton, J.J. (1992) *Recent Developments in the Regulation and Supervision of US Finanancial Institutions: The Evolution of Capital Adequacy Standards and the Financial Institutions Reform, Recovery, and Enforcement Act of 1989*, Bangor: Institute of European Finance.

Oatley, T. and Nabors, R. (1998) "Redistributive Cooperation: Market Failure, Wealth Transfers, and the Basle Accord," *International Organization*, 52, 1, 35–54.

Pattison, J.C. (2006) "International Financial Cooperation and the Number of Adherents: The Basel Committee and Capital Regulation," *Open Economies Review*, 17, 4–5, 443–458.

Pecchioli, R.M. (1987) *Prudential Supervision in Banking*, Paris: Organization for Economics Cooperation and Development.

Peek, J. and Rosengren, E. (1995) "The Capital Crunch: Neither a Borrower nor a Lender Be," *Journal of Money, Credit and Banking*, 27, 3, 625–638.

Peek, J. and Rosengren, E.S. (1999) "Japanese Banking Problems: Implications for Lending in the United States," *New England Economic Review*, January/February, 25–35.

Peltzman, S. (1976) "Toward a More General Theory of Regulation," *Journal of Law and Economics*, 19, 2, 1–40.

Peltzman, S. (1993) "George Stigler's Contribution to the Economic Analysis of Regulation," *Journal of Political Economy*, 101, 51, 818–832.

Persson, T. and Tabellini, G. (2003) *The Economic Effects of Constitutions*, London: The MIT Press.

Posner, R. (1974) "Theories of Economic Regulation," *Bell Journal of Economics*, 5, 335–358.

Pressman, J. and Wildavsky, A. (1973) *Implementation*, Berkeley, CA: University of California Press.

PriceWaterhouse (1991) *Bank Capital Adequacy and Capital Convergence*, London: PriceWaterhouse.

Putnam R. (1988) "Diplomacy and Domestic Politics: The Logic of Two-Level Games," *International Organization*, 42, 3, 427–460.

Quinn, D.P. and Inclán, C. (1997) "The Origins of Financial Openness: A Study of Current and Capital Account Liberalization," *American Journal of Political Science*, 41, 3, 771–813.

Rabobank International (1999) *Bank Capital: A Simple Guide to a Complex Area*.

Reinicke, W.H. (1995) *Banking, Politics, and Global Finance: American Commercial Banks and Regulatory Change, 1980–1990*, Aldershot: Edward Elgar.

Reinicke, W.H. (1998) *Global Public Policy: Governing Without Government?*, Washington, DC: Brookings Institution Press.

Remmer, K.L. (1991) "The Political Impact of Economic Crisis in Latin America in the 1980s," *American Political Science Review*, 85, 3, 777–800.

Rogers, D. (1993) *The Future of American Banking: Managing for Change*, London: McGraw-Hill, Inc.

Rosenbluth, F.M. (1989) *Financial Politics in Contemporary Japan*, London: Cornell University Press.

Rosenbluth, F.M. (1993) "Financial Deregulation and Interest Intermediation," in G.D. Allinson and Y. Sone, eds, *Political Dynamics in Contemporary Japan*, London: Cornell University Press.

Rosenbluth, F. and Schaap, R. (2001) *The Domestic Politics of Banking Regulation*, Paper Presented to the Annual Conference of the American Political Science Association.

Rossman, G.B. and Wilson, B.L. (1985) "Numbers and Words: Combining Quantitative and Qualitative Methods in a Single Large-Scale Evaluation Study," *Evaluation Research*, 9, 5, 627–643.

Rudolph, B. (1990) "Capital Requirements of German Banks and the European Economic Community Proposals on Banking Supervision," in J. Dermine, ed., *European Banking in the 1990s*, Oxford: Basil Blackwell Ltd.

Sabatier, P.A. (1986) "Top-Down and Bottom-Up Approaches to Implementation Research: A Critical Analysis and Suggested Synbook," *Journal of Public Policy*, 6, 21–48.

Sabatier, P.A. and Mazmanian, D.A. (1981) "The Implementation of Public Policy: A Framework of Analysis," in P.A. Sabatier and D.A. Mazmanian, eds, *Effective Policy Implementation*, Lexington, MA: Lexington Books.

Santos, J.A.C. (2000) *Bank Capital Regulation in Contemporary Banking Theory: A Review of the Literature*, BIS Working Paper 90.

Sawabe, N. (1995) *Reregulating the Japanese Banking in the International Political Economy: Making of the Basle Accord*, Working Paper, Ritsumeikan University, October.

Schoppa, L.J. (1993) "Two-Level Games and Bargaining Outcomes: Why Gaiatsu Succeeds in Japan in Some Cases but Not Others," *International Organization*, 47, 3, 353–386.

Schroder, M. and Sims, G.T. (2003) "Banks in U.S. Say Rules Hurt Them vs. Europe," *Wall Street Journal Europe*, 28 February–2 March.

Scott, H.S. (1995) "Implications of the Basle Capital Accord," *Saint Louis University Law Journal*, 39, 3, 885–896.

Scott, H. and Iwahara, S. (1994) *In Search of a Level Playing Field: The Implementation of the Basle Capital Accord in Japan and the US*, Occasional Paper 46, Washington, DC: Group of Thirty.

Scott, H.S. and Wellons, P.A. (1995) *International Finance: Transactions, Policy, and Regulation*, Westbury, NY: Foundation Press.

Seeliger, R. (1996) "Conceptualizing and Researching Policy Convergence," *Policy Studies Journal*, 24, 2, 287–306.

Shelton, D., ed. (2000) *Commitment and Compliance: The Role of Non-Binding Norms in the International Legal System*, Oxford: Oxford University Press.

Sheng, A. (1995) *Bank Restructuring*, Washington, DC: The World Bank.

Simmons, B.A. (1994) *Who Adjusts? Domestic Sources of Foreign Economic Policy During the Interwar Years*, Princeton, NJ: Princeton University Press.

Simmons, B.A. (2000) "International Law and State Behavior: Commitment and Compliance in International Monetary Affairs," *American Political Science Review*, 94, 4, 819–835.

Simmons, B.A. (2001) "The International Politics of Harmonization: The Case of Capital Market Regulation," *International Organization*, 55, 3, 589–620.

Sinclair, T.J. (1994) "Passing Judgement: Credit Rating Processes as Regulatory Mechanisms of Governance in the Emerging World Order," *Review of International Political Economy*, 1, 1, 134–159.

Singer, D.A. (2002) "Prudential Markets: A New Look at the Regulator's Dilemma in Banking and Securities," paper presented at the American Political Science Annual Conference.

Slaughter, A.-M. (2000) "Governing the Global Economy Through Government Networks," in M. Byers, ed., *The Role of Law in International Politics*, Oxford: Oxford University Press.

Stein, A. (1983) "Coordination and Collaboration: Regimes in an Anarchic World," in S. Krasner, ed., *International Regimes*, Ithaca, NY: Cornell University Press, pp. 115–140.

Stigler, G. (1971) "The Economic Theory of Regulation," *Bell Journal of Economics*, 2, 3–21.
Stigler, G.J. and Friedland, C.J. (1962) "What Can Regulators Regulate? The Case of Electricity," *Journal of Law and Economics*, 5, 1–16.
Story, J. (1997) "Globalisation, the European Union and German Financial Reform: The Political Economy of Finanzplatz Deutschland," in G.R.D. Underhill, ed., *The New World Order in International Finance*, London: Macmillan Press Ltd.
Tabachnick, B.G. and Fidell, L.S. (1989) *Using Multivariate Statistics*, New York: HarperCollins Publishers.
Tamura, K. (2002) *The Political Problem for the Japanese Implementation of the Basle Capital Accord: Domestic Politics and International Regulatory Standards*, mimeo, London School of Economics.
Tamura, K. (2003a) "Preference Formation, Negotiations, and Implementation: Japan and the Basle Capital Accord," PhD dissertation, London School of Economics.
Tamura, K. (2003b) "A Regulator's Dilemma and Two-level Games: Japan in the Politics of International Banking Regulation," *Social Science Japan Journal*, 6, 221–240.
Thomas, R.M. (2003) *Blending Qualitative and Quantitative Research Methods in Theses and Dissertations*, London: Corwin Press.
Thomsen, S. and Pedersen, T. (1996) "Nationality and Ownership Structures: The 100 Largest Companies in Six European Nations," *Management International Review*, 36, 149–166.
Tobin, G. (1991) "Global Money Rules," PhD dissertation, Harvard University.
Underdal, A. and Hanf, K. (1995) "Domesticating International Commitments," *The International Politics of Environmental Management*, Dordrecht, The Netherlands: Kluwer Academic Publishers.
Underhill, G.R.D. (1992) "Private Markets and Public Responsibility in a Global System: Conflict and Co-operation in Transnational Banking and Securities Regulation," in G.R.D. Underhill, eds, *The New World Order in International Finance*, New York: St. Martin's Press.
US House of Representatives Committee on Banking, Finance, and Urban Affairs (1982) *International Financial Markets and Related Matters*, 97th cong., 2nd sess., 21 December.
Van Meter, D. and Van Horn, C. (1975) "The Policy Implementation Process: A Conceptual Framework," *Administration and Society*, 6, 445–488.
Verdier, D. (2002) *Moving Money: Banking and Finance in the Industrialized World*, Cambridge: Cambridge University Press.
Vernon, R., Spar, D.L., and Tobin, G. (1991) *Iron Triangles and Revolving Doors: Cases in US Foreign Economic Policymaking*, London: Praeger.
Wagster, J.D. (1996) "Impact of the 1988 Basle Accord on International Banks," *Journal of Finance*, 51, 1321–1346.
Wagster, J., Kolari, J., and Cooper, K. (1996) "Market Reaction to National Discretion in Implementing the Basle Accord," *The Journal of Financial Research*, XIX, 3 (Fall), 339–357.
Walter, A. (2000) "Globalization and Policy Convergence: The Case of Direct Investment Rules," in R.A. Higgott, G.R.D. Underhill, and A. Beiler, eds, *Non-State Actors and Authority in the Global System*, London: Routledge.
Walter, A. (2002) "Financial Liberalization and Prudential Regulation in East Asia: Still Perverse?" unpublished manuscript, London School of Economics.
Waltz, K. (1979) *Theory of International Politics*, Boston, MA: Addison-Wesley.
Ward, J. (2002) *The New Basel Accord: What Is in It and Is It Any Good?* Paper

202 Bibliography

Presented to the International Financial Regulation seminar, ESRC Centre for Business Research, Cambridge University, 23 January.

Welch, D. (1992) "The Organizational Process and Bureaucratic Politics Paradigms: Retrospect and Prospect," *International Security*, 17, 2, 112–146.

White, L.J. (1992) "The United States Savings and Loan Debacle: Some Lessons for the Regulation of Financial Institutions," in Dimitri Vittas, ed., *Financial Regulation: Changing the Rules of the Game*, Washington, DC: The World Bank.

Wilson, N. (1989) "Read to Go–France's First Securitisation Issues Has Yet to be Made," *American Banker*, 1 December.

Woolcock, S. (1996) "Competition Among Rules in the Single European Market," in W. Bratton, J. McCahery, S. Piciotto, and C. Scott, eds, *International Regulatory Competition and Coordination*, Oxford: Clarendon Press.

World Development Indicators (2001) World Bank, CD.

Wright, R. (1994) "The Fed Fights Back," *The Banker*, March, 43–44.

Yellen, J.L. (2000) "The 'New' Science of Credit Risk Management at Financial Institutions," in D.B. Papadimitriou, ed., *Modernizing Financial Systems*, London: Macmillan Press.

Young, O.R. (1999) *Governance in World Affairs*, London: Cornell University Press.

Zimmer, S.A. and McCauley, R.N. (1991) "Bank Cost of Capital and International Competition," *Federal Reserve Bank of New York Quarterly Review*, Winter, 33–59.

Journal and newspaper articles (unsigned)

"Is There a Credit Crunch?" *Banking World*, May 1991.

"Rep. Moran Seeks Cut in Capital Requirement for CRE," *National Mortgage News*, 24 February 1992.

"Basel Committee Issues Interpretation on Tier1 Eligibility," *M2 Press Wire*, 29 October 1998.

"Japan Banking 'Shokku' Continues," *Retail Banking International*, 18 June 1999.

American Banker

"Preferred Stock Comes of Age," *American Banker*, 31 March 1983.

"Bankers Ink Risk-Based Capital Plan: Changes Made in the Definition of Capital, Mortgage Risks," *American Banker*, 12 July 1988.

"Merrill Finds $300 Million 'Hidden' at Japan's Banks," *American Banker*, 29 September 1989.

"Builders Seek Easier Capital Rule," *American Banker*, 2 October 1991.

"Basel Group Thwarted by Its Members," *American Banker*, 31 December 1991.

"The Banks Bounce Back," *American Banker*, March 1993.

"The Walls Come Down," *American Banker*, June 1995.

"Greenspan Tells Regulators to Stop Playing Politics with Capital Rules," *The American Banker*, 7 May 1999.

The Banker

"Japan Focus: Smart Moves," *The Banker*, 1 January 1989.

"Funds Costlier for Japan's Banks," *The Banker*, 16 October 1990.

"Asia: Welcome to Hard Times," *The Banker*, 1 January 1992.
"The Banks Bounce Back," *The Banker*, March 1993.
"Japan: The Banks Feel the Pain," *The Banker*, 1 January 1994.
"Japan: A Clean Slate," *The Banker*, 1 January 1996.
"Notes: Japan Makes a Dash for Big Bang in 2001," *The Banker*, 1 June 1997.
"Basel Committee Agrees to Relaxation," *The Banker*, May 1998.
"The Bottom Line," *The Banker*, 1 September 1995.
"Congress Finally Bows to the Inevitable," *The Banker*, 1 December 1999.
"Japan in Tight Corner over Bad Debts," *The Banker*, November 2002.

The Economist

"Banks and Politicians Want to Weaken Capital Standards for Banks. Regulators Should Say No," *The Economist*, 26 October 1991.
"Time to Leave: the Worship of Basle" *The Economist*, 2 May 1992.
"What's Cooking in Basle," *The Economist*, 17 April 1999.
"German Banks Under Fire," *The Economist*, 22 May 1999.
"Japanese Banks: Abandon Hope," *The Economist*, 22 September 2001.
"A Survey of Global Finance," *The Economist*, 3 May 2003.

Euromoney

"Naughty Germans," *Euromoney*, April 1997.
"Bank Capital Raising: Squeezing More into Tier One," *Euromoney*, March 1998.
"Bank Portfolio Management: Learning to Play Around with Loans," *Euromoney*, May 1999.
"Risk Scientists Look Beyond Their Silos," *Euromoney*, May 1999.

Financial Regulation Report

"Japanese Banks Need Dollars 50 bn to Meet Basle Standards," *Financial Regulation Report*, 1 June 1988.
"The Level Playing Field Revisited," *Financial Regulation Report*, 1 June 1994.

Financial Times

"Harassed Regulatory Try to Draw the Line," *Financial Times*, 6 April 1998.
"US–German Animosity Stalls Bank Capital Talks," *Financial Times*, 13 May 1999.
"EU Warned on Derivates Rules," *Financial Times*, 2 February 2004.
"French Call IASB to Account," *Financial Times*, 2 February 2004.

Global Risk Regulator

"Japanese Banks Have Negative Capital," *Global Risk Regulator*, January 2003.
"Stripped Down Basel II Accord Likely," *Global Risk Regulator*, February 2003.

Wall Street Journal

"Big Savings Seen in Revised Capital Guidelines: Bankers Breathe Sigh of Relief over Compromise on Cumulative Preferred Stock," *American Banker*, 23 August 1988.

"Banks' Weaknesses Are a Regulatory Illusion," *Wall Street Journal*, 7 February 1991.

"Bank Regulators Seek to Loosen Capital Rules," *Wall Street Journal*, 24 December 1991.

Index

aggregate introduction, case studies 97–9
Alexander. K. 23, 24, 35
American Banker 104
American Bankers Association 111
arbitrage incentives 106
Asia Pacific, univariate analysis of regional effects hypothesis 62
Association Française des Etablissements de Crédit (AFEC), France 130
asymmetric negotiating authority 22
Australia: comparative descriptive statistics 54, 55, 59; data sources 71; Tier1 capital definitions 57; Tier2 capital definitions 56
Austria: comparative descriptive statistics 54, 55, 59; data sources 71; Tier1 capital definitions 57; Tier2 capital definitions 56

Bank for International Settlements (BIS) 118; Core principles for Banking Supervision 180n2
Bank Holding Companies (BHCs) 112, 117–18
Bank of England 7, 23, 103, 109, 184–5n11
Bank of Japan (BOJ) 18, 114, 147, 148, 149, 158
bank preferences; case studies 113–14, 120, 137–8, 156–7, 162–3; overview 38–42; quantitative study 64–6; quantitative tests 74–91; summary 169–70
bank-centred model, France 129
bank-oriented financial system, Germany 131
Banker, The 14, 65, 143
Banking Act (1961), Germany 131
Banking Advisory Committee (BAC), EC 18

banking crisis, Japan 157–9
Banking Reform Act (1984), France 130
Banque Indosuez 127
Banque Nationale de Paris (BNP) 127
Baron, D.P. 39
Barsoon, P.N. 168, 175
Barth, J.R. 44, 66, 67, 99, 160
Basel Accord (1988): areas of permitted discretionary implementation 51–63; comparison with EU directives 68; comparison with US–UK Accord 19; and degrees of compliance 35–6; hypotheses on implementation 46; negotiation of 13–20, 107–9; overview of 1–8; as "soft law" 23–7; theoretical perspectives on 20–7; theories of compliance with 36–45
Basel Committee on Banking Supervision (BCBS): concern with Japanese policies 160; economic pressure for multilateral agreement 18; issue of amendments 6–7; negotiations compared to EC 124–6; negotiations on US Tier1 118; overview 1, 179n1–2
Basic Law, Germany 131
Belgium: capital asset ratios 14; comparative descriptive statistics 54, 55, 59; data sources 72; pre-Basel capital adequacy regulations 16; pre-Basel capital regulatory index 64; Tier1 capital definitions 57; Tier2 capital definitions 56
bilateral capital adequacy agreement, US–UK 17–18, 22–3, 118–19, 146–7, 150, 180n26, 184–5n11
binary compliance variables 30–6
binary implementations variables 173–4
bivariate correlations: analysis of first period of implementation 76–8; analysis

206 *Index*

bivariate correlations *continued*
  of second period of implementation 84–7
bootstrap method 78, 183–4n1, 184n2
Botcheva, L. 30, 31–2, 173
Bundesbank, Germany 19, 130, 138
Bundesverbank Deutscher Banken (BDB) 132
Bush, George W. 114, 115, 121

Calomiris, C.W. 184n7
Canada: capital asset ratios 14; comparative descriptive statistics 54, 55, 59; data sources 72; pre-Basel capital adequacy regulations 16; pre-Basel capital regulatory index 64; Tier1 capital definitions 57; Tier2 capital definitions 56
Capital Adequacy Directive (CAD), EC 126, 139, 140
capital adequacy ratios (CARs): France 134; Germany 132; Japan 158; US 110
capital asset ratios, compliance effects 38–9; France 127, 134, 143; G-10 banks 13, 14; Germany 136–7, 143; Japan 149, 150, 151, 153–4, 160; US 104
capital regulation index (CREG): coding 69–71; comparisons for case study countries 98; first period 53–8, 75–83; second period 58–63, 83–90; summary of findings 166–7, 176–7, 178
capital standards, US loosening of 119–20
capital-to-risk-adjusted-assets approach 105
Caprio, G. Jr. 44, 66, 67, 99, 160
"capture" theory 38, 114, 121, 138–9
case studies: aggregate introduction to the cases 97–9; goals of qualitative research 93–5; methodology 95–7; overview 5
Casserley, Dominic 13
Chicago School 38
Citibank 112
Citicorp 119
Coleman, W.D. 129, 176
Comité de la Réglementation Bancaire (CRB), France 130
Comité des Etablissements de Crédit (CEC), France 130
Commission Bancaire (CB), France 130
Compagnie Bancaire 127
comparative politics 30
compliance: theorizing degrees of 29–36; with Basel Accord 36–45
construction methods 51–3

"constructive ambiguity" 24
Continental Illinois 108
convergence 24–6; effects 32, 33; first period 166–7; second period 167
Cooke, Peter 15, 179n2
Cooper, K. 152
correlation coefficients: CREG 76, 79, 85, 86; independent variables 76; stability 84
corruption hypothesis 43–4
counterparty risks 104–5
Crédit Agricole 117, 127, 141
Credit Law, Germany 138
Crédit Lyonnais 98, 117, 127, 130, 134, 141
credit risks, management of 119
Cronbach alpha 52
cumulative preferred stock 112

Dahl, D. 180n22
Dai-Ichi Kangyo Bank 147, 152
Daiwa Bank 160
Dale, R. 16, 20, 65
data collection 51, 52–3
data sources, quantitative database 71–3
dated debt securities 118
Davison, A.C. 184n2
De Boissieu, C. 129
De Nederlandsche Bank 158
deductions from capital 70
deductivist approach 94–5
deferred tax assets 159
definitions: Tier1 capital 69; Tier2 capital 69–70
demand-side model 38–42
Demirgüç-Kunt, A. 67
democracy hypothesis 43–4
Denmark: comparative descriptive statistics 54, 55, 59; data sources 72; Tier1 capital definitions 57; Tier2 capital definitions 56
dependent variables 177–8
deposit rate controls, Japan 148
derivatives methods 120
Deutsche Bank 118
Development of financial liberalization and its environmental arrangements (Ministry of Finance, Japan) 149
dichotonious conceptualisation of implementation 30–1
differentiated compliance indicators 32, 35–6, 178
differentiated compliance variables 174
discretionary implementation areas, Basel Accord 51–63

divergence: effects 32, 33; first period 166–7; second period 167
double-gearing 159, 161, 162
Downs, G.W. 168, 175
dummy indicators 173–4

econometric studies 26
economic growth, US 115–16
economic stability hypothesis: case studies 102, 113, 121, 138, 142, 162–3; comparative statistics 97–9; overview 42–3; quantitative tests 76–83
Efron, B. 183–4n1
electoral cycles hypothesis 121, 190n3; summary 170–1
Enforcement School 30, 31, 174, 175–6
equities market, Japan 152
equity costs 148
Europe, univariate analysis of regional effects hypothesis 62
European Community (EC): implementation 124–6; overview 123–4; second implementation period (1993–2000) 139–43; variance of CREG scores versus non–EU 63; *see also* Banking Advisory Committee (BAC); Own Funds Directive
European Union (EU): approach to capital adequacy standards 123–4; comparison of directives with Basel framework 68; issue of amendments 6–7
European Union Banking Advisory Committee (BAC) 124–5; exam procedures, US 109–10
Evans, P.B. 182–3n44
explanatory variables, measurement and description 63–7

Fallacies about the effects of market risk management systems (Bank of England) 7
Federal Bankers' Associations of Japan (FBAJ) 149, 150
Federal Banking Supervisory Authority (FBSA), Germany 130 131–2, 135–6, 137, 138, 140
Federal Deposit Insurance Corporation (FDIC) 101, 105–6, 108–9, 110–11, 112, 114, 120
Federal Home Loan Bank Board 107
Federal Home Loan Mortgage Corporation (Freddie Mac) 111
Federal National Bank of Bellaire, Texas 185n31

Federal Reserve, US 101, 105–18, 120; and US–UK Accord 22–3, 103; concern with Japanese policies 160; requirements from foreign banks 45; studies by 41
Federal Savings & Loan Corporation, US 107
Feldstein, Martin 186n44
Ferry, J. 4, 7
financial engineering 134
Financial Institutions Reform, Recovery, and Enforcement Act (1989), US 107
financial integration 21
financial product innovation capacity, France 129
Finland: comparative descriptive statistics 54, 55, 59; data sources 72; Tier1 capital definitions 57; Tier2 capital definitions 56
First Banking Co-ordination Directive (1977), EU 124
first period implementation (1988–1992) 53–8; analysis of implementation 75–83; convergence/divergence 166–7; France 133–5, 137–9; Germany 135–9; Japan 152–7; US 109–14
France: background to implementation 126–30; capital asset ratios 14; comparative descriptive statistics 54, 55, 59; cost of equity 148; data sources 72; first implementation period (1988–1992) 133–5; introduction to case study 97–9; overview 123–4; pre-Basel capital adequacy regulations 16; pre-Basel capital regulatory index 64; second implementation period (1993–2000) 141–2; summary of findings 166–72; Tier1 capital definitions 57; Tier2 capital definitions 56
Frankfort-Nachmias, C. 183n8
Free Democratic Party, Germany 132
Fukao, M. 146, 154, 159, 162
"functional equivalents" scheme 15–17
funding crisis, US 101–2

G-10: Basle Accord agreement 1; capital asset ratios 13, 14; cost of equity 148; US–UK market power over 11–12, 21–3
Gamble, A. 4, 50, 52, 53–4, 71–3
Generally Accepted Accounting Principles (GAAPs), US 110, 118, 128
George, A. 95

Germany: background to implementation 130–3; capital asset ratios 14; comparative descriptive statistics 54, 55, 59; cost of equity 148; data sources 72; first implementation period (1988–1992) 135–7; introduction to case study 97–9; objection to freedom of US holding companies 117–18; overview 123–4; pre-Basel capital adequacy regulations 16; pre-Basel capital regulatory index 64; second implementation period (1993–2000) 140–1; summary of findings 166–72; Tier1 capital definitions 57; Tier2 capital definitions 56
Gilpin, R. 176, 181n1
Glass-Steagall Act (1993), US 116, 119
goodwill 112
government ownership hypothesis: case studies 128–9, 137, 142; comparative statistics 97–9; overview 44–5; quantitative tests 76–91
Great Depression 113
Greenspan, Alan 112, 113, 115, 141
Groupe CIC 127
Groupe des Banques Populaires 127

Haggard, S. 182–3n44
Hall, M.J.B. 52, 147, 155
"hard law" 23–4
Hashimoto, Ryutaro 161
hegemonic influences hypothesis: case studies 103, 139; comparative statistics 97–9; overview 45
hegemony hypothesis 61–3, 139
Henisz, W.J. 67
"hidden defection," Japan 159, 162
hidden reserve holdings 136
Hinkley, D.V. 184n2
history, US capital adequacy regulation 103–7
Ho, Daniel 35–7, 38, 42, 43–4, 67, 168, 173–4, 182–3n44
House of Representatives Banking Committee 108
hypotheses on implementation 46
hypothesis review: first period of implementation 113–14, 137–9, 156–7; second period of implementation 120–1, 142–3, 162–3

implementation: analysis of first period 75–83; analysis of second period 83–90; differentiated approach to study of 172–6; EC 124–6; existing approaches to 29–35; first period of 53–8; France 133–5, 137–9, 141–3; Germany 135–9, 140–1, 142–3; Japan 152–63; measurement and description 50–63; second period 58–63; theories of 37–45; US 109–21
ING Barings 161
insolvencies, US 107–8
Institutionalist theory 21–2, 29–30, 31–2
interest group theory 38
internal modelling 119–20
international ambitions, banks 41
international expansion, Japan 147–8, 156, 157
international exposure hypothesis: case studies 157; comparative statistics 97–9; overview 42–3, 44–5; quantitative tests 76–91; summary 162, 170, 176
international institutions 181n1
International Lending Supervision Act (ILSA) 17, 108, 109–10, 113
international market failure 11, 21
international markets, exposure to 41
International Monetary Fund (IMF) 108, 160, 173
International Organization of Securities Commissions (IOSCO) 173
Ireland: comparative descriptive statistics 54, 55, 59; Tier1 capital definitions 57; Tier2 capital definitions 56
Italy: capital asset ratios 14; pre-Basel capital adequacy regulations 16

Japan Center for Economic Research 159, 160
Japan: background to implementation 146–51; capital asset ratios 14, 18; comparative descriptive statistics 54, 55, 59; cost of equity 148; data sources 72; first period implementation (1988–1992) 152–7; introduction to case study 97–9; opt-in to US–UK Accord 18, 23, 118–19, 146–7, 150; overview 145–6; pre-Basel capital adequacy regulations 16; pre-Basel capital regulatory index 64; second period implementation (1993–2000) 157–63; summary of findings 166–72; Tier1 capital definitions 57; Tier2 capital definitions 56
Joint-gains theory 21–2
Josselin, D. 125

Kane, E.J. 129, 185n20
Kapstein, E. 21, 42–3, 105, 146, 180n23, 180n26, 184–5n11
King, G. 83, 88
Knights, D. 39
Kolari, J. 152
Krueger, Anne 84

Landesbank 118
large-scale credits ceilings 131–2
lax interpretation 38–42
legal enforcement 24
Leigh-Pemberton, Robin 17
Lesser-developed countries (LDCs): debt crisis 16, 21, 108, 187n7; loans to 13–14, 107–8, 127, 128
leverage ratios 186n44
Levine, R. 44, 66, 67, 99, 160
Liberal Democratic Party (LDP), Japan 149, 161
liberalization, Japan 147–9
loan–loss reserves: France 128; Germany 133; US 108–9, 111
logistical regression models 35–6
London inter-bank bid rate (LIBID) 155
Luxembourg: comparative descriptive statistics 54, 55, 59; data sources 73; pre-Basel capital adequacy regulations 16; pre-Basel capital regulatory index 64; Tier1 capital definitions 57; Tier2 capital definitions 56

Maccario, A. 148
macroeconomic instability hypothesis: case studies 157, 162–3; quantitative studies 66; quantitative tests 74–91; summary 169
Management School 30, 31, 174–6
market supervision hypothesis: case studies 120–1, 162; comparative statistics 97–9; compliance effects 39–41; summary 169–70, 171
market value, Japanese bank shares 154
Marshall, J. 179n1
Martin, L.L. 30, 31–2, 173
Matten, C. 180n22, 189n17
measurement, implementation 50–63; explanatory variables 63–7; overview 183n8
Merrill Lynch Capital Markets study 151
methodology: case studies 95–7; review of 176–7
microeconomic effects, Japan 152–3, 158–9

"minimum harmonization" 24
Ministry of Finance, Japan 147, 148, 149–50, 152, 153–4, 156, 159–61
Mooney, C.Z. 183–4n1
Moran, M. 176
Morgan, G. 39
mortgage loans, US 110, 111, 115
multi-nationalization of banking 14–15
multivariate analysis: analysis of first period of implementation 78–83; analysis of second period of implementation 87–9
Murray-Jones, A. 4, 50, 52, 53–4, 71–3
"mutual recognition" framework, EC 143

Nabors, R. 21, 22, 23, 25, 40, 99, 123, 127, 135, 137, 146–7, 150–1, 165, 187n7, 189n20
Nachmias, D. 183n8
National Mortgage Association (Ginnie Mac), US 111
national treatment 148
nationalization, France 129
negotiation, Basel Accord 13–20, 107–9
Netherlands: comparative descriptive statistics 54, 55, 59; data sources 73; pre-Basel capital regulatory index 64; Tier1 capital definitions 57; Tier2 capital definitions 56
New Zealand: comparative descriptive statistics 54, 55, 59; data sources 73; Tier1 capital definitions 57; Tier2 capital definitions 56
Nikkei 225 index 152, 153, 154, 158
"no law" 24
non-bank financial institutions, US 116–17
non-performing loans (NPLs), Japan 156, 158, 159, 161–2
non-risk sensitive capital-to-assets approach 105
North America, univariate analysis of regional effects hypothesis 62
North, D. 182–3n44
Norton, J.J. 99, 104, 106

Oatley, T. 21, 22, 23, 25, 40, 99, 123, 127, 135, 137, 146–7, 150–1, 165, 187n7, 189n20
objectives, Basle Accord 13
off-balance sheet (OBS): assets 20, 51–63, 166; comparative descriptive statistics 53; risk weights 70–1

Office of the Comptroller of the Currency (OCC), US 101, 105–6, 108–9, 110–11, 112, 114; *OCC v. Federal National Bank of Bellaire, Texas* (1983) 185n31
Office of Thrift Supervision (OTS), US 118
on-balance sheet: assets 20, 51–63; risk weights 70
ordered probit regression results 88
ordinal scale 52
ordinary least squares (OLS) regression 78–83, 87
Organization for Economic Cooperation and Development (OECD) 20
Organization of Petroleum Exporting Countries (OPEC) 13
"organized liberalism" 130–1
over-capitalization 119
over-compliance 31
Own Funds Directive, EC 40, 125–6, 133, 135, 137, 139, 187n31

Paribas 127
path dependence 38–40, 64–6, 82, 85, 120, 137–8; summary 167–8, 169, 175
Pattison, J.C. 23
Pecchioli, R.M. 65
Peek, J. 155
Persson, T. 190n3
policymaking, demand-side model 38–42
political fragmentation hypothesis: case studies 104–5, 114, 121, 137, 138–9, 143; comparative statistics 97–9; overview 43–4, 182–3n44; quantitative studies 66–7; quantitative tests 74–91; summary 170
political institutions theory 43–4
political management, impediments to compliance 30
political power of banks, France 129–30
politicization of capital regulation, US 107–9
pre-Basel regime hypothesis: comparison of 16, 97–9: compliance 39–41; index comparisons with CREG 77; quantitative tests 74–91; study of 22
Pressman, J. 30
PriceWaterhouse 4, 50, 52, 53–4, 71–3, 150, 187n31
Private Monitoring Index 66
profitability influence of capital standards 25–6
public choice theory 22
public policy research 30

qualitative research: appropriateness 163; goals 93–5; overview 4; summary 176–7
quantitative tests, implementation: analysis of first period implementation 75–83; analysis of second period implementation 83–90; overview 3–4, 74–5, 183–4n1-2; summary 176–7

Rabobank International 189n17
rationalist school 29, 174
real-estate investment trusts (REITS), US 107–8
realist school 29, 45, 174
recession: Japan 154, 162–3; US 102
redistributive theory 22–3, 25, 150–2
regional imitation hypotheses testing 61–3
regional influences hypothesis: case studies 114, 142–3; comparative statistics 97–9; overview 43–5; quantitative studies 61–3
"regulator's dilemma" 21–3, 24–5, 42–3
regulatory advantages, domestic banks 15
regulatory capital definitions: EU 125, 140–1; FDIC/Federal Reserve/Basel Accord comparison 106; US 110, 111–12, 116, 118–19; summary 166–7
regulatory discretion 20
"regulatory rent" 159–60
Reinicke, W.H. 185n20, 187n7
reputational effects of non-compliance 40–1
research findings: implications for future research 177–8; implications of 172–6; methodology review 176–7; summary of 166–72
reunification, Germany 137, 138
revaluation reserves 114, 133, 134, 151, 189n20
risk weights assets (RWA): Basel Accord 20, 51–63; comparative descriptive statistics 53; France 127–8, 134–5; Germany 140–1; Japan 154–5, 158–9; overview 180n22, 181n30, 184–5n11; US 110, 180n23
risk-taking, commercial banks 13–14
risk-weighted capital adequacy standard: need for 17; US 108
Rocke, D.M. 168, 175
Rome Treaty (1958) 18
Rosenbluth, F.M. 190n3
Rosengren, E.S. 155
Rossman, G.B. 93
rule of law hypothesis 43–4

St Germain, Ferdinand 108
Salomon Brothers 112
Savings and Loan crisis, US 111
Sawabe, N. 145, 147, 149
Schapp, R. 190n3
Scott, H. 25
second period of implementation (1993–2000) 58–63: analysis of implementation 83–90; convergence/divergence 167; France 141–3; Germany 140–1, 142–3; Japan 157–63; US 114–21
Securities and Exchange Commission, US 116
Seidman, L. William 112
Senate Banking Committee 110
sensitivity analysis 89–90
sensitivity exams 83
SG Groupe Ecureuil 12
Shrieves, R.E. 180n22
silent participations 118
Simmons, Beth 40, 44–5, 142
Singer, D.A. 21, 42–3
Sironi, A. 148
small- and medium sized enterprises (SMEs), Japan 156, 161
SMH-Bank 132
Société Générale 130
"soft law": Basle Accord as 23–7; interpretations of 167–71; overview 5–6
Solvency Ratio Directive, EC 126, 135, 137
Spain: comparative descriptive statistics 54, 55, 59; data sources 73; Tier1 capital definitions 57; Tier2 capital definitions 56
Spar, D.L. 109
stability, Japanese banks 155–6
standardization 95
status quo 39–41, 136, 176
stock prices, effects of Basel Accord 26
Story, J. 131, 138, 187n31
strict interpretations 38–42, 74–91; summary 167–72
subordinated debt, Tier2 56–7
"super-regional" banks 120
Sweden: comparative descriptive statistics 54, 55, 59; data sources 73; Tier1 capital definitions 57; Tier2 capital definitions 56
Switzerland: capital asset ratios 14; comparative descriptive statistics 54, 55, 59; data sources 73; pre-Basel capital adequacy regulations 16; pre-Basel capital regulatory index 64; Tier1 capital definitions 57; Tier2 capital definitions 56

Takellini, G. 190n3
Tamura, K. 4, 145, 149, 150, 151, 156, 161, 162, 163, 189n20
tax-deductible preferred stock 116–18, 120, 141–2
tax-shielded preferred stock 114, 116
test-retest method 52
theoretical perspectives, Basel Accord 20–7
theories of compliance with Basel Accord 36–45
theories of implementation 37–45
theorizing, degrees of compliance 29–36
Tibshirani, R.J. 183–4n1
Tier1 capital 51–63; Basel Accord 19–20; capital assets ratios, US banks 116; capital definitions 57–8; comparative descriptive statistics 53; compared to EU directives 68; indicators 77–8, 79, 85–9; US–UK Accord 17–18
Tier2 capital 51–63: Basel Accord 19–20; capital definitions 56–7; comparative descriptive statistics 53; compared to EU directives 68; indicators 77–8, 79, 85–9; US–UK Accord 17–18
Tobin, G. 109
two-tier framework, arbitrage incentives 106
two-tiered mutual recognition framework: Basel Accord 19–20, 22–3; US–UK Accord 17

UK: capital asset ratios 14; comparative descriptive statistics 54, 55, 59; data sources 73; market power 11–12, 21; pre-Basel capital adequacy regulations 16; pre-Basel capital regulatory index 64; Tier1 capital definitions 57; Tier2 capital definitions 56; see also US–UK Accord
Underdal, A. 34, 39
undisclosed reserves 133
Uniform Interagency Bank Rating System, US 105
univariate statistical analyses 3–4
unrealised capital gains: France 40, 128; Japan 18, 149, 150, 151; overview 189n17
unrealised securities: Japan 154–5; summary 168–9

unweighted capital ratios, Japan 151
US: background to implementation 103–9; capital asset ratios 14; comparative descriptive statistics 54, 55, 59; cost of equity 148; data sources 73; "first mover" advantage 45; first period implementation (1988–1992) 109–14; introduction to case study 97–9; Japanese banks in 147–8; market power 11–12, 21, 22; occupation of Japan 147; overview 101–3; pre-Basel capital adequacy regulations 16; pre-Basel capital regulatory index 64; second period implementation (1993–2000) 114–21; summary of findings 166–72; Tier1 capital definitions 57; Tier2 capital definitions 56; univariate analysis of hegemonic hypothesis 61
US–UK Accord 17–18, 22–3, 118–19, 146–7, 150, 180n26, 184–5n11; comparison with Basel Accord 19

Verdier, D. 75, 183–4n1
Vernon, R. 109

Wagster, J. 26, 145, 152–3, 170
Walter, A. 42
wealth redistributive effects 135–6
Weingast, B. 182–3n44
Wildavsky, A. 30
Wilson, B.L. 93
Woolcock, S. 24
World Bank 24

Yoshimasa, Noishimura 156

Zazzara, C. 148

eBooks – at www.eBookstore.tandf.co.uk

A library at your fingertips!

eBooks are electronic versions of printed books. You can store them on your PC/laptop or browse them online.

They have advantages for anyone needing rapid access to a wide variety of published, copyright information.

eBooks can help your research by enabling you to bookmark chapters, annotate text and use instant searches to find specific words or phrases. Several eBook files would fit on even a small laptop or PDA.

NEW: Save money by eSubscribing: cheap, online access to any eBook for as long as you need it.

Annual subscription packages

We now offer special low-cost bulk subscriptions to packages of eBooks in certain subject areas. These are available to libraries or to individuals.

For more information please contact webmaster.ebooks@tandf.co.uk

We're continually developing the eBook concept, so keep up to date by visiting the website.

www.eBookstore.tandf.co.uk